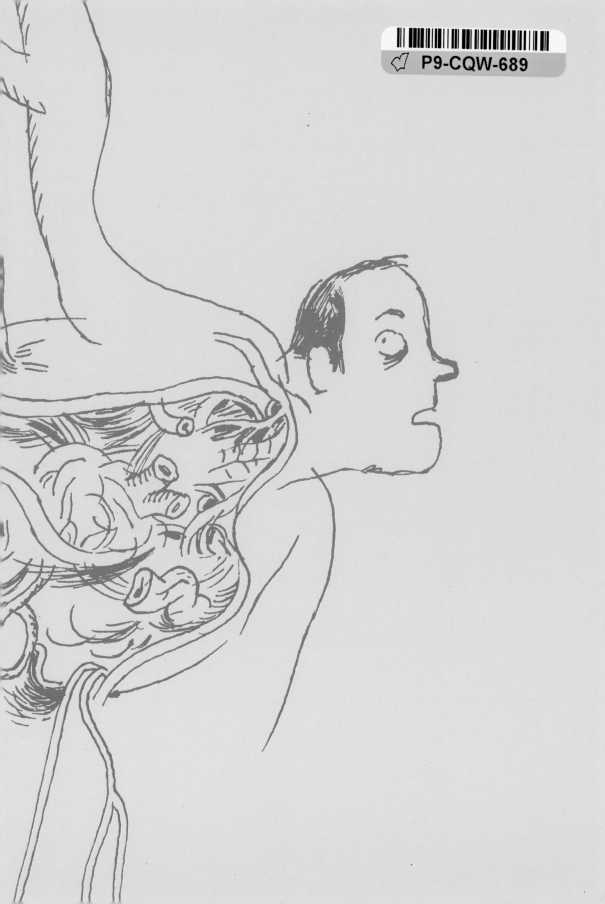

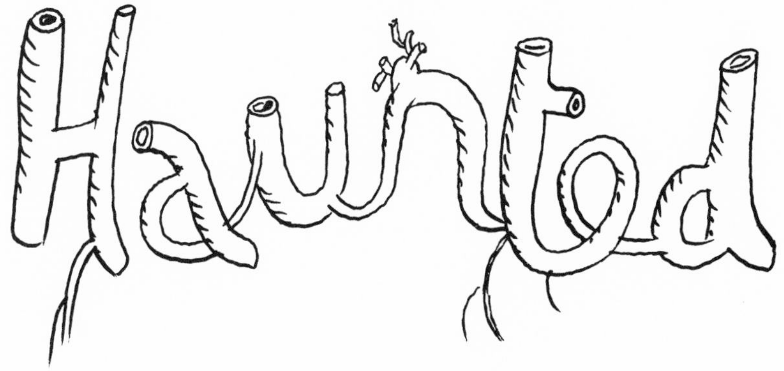
Haunted

Philippe Dupuy

Haunted

Drawn & Quarterly
Montréal

For Loo

Thanks to Charles, Blutch, Jean-Louis, Tessa, Valentin, Noémie, Agnès, Nath and Jean-Pierre Bigeault.

During the night of May 14th to May 15th 2004, I saw a number
of paintings in a dream. I don't know who painted them. They were
portraits. Faces without eyes. Instead of a gaze, scarred emptiness.

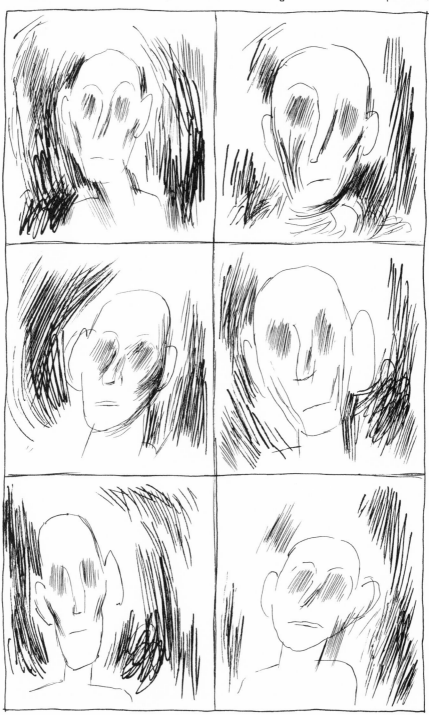

Run Movie 1 Jogging

Starting on May 15,th 2004, I set myself to Running for an hour almost every morning.

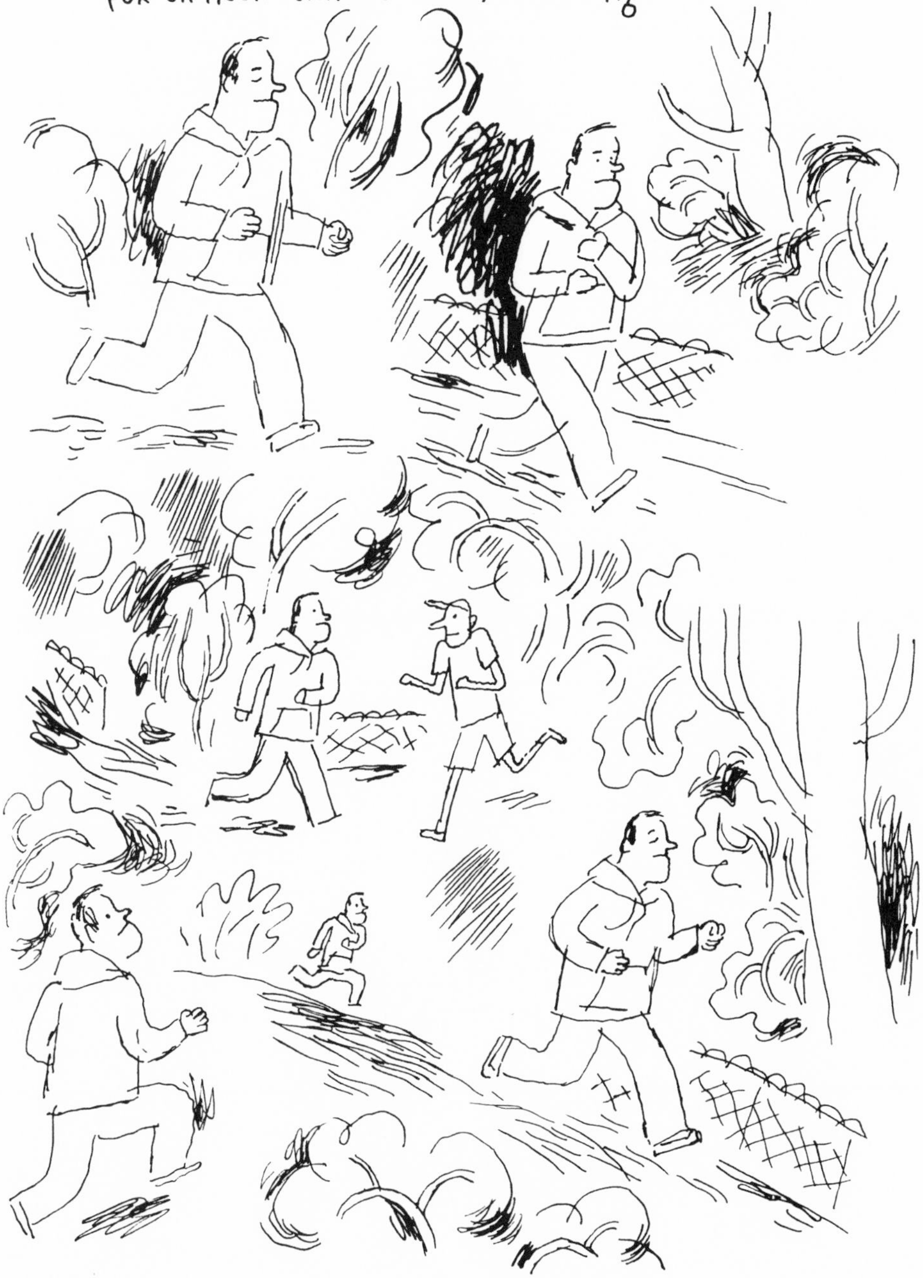

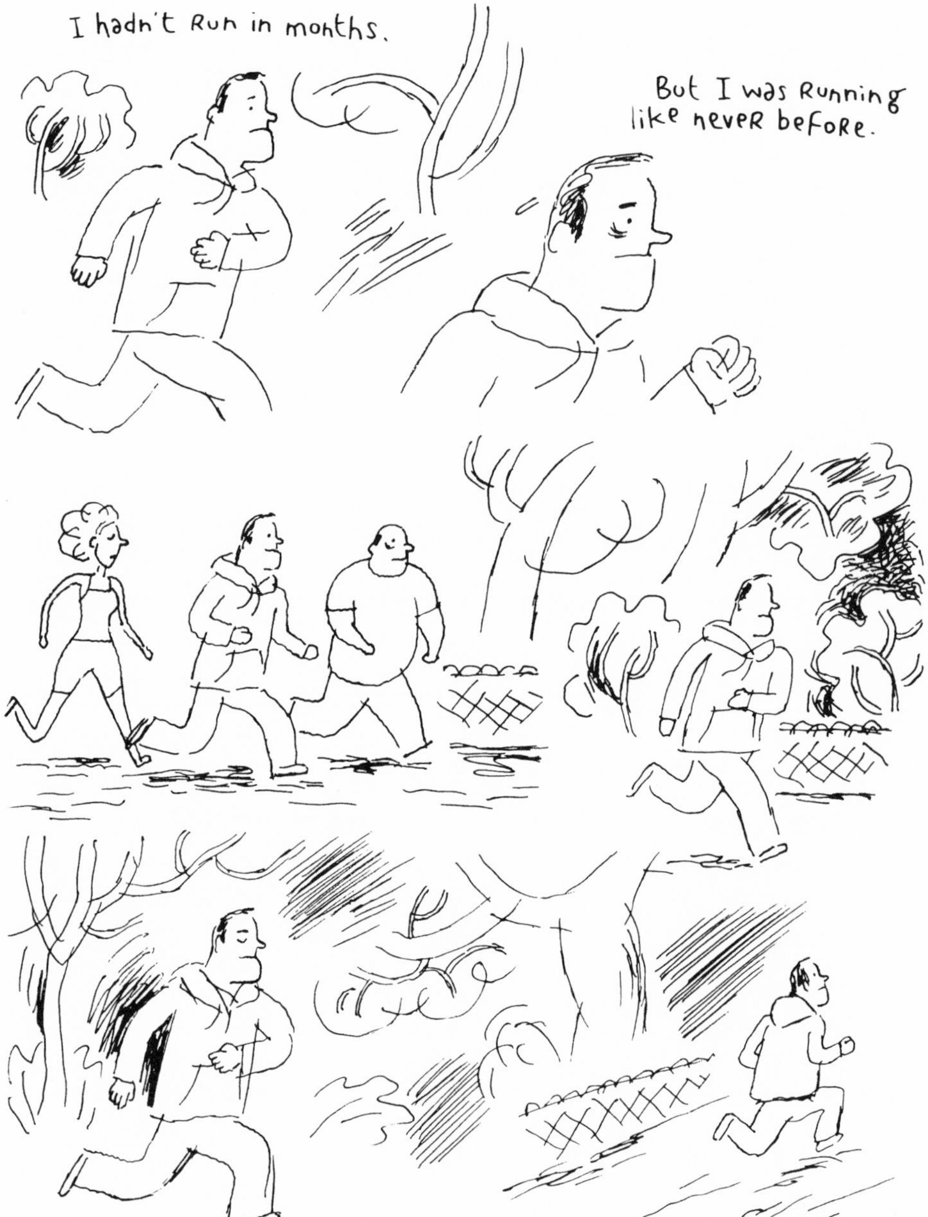
I hadn't Run in months.
But I was Running like never before.

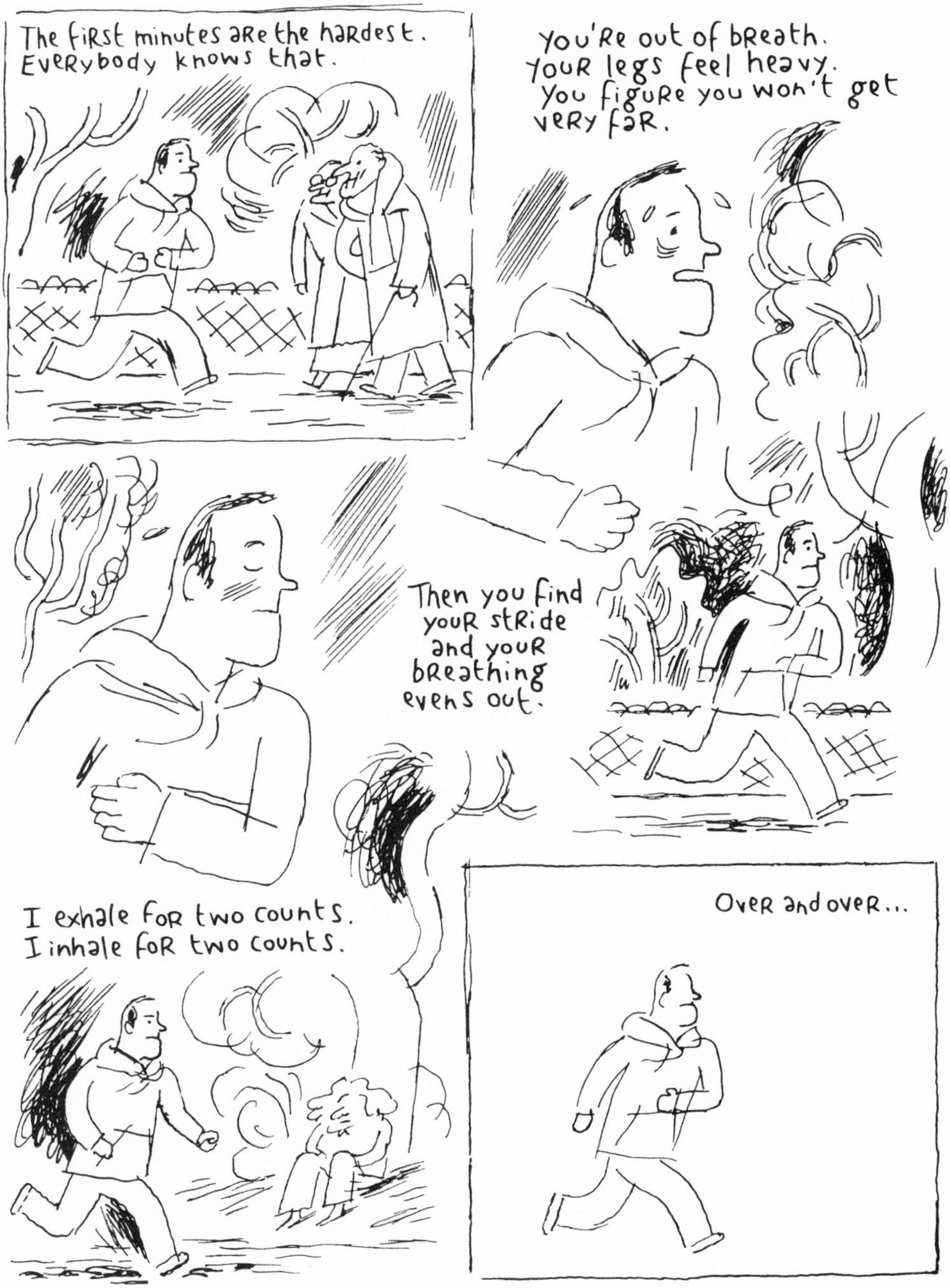
The first minutes are the hardest.
Everybody knows that.
You're out of breath.
Your legs feel heavy.
You figure you won't get
very far.
Then you find
your stride
and your
breathing
evens out.
I exhale for two counts.
I inhale for two counts.
Over and over...

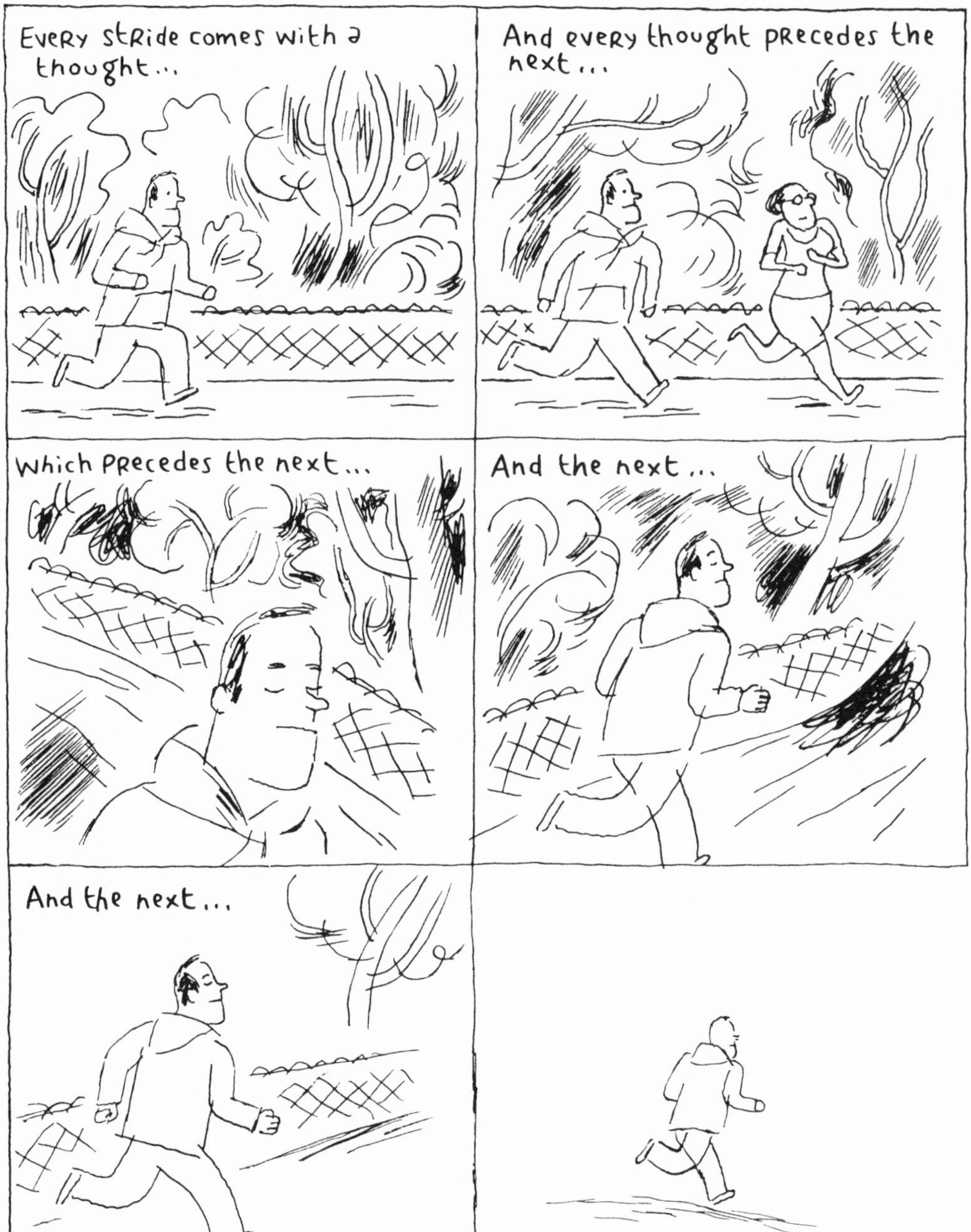
Every stride comes with a thought...
And every thought precedes the next...
Which precedes the next...
And the next...
And the next...

the dog

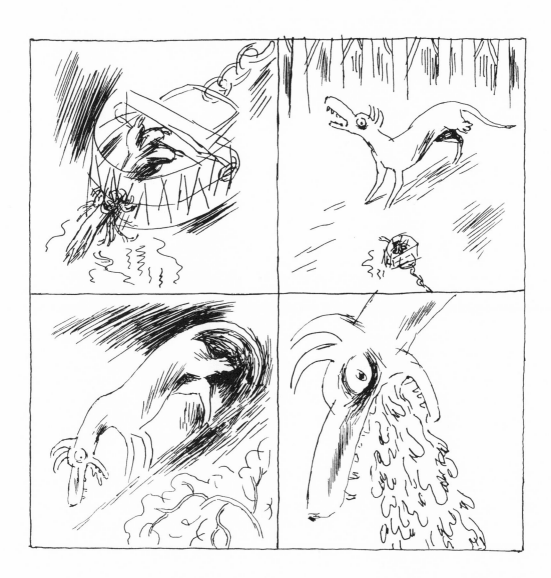

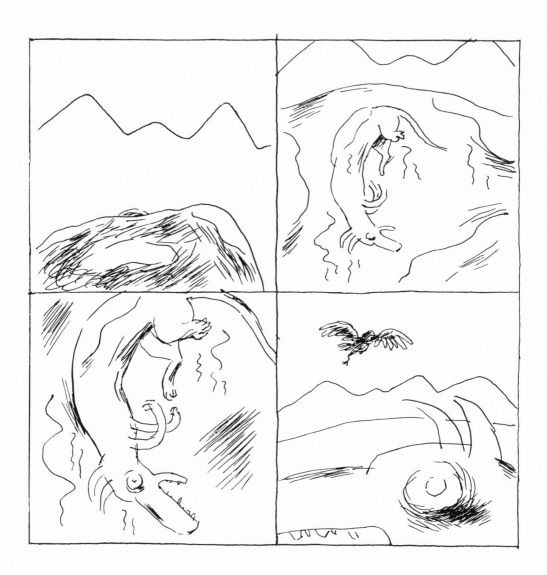

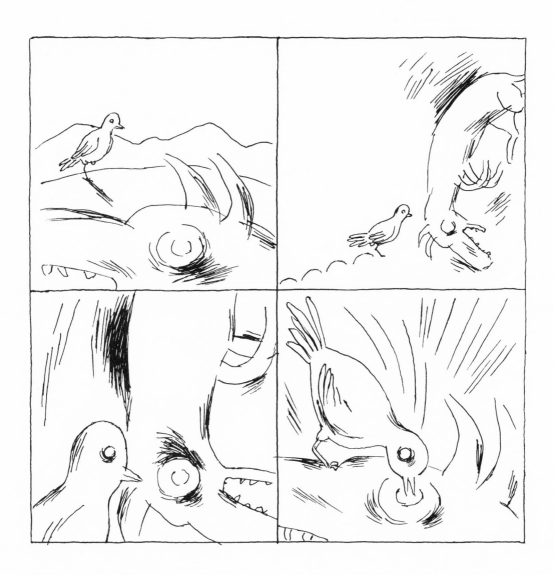

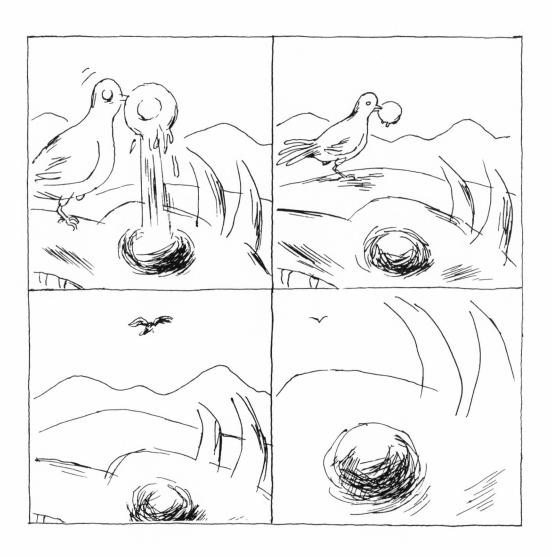

Run Movie 2 Hands

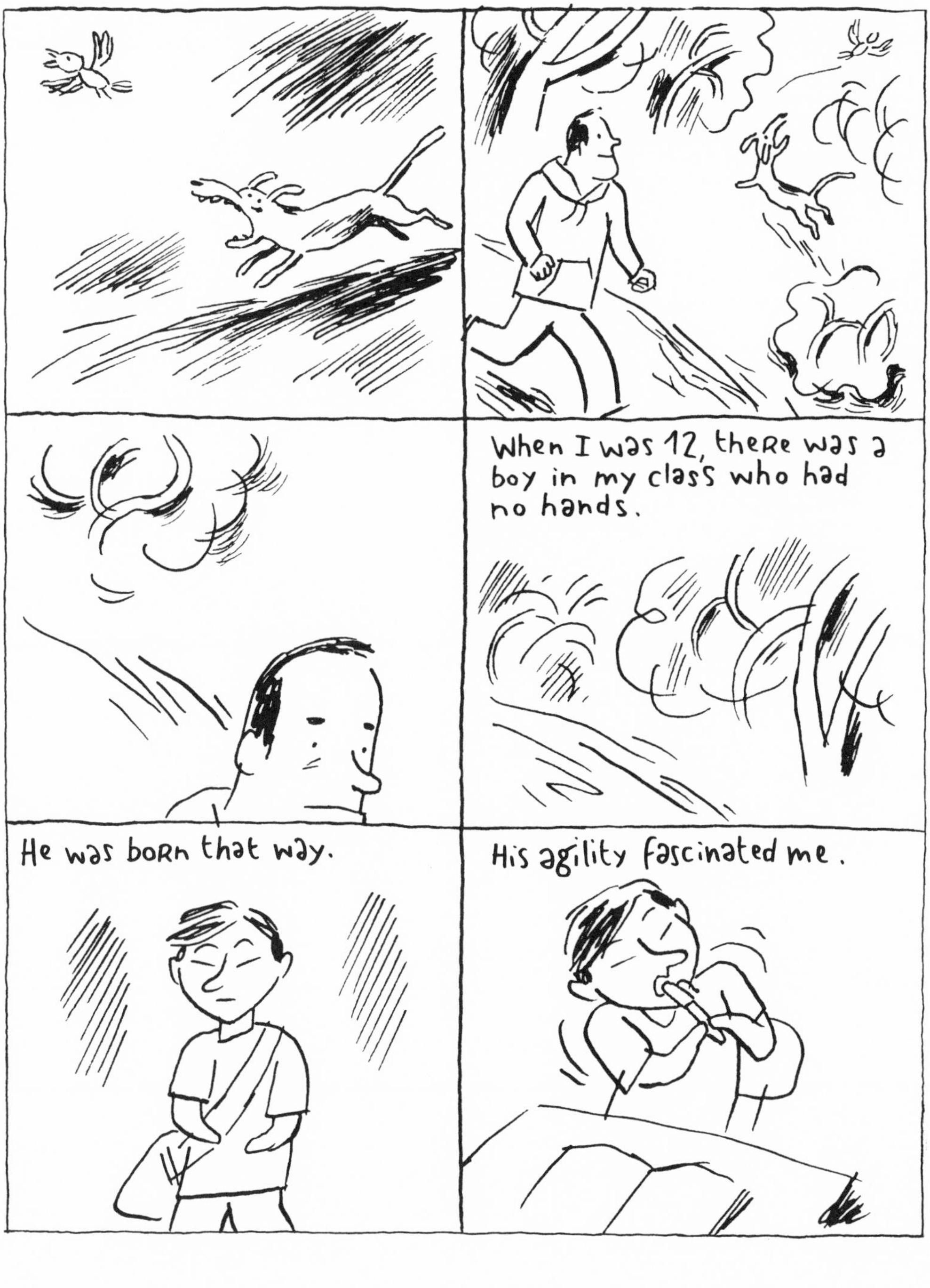
When I was 12, there was a boy in my class who had no hands.
He was born that way.
His agility fascinated me.

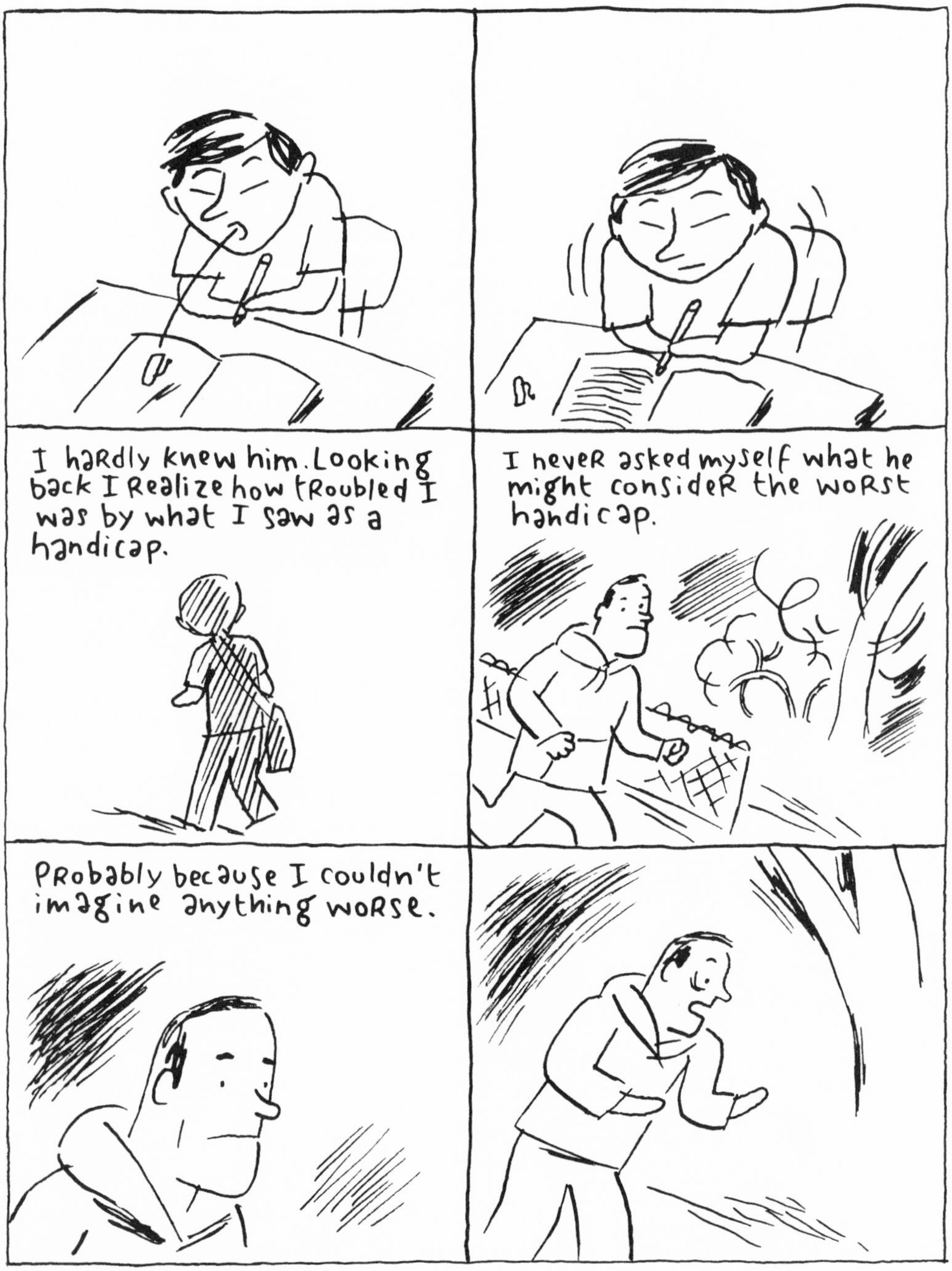
I hardly knew him. Looking back I realize how troubled I was by what I saw as a handicap.
I never asked myself what he might consider the worst handicap.
Probably because I couldn't imagine anything worse.

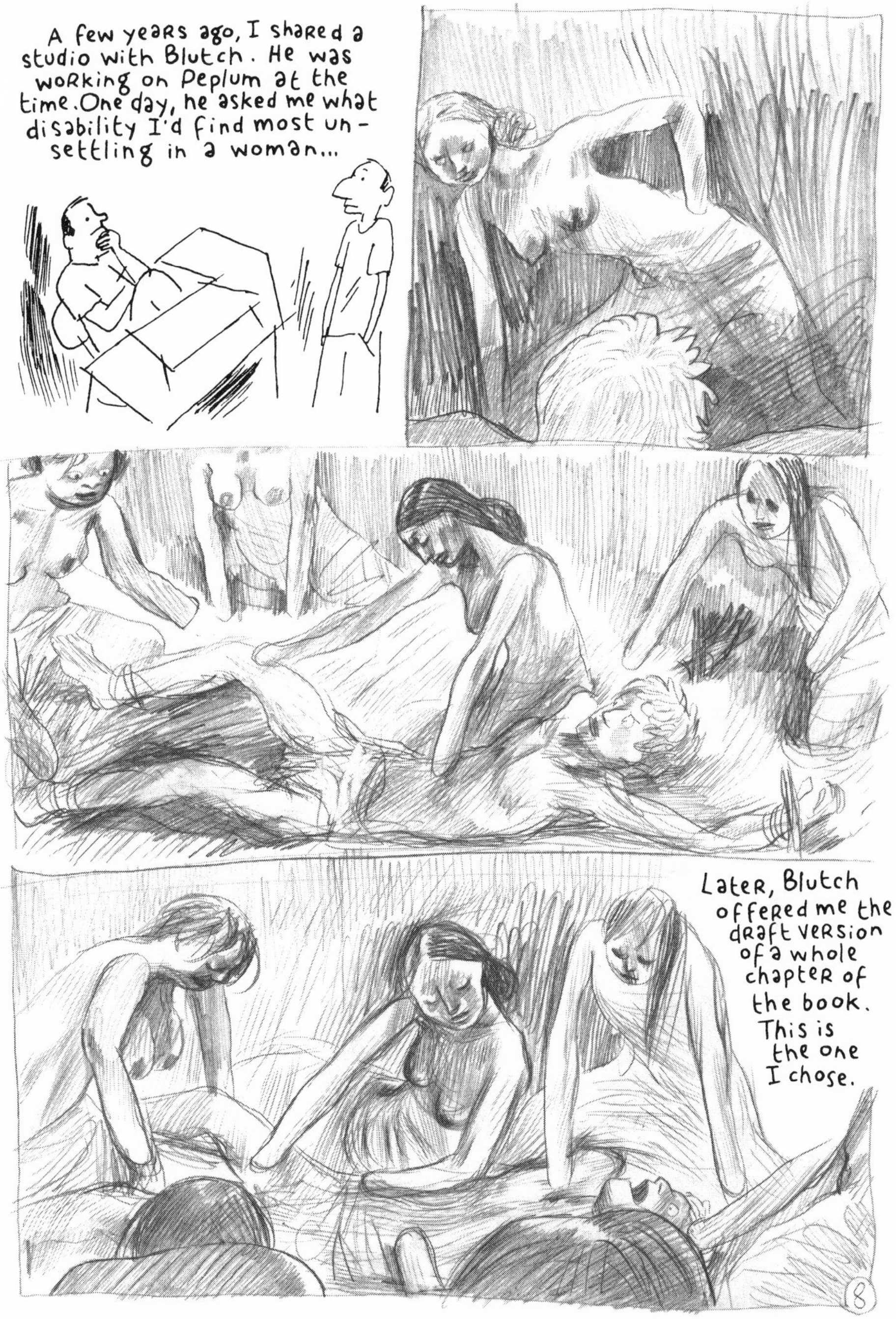
A few years ago, I shared a studio with Blutch. He was working on Peplum at the time. One day, he asked me what disability I'd find most unsettling in a woman...
Later, Blutch offered me the draft version of a whole chapter of the book. This is the one I chose.
8

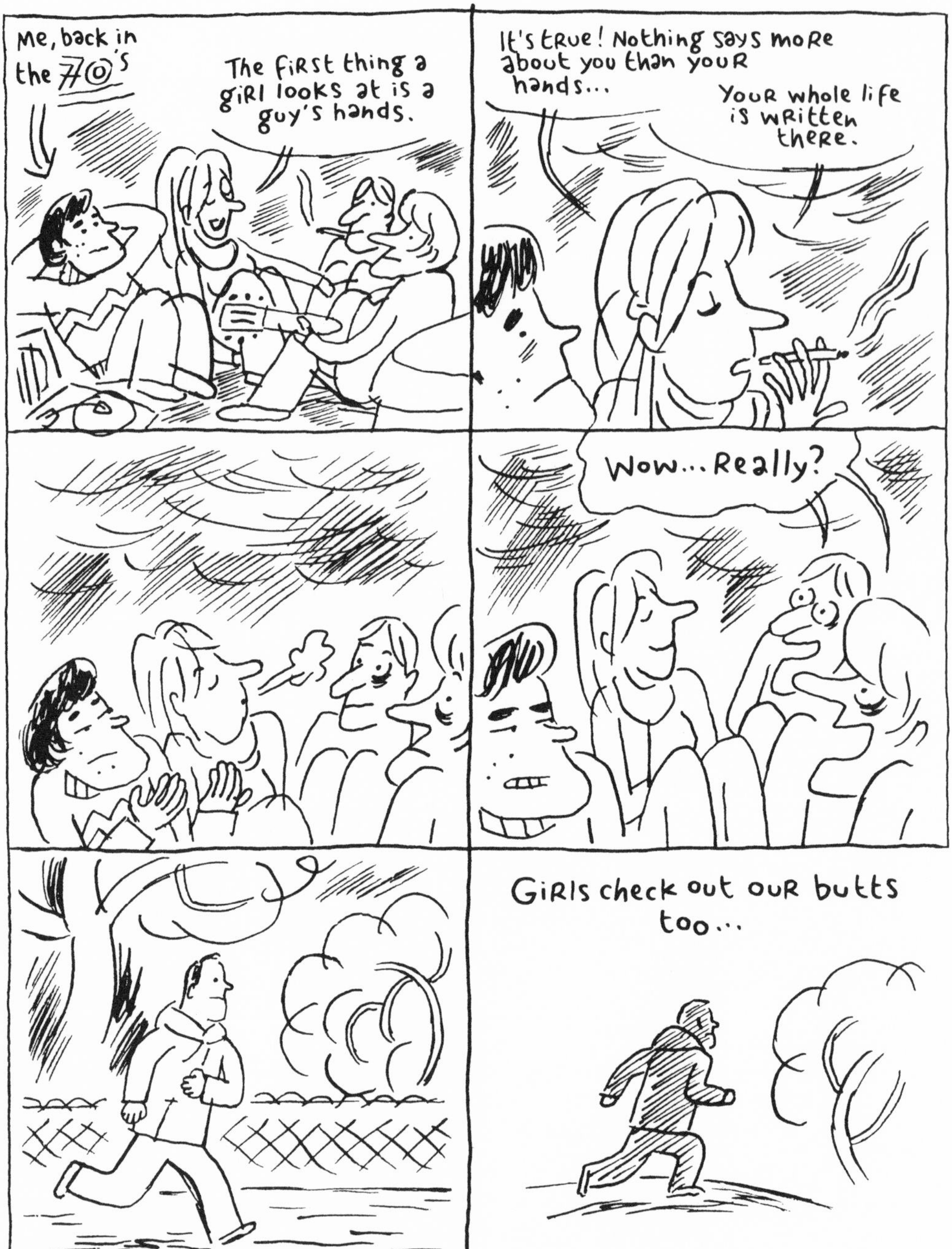
Me, back in the 70's
The first thing a girl looks at is a guy's hands.
It's true! Nothing says more about you than your hands...
Your whole life is written there.
Wow... Really?
Girls check out our butts too...

the dReam

I'm at my bedroom window.
I'm watching a strange commotion down in the street.

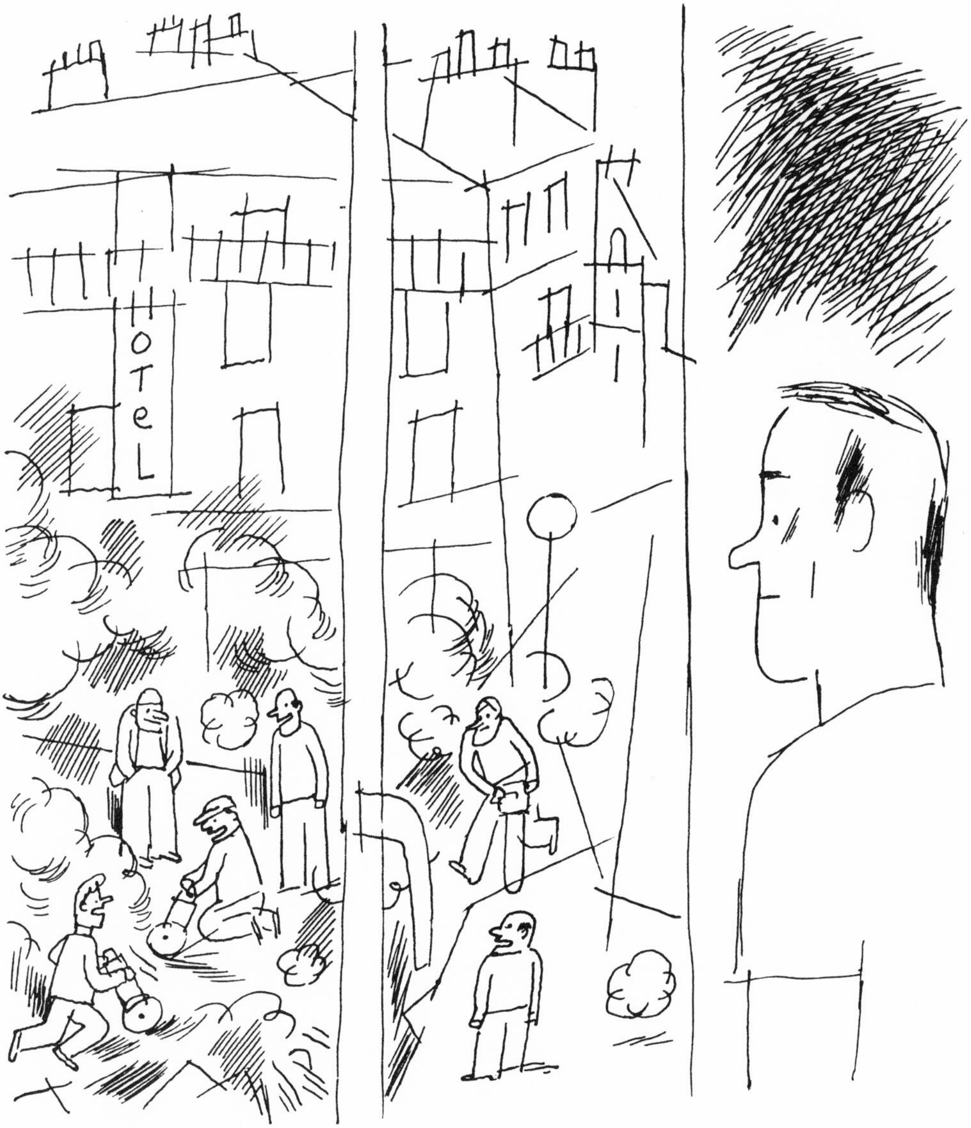
HOTEL

Men are sawing into the pavement, tearing it open.
Others are looking on.
They seem elated somehow.

As their machinery cuts into the asphalt, it grinds out the tune to *Happy Birthday to you*.

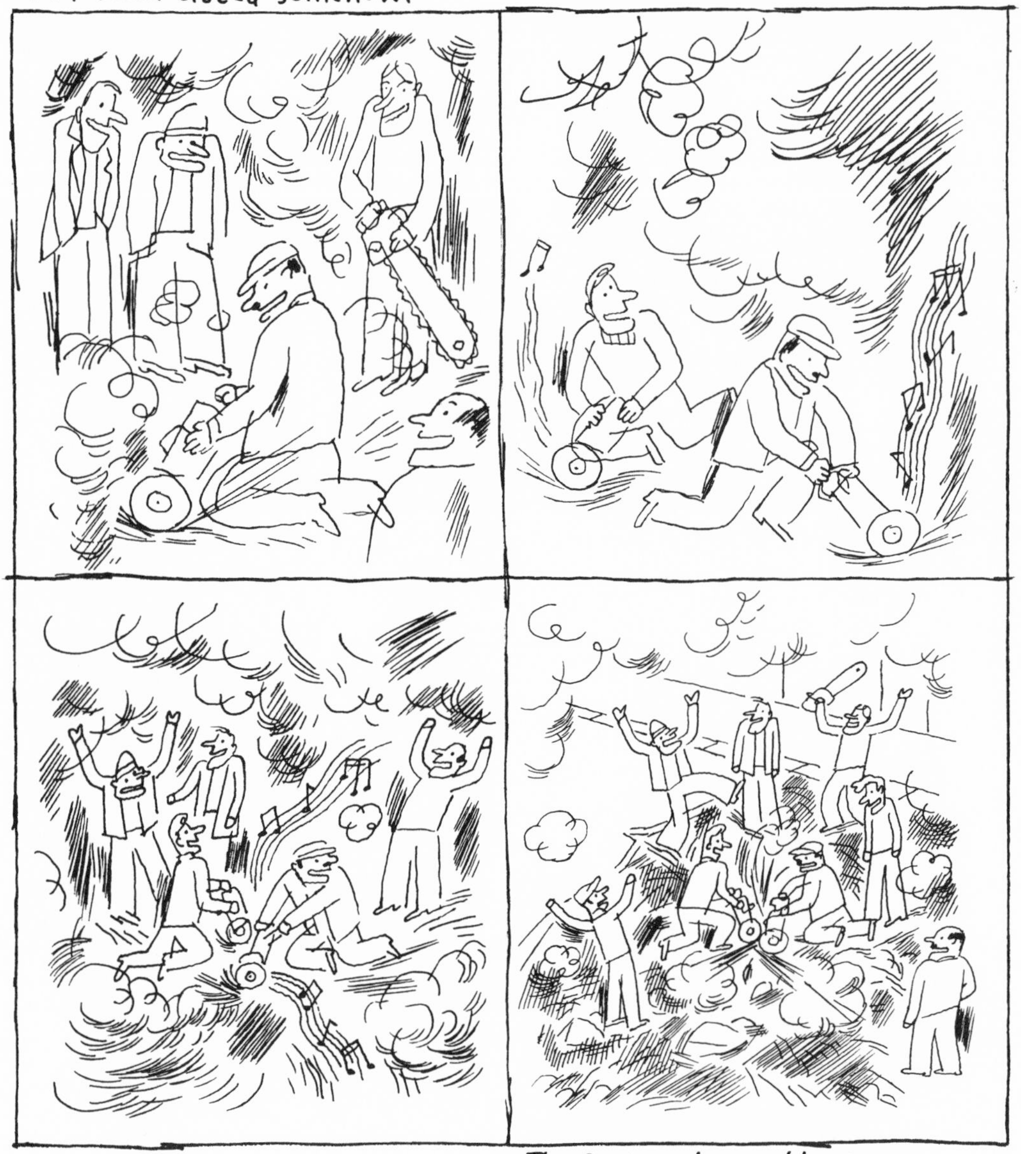

The pavement is getting more and more broken up.
I tell myself they're crazy and don't realize what they're doing.

I sense imminent disaster.

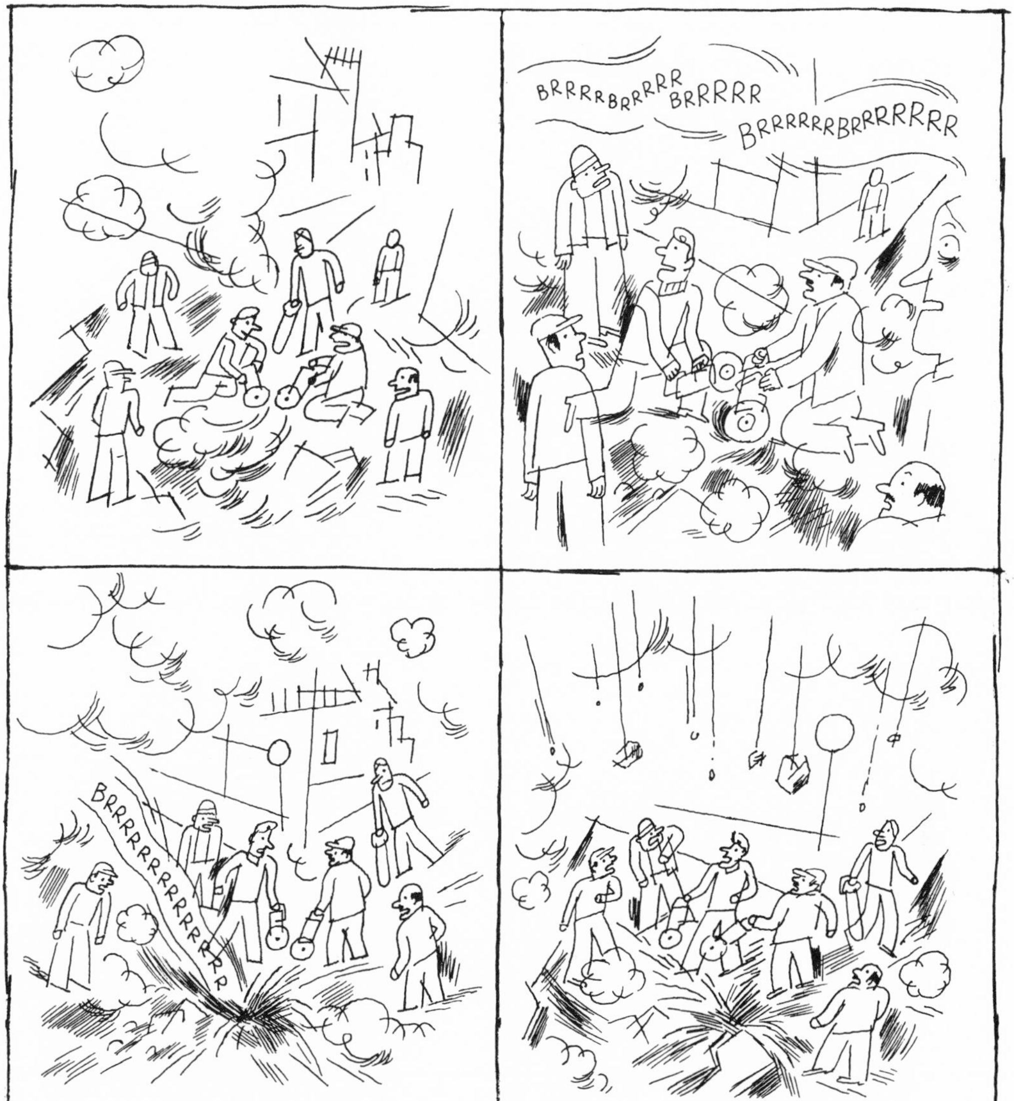
BRRRRBRRRRR BRRRRR
BRRRRRRBRRRRRRR
BRRRRRRRRRRRRR

Suddenly, a section of pavement starts to give way.

The buildings heave.

Everybody panics.

In the middle of the street, a man disappears down a crack.

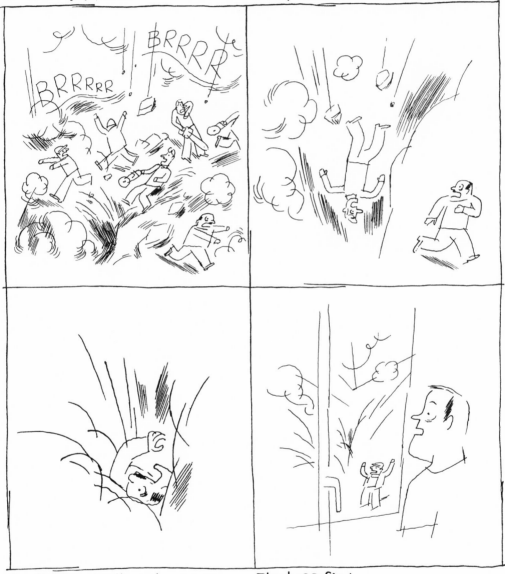

Another is swallowed up by the collapsing ground.

I'm horrified.
I tell myself I should do something fast. I should call for help.

But I can't.
I don't know the number...

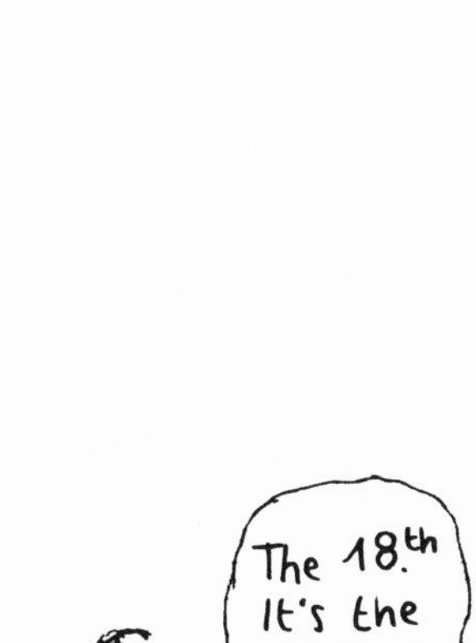
The 18.th
It's the
18th !

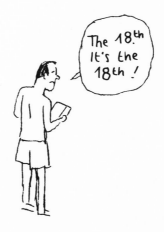

Run Movie 3 the museum

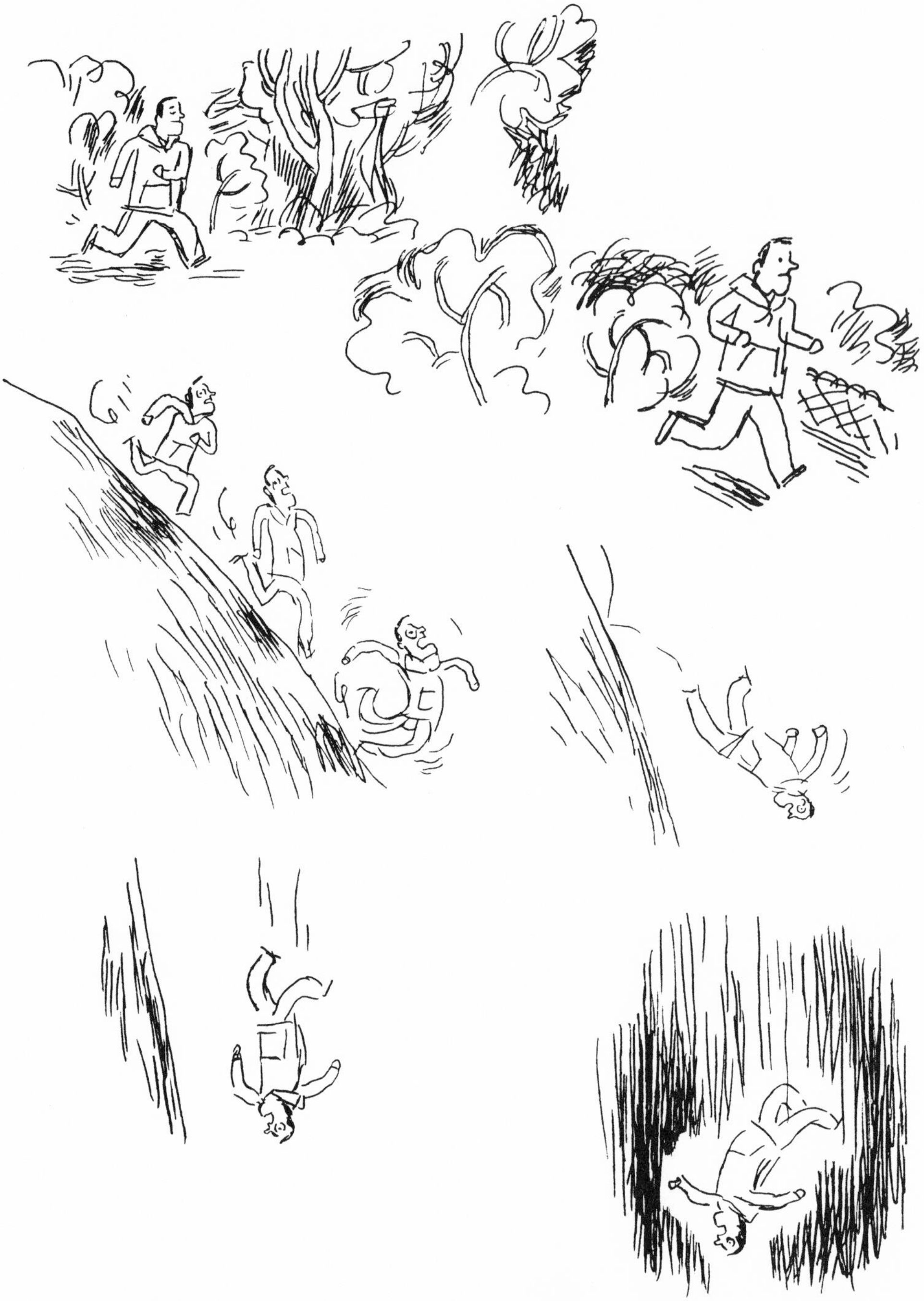

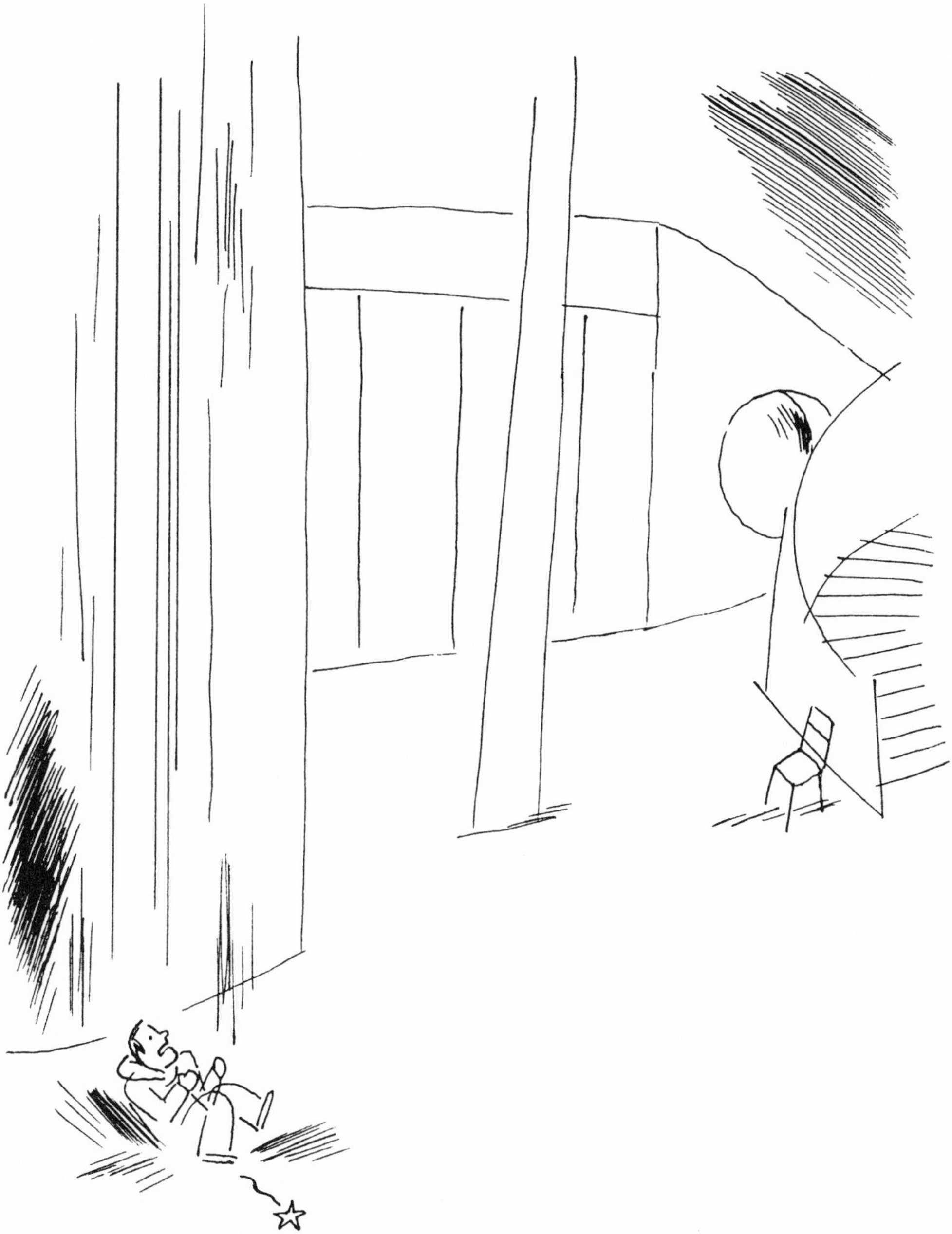

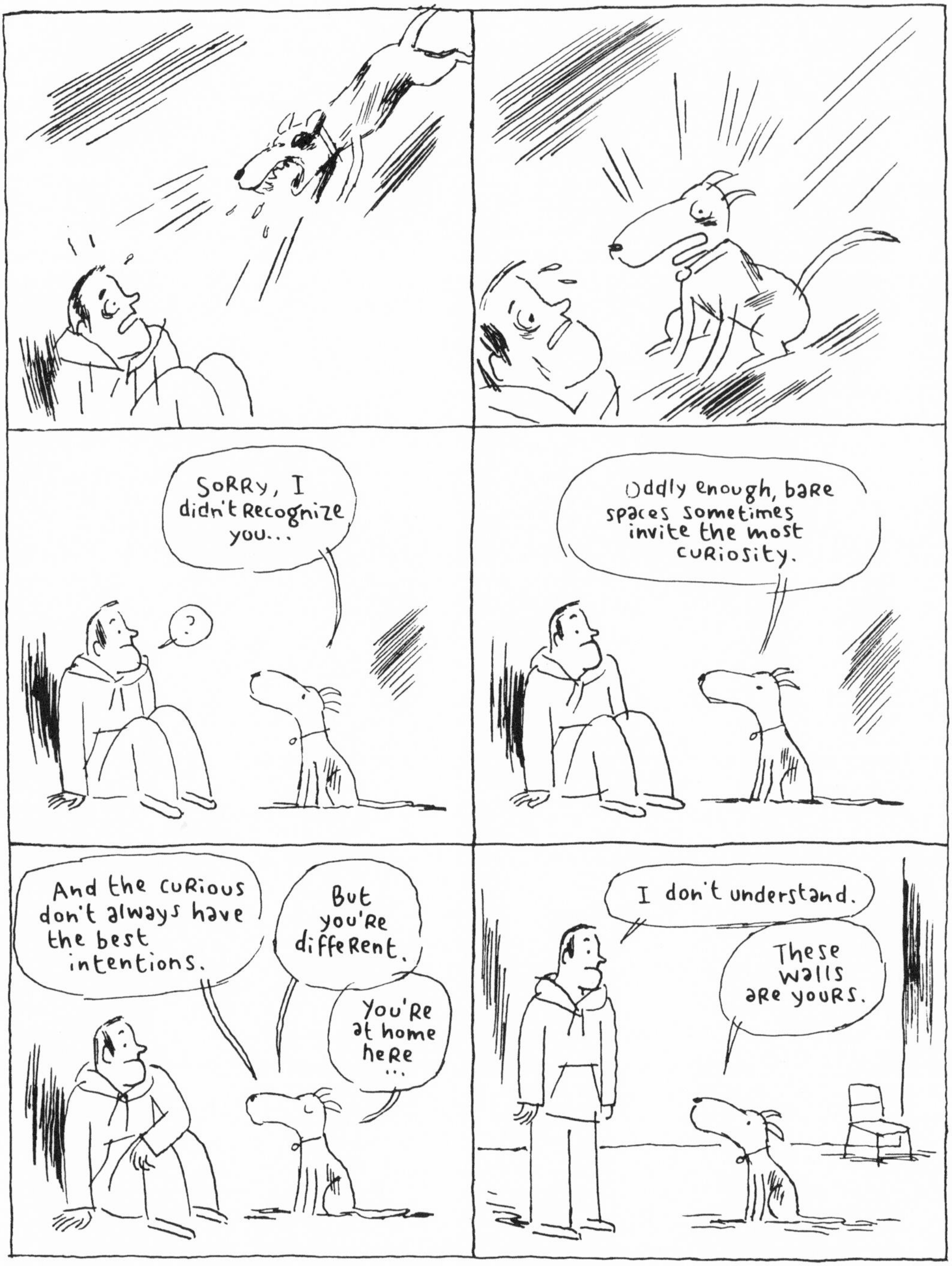
SORRY, I didn't Recognize you...
?
Oddly enough, bare spaces sometimes invite the most curiosity.
And the curious don't always have the best intentions.
But you're different.
You're at home here ...
I don't understand.
These walls are yours.

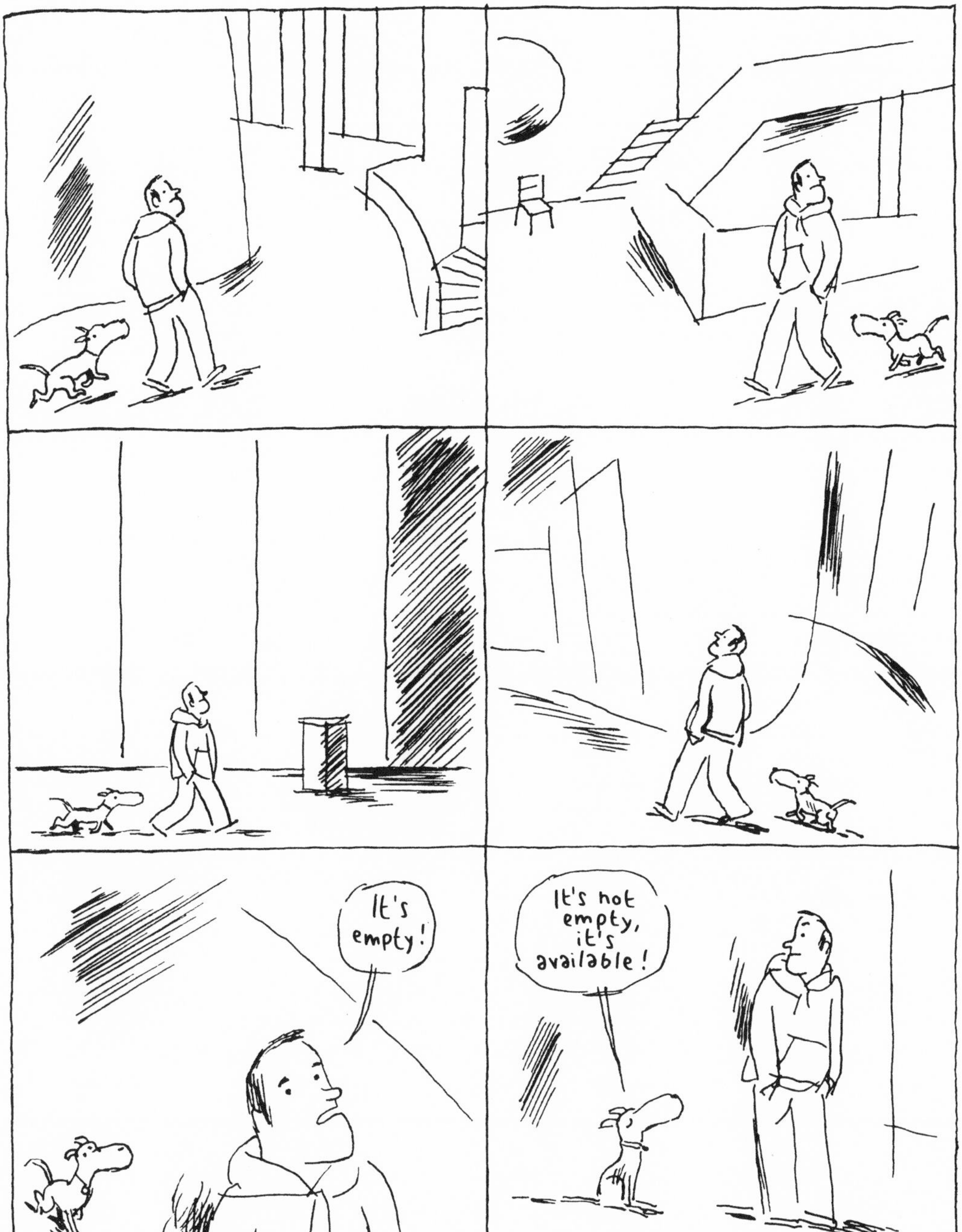
It's empty!
It's not empty, it's available!

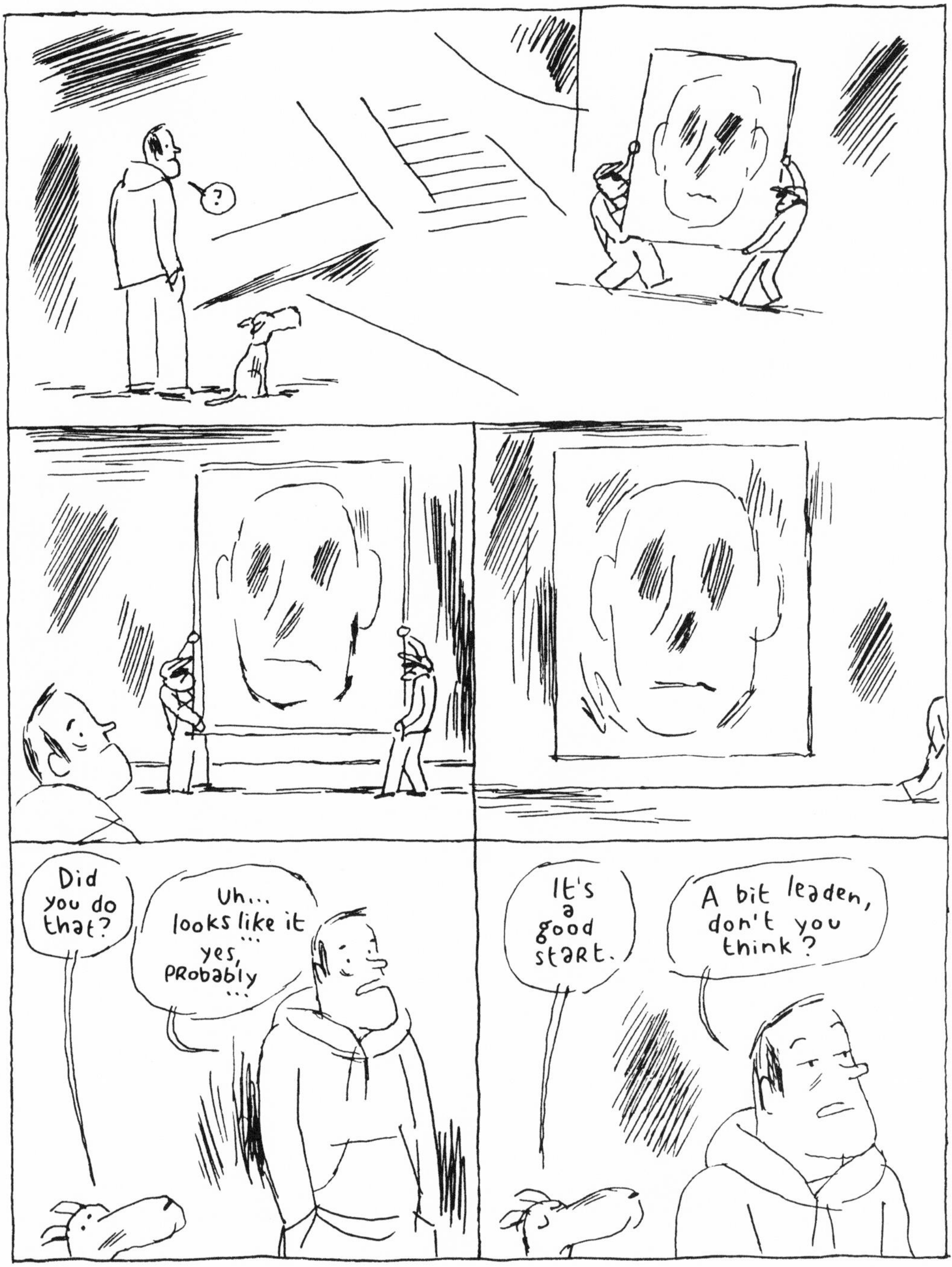
?
Did you do that?
Uh... looks like it ... yes, probably ...
It's a good start.
A bit leaden, don't you think?

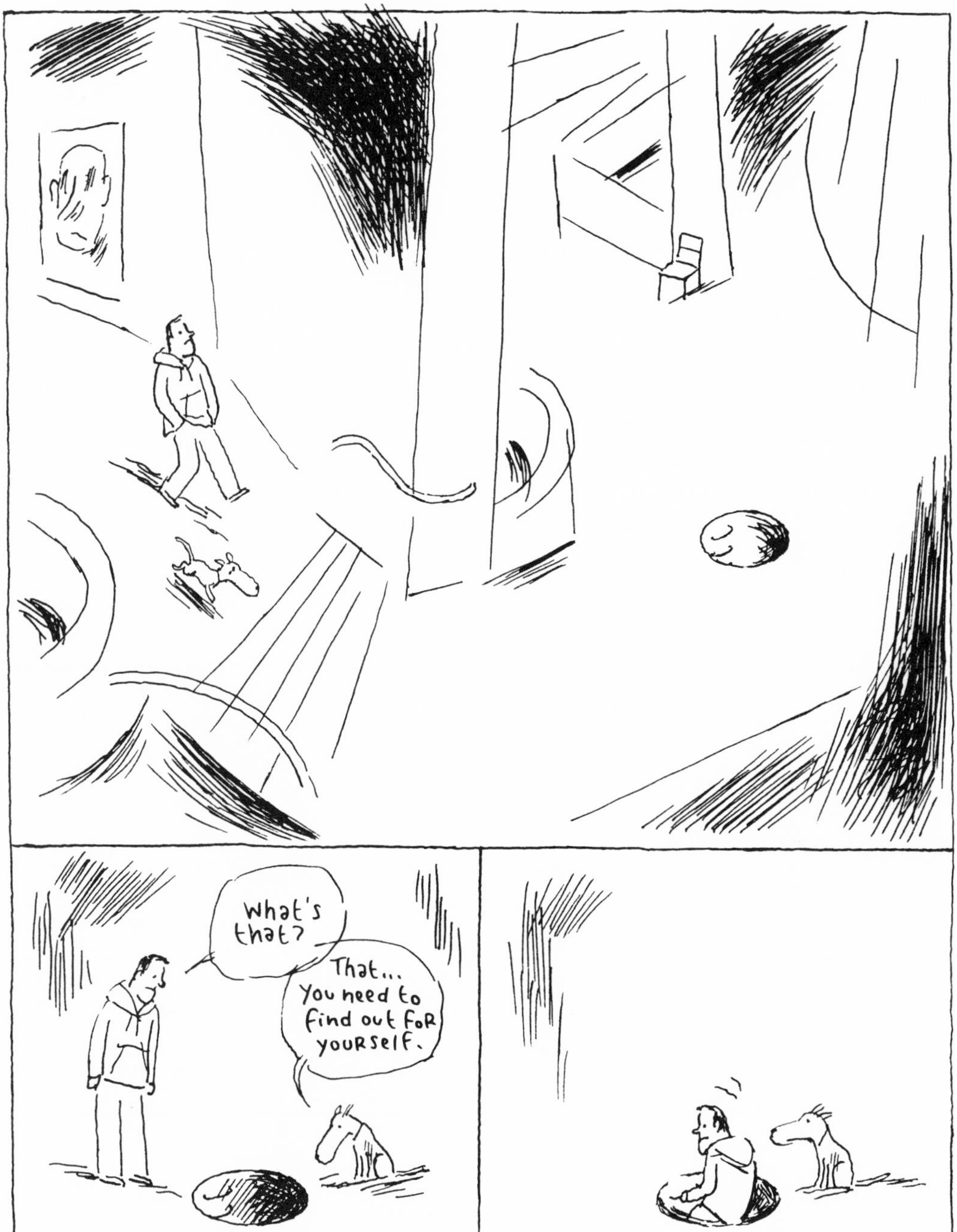
What's that?
That... You need to find out for yourself.

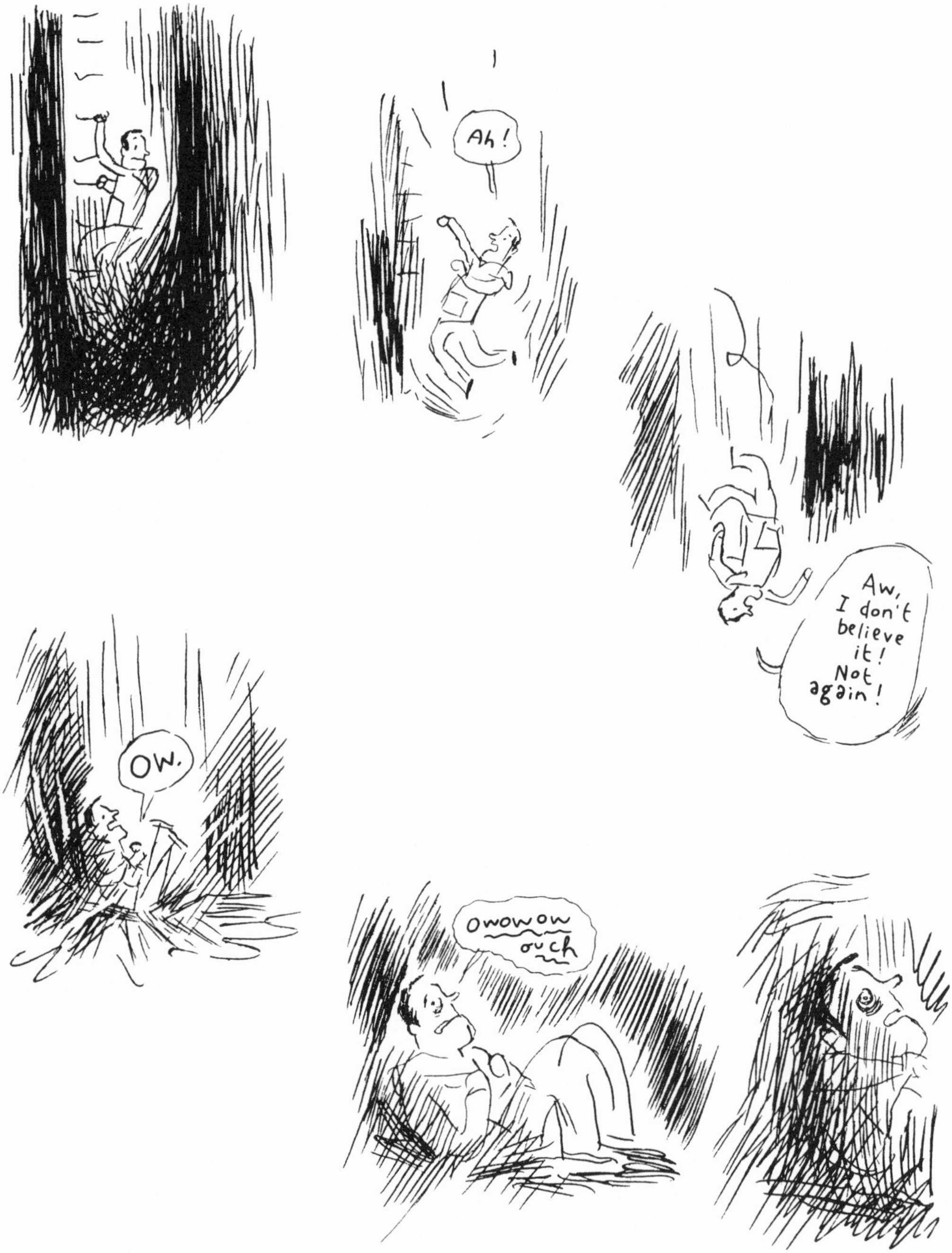
Ah!
Aw, I don't believe it! Not again!
OW.
owowow ouch

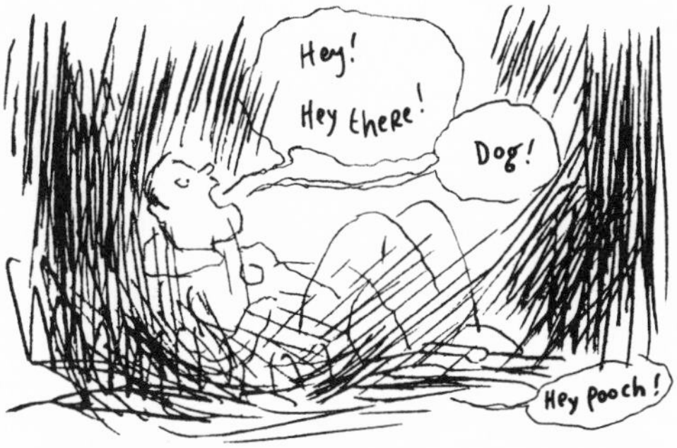
Hey!
Hey there!
Dog!
Hey pooch!

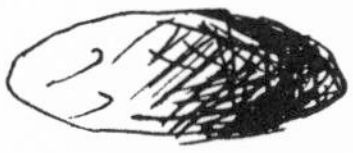

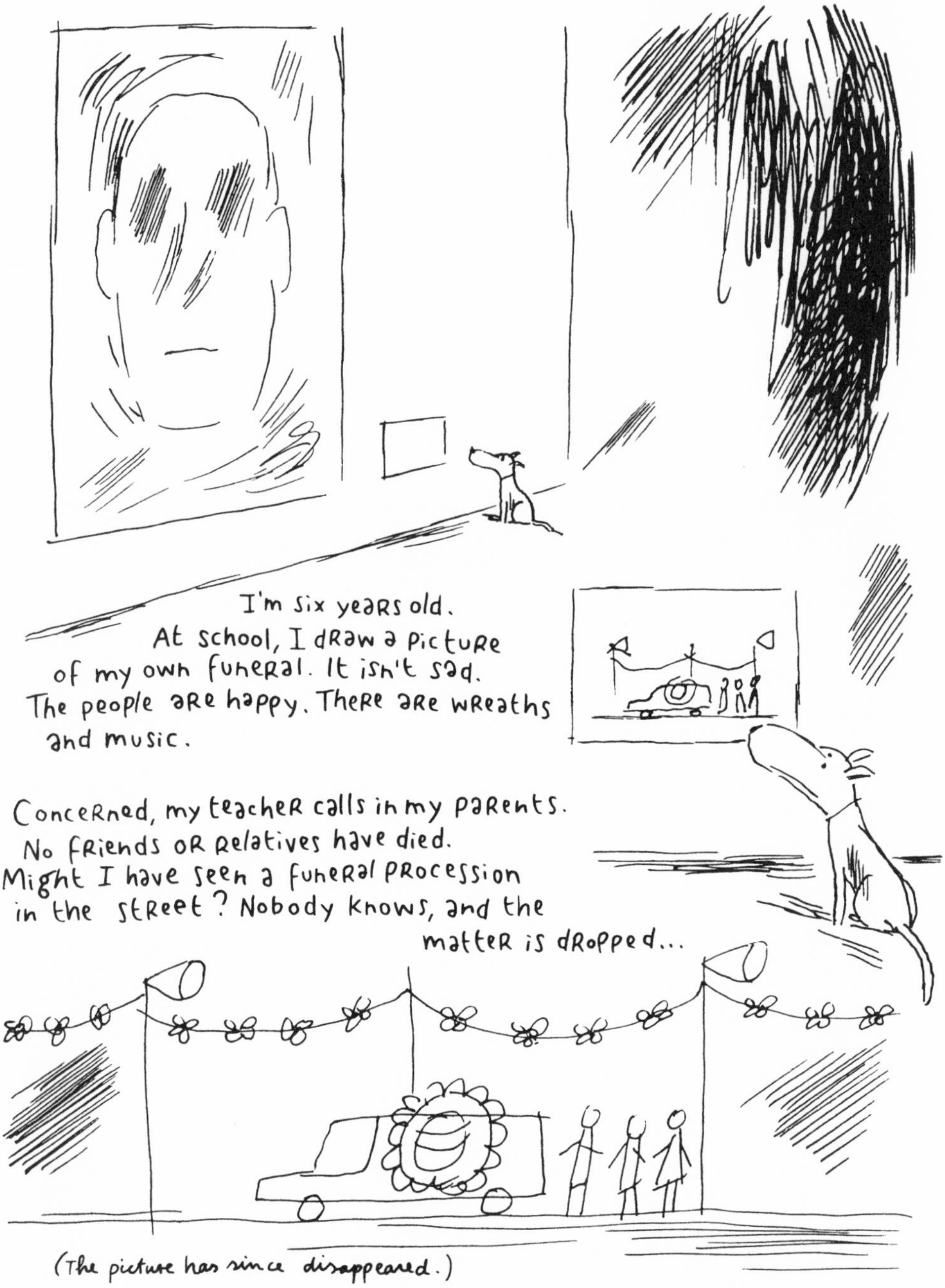
I'm six years old.
At school, I draw a picture of my own funeral. It isn't sad.
The people are happy. There are wreaths and music.
Concerned, my teacher calls in my parents.
No friends or relatives have died.
Might I have seen a funeral procession in the street? Nobody knows, and the matter is dropped...
(The picture has since disappeared.)

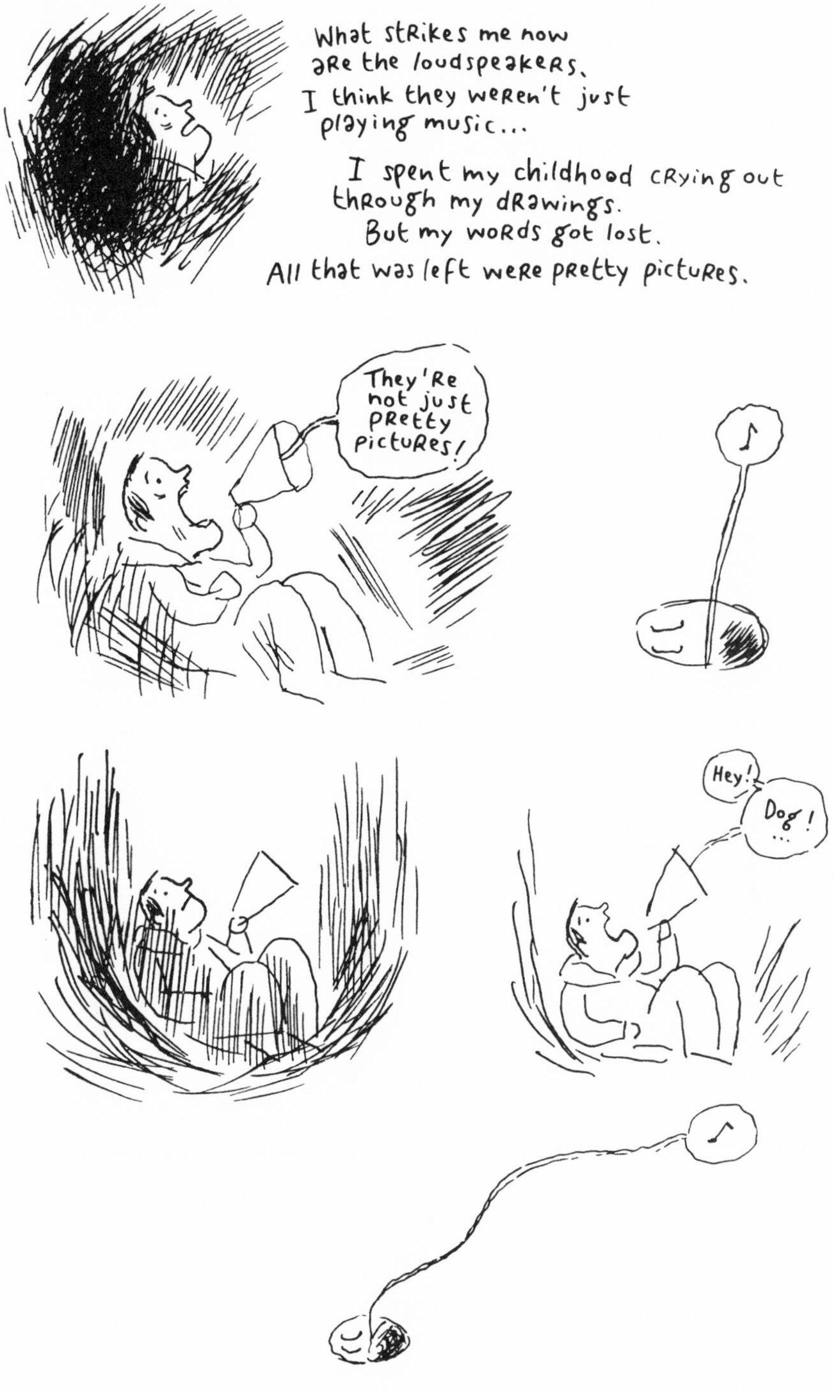
What strikes me now are the loudspeakers. I think they weren't just playing music...
I spent my childhood crying out through my drawings.
But my words got lost.
All that was left were pretty pictures.
They're not just pretty pictures!
Hey!
Dog! ...

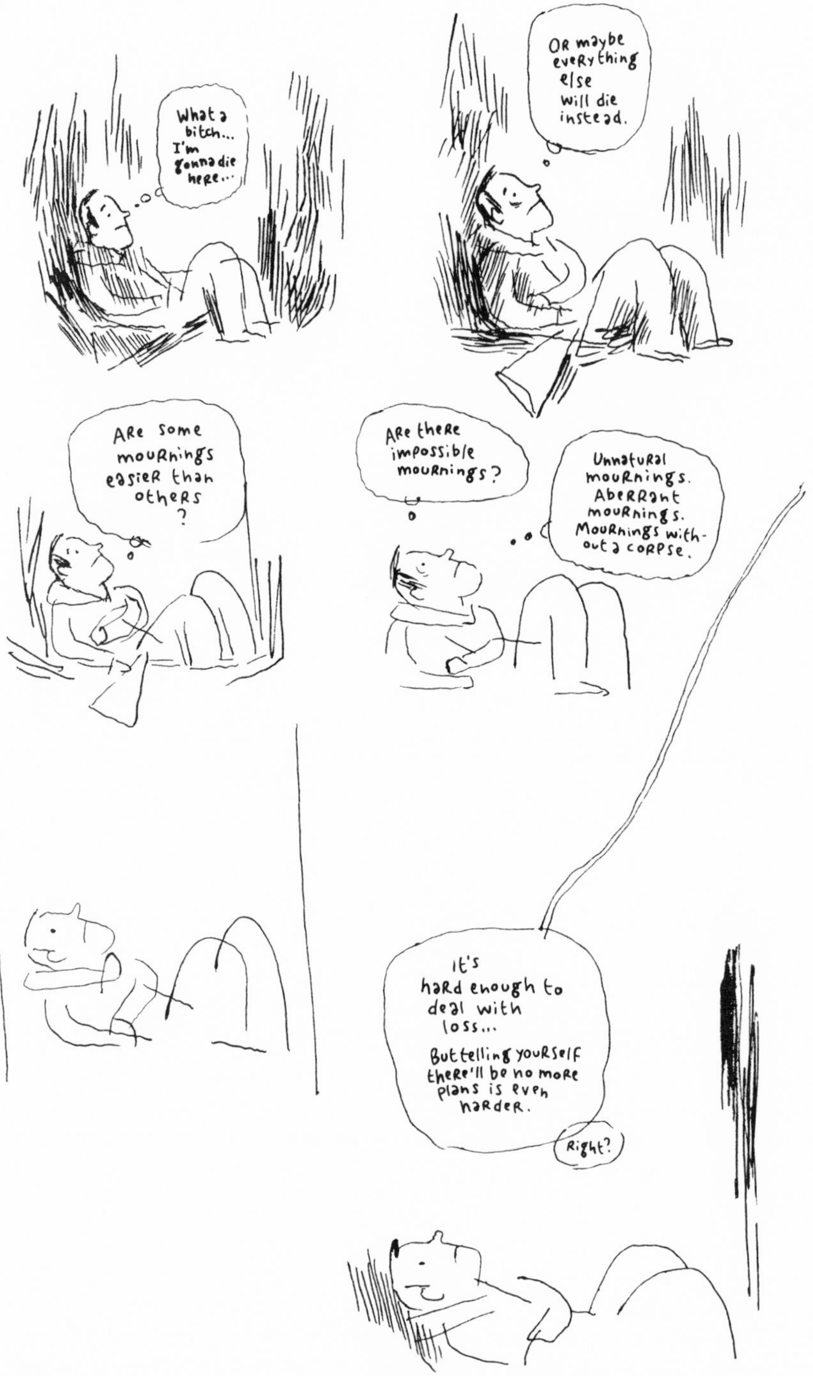
What a bitch... I'm gonna die here...
Or maybe everything else will die instead.
Are some mournings easier than others?
Are there impossible mournings?
Unnatural mournings. Aberrant mournings. Mournings without a corpse.
It's hard enough to deal with loss...
But telling yourself there'll be no more plans is even harder.
Right?

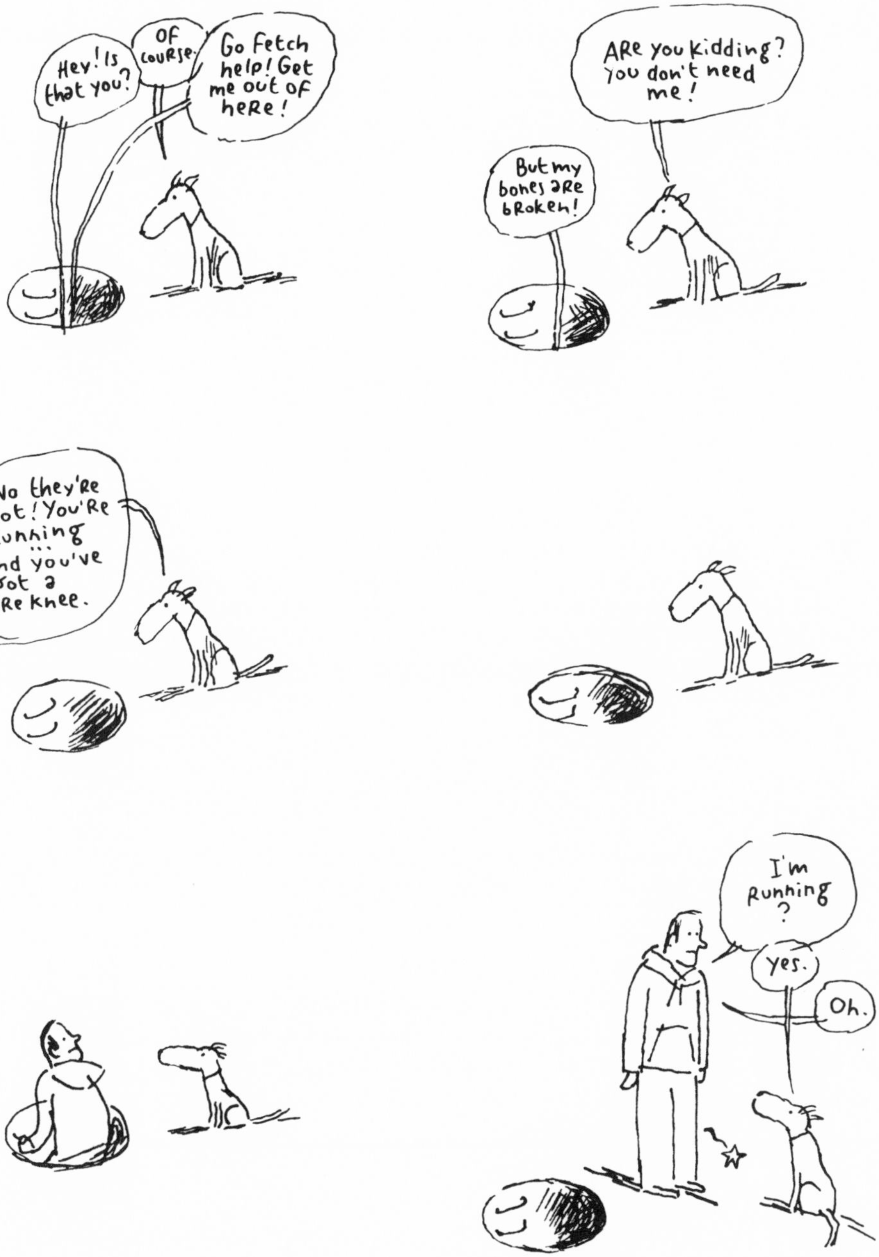
Hey! Is that you?
Of course.
Go fetch help! Get me out of here!
Are you kidding? You don't need me!
But my bones are broken!
No they're not! You're running ... and you've got a sore knee.
I'm running?
Yes.
Oh.

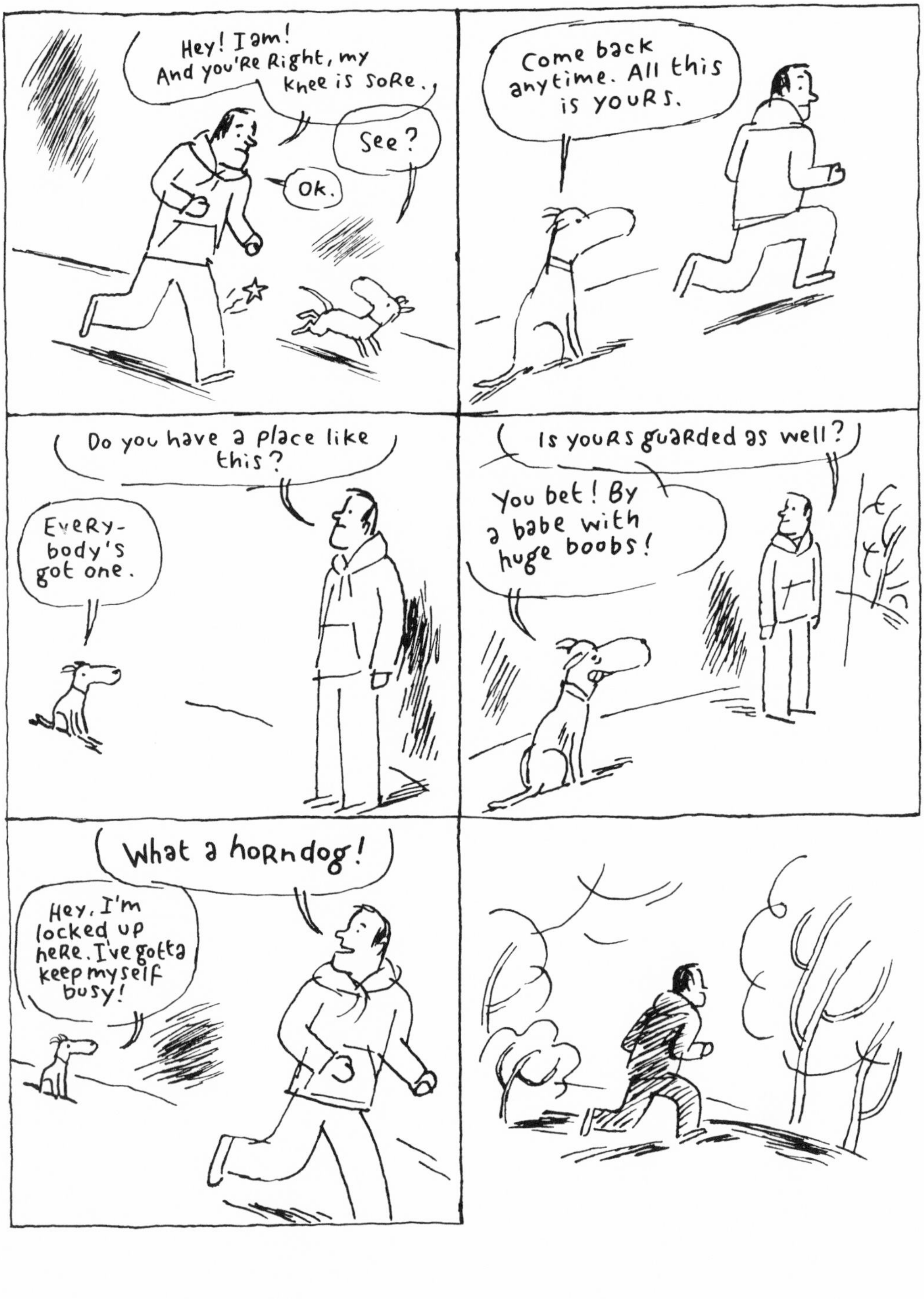
Hey! I am! And you're Right, my knee is sore.
See?
Ok.
Come back anytime. All this is yours.
Do you have a place like this?
Every-body's got one.
Is yours guarded as well?
You bet! By a babe with huge boobs!
What a horndog!
Hey, I'm locked up here. I've gotta keep myself busy!

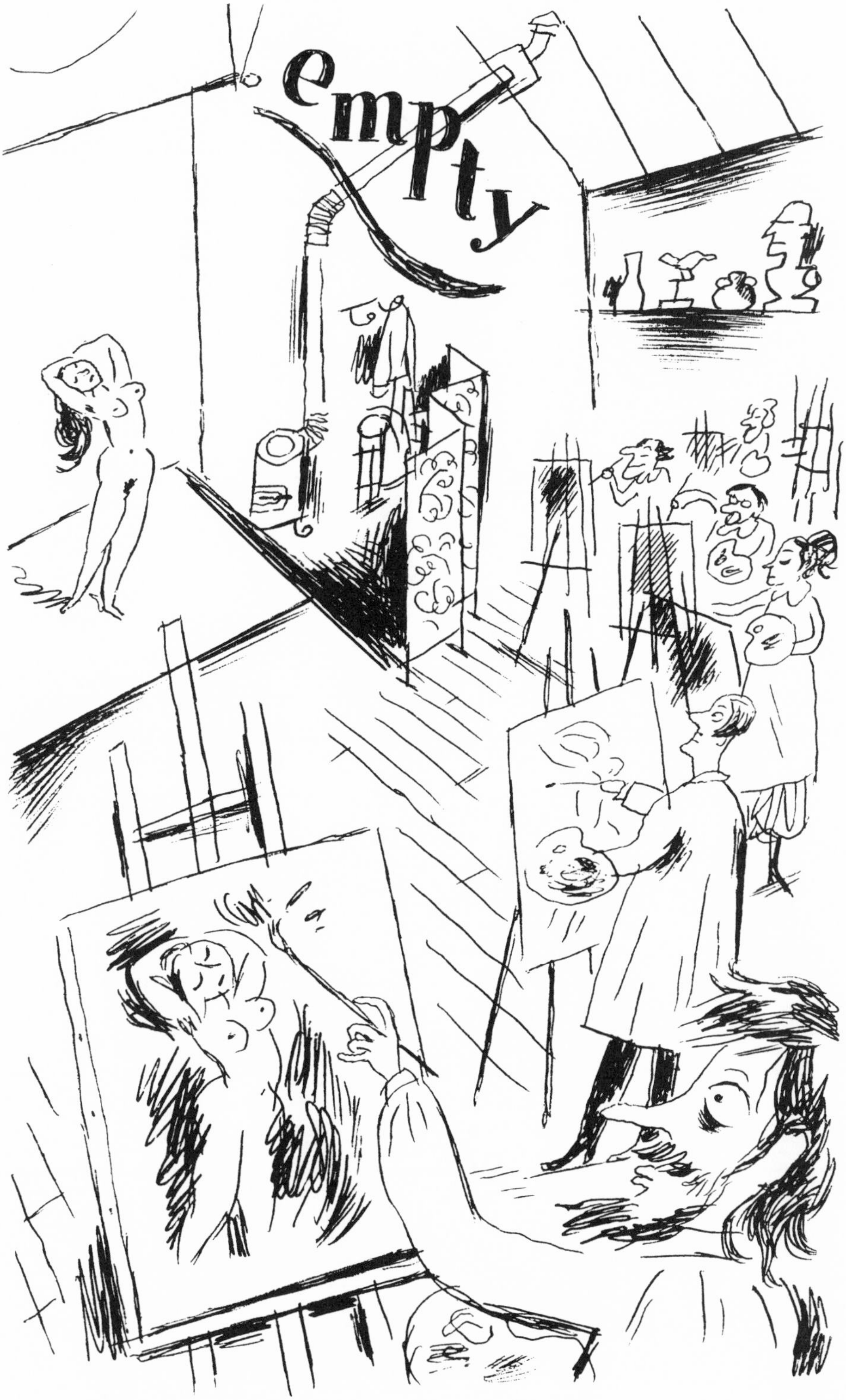
empty

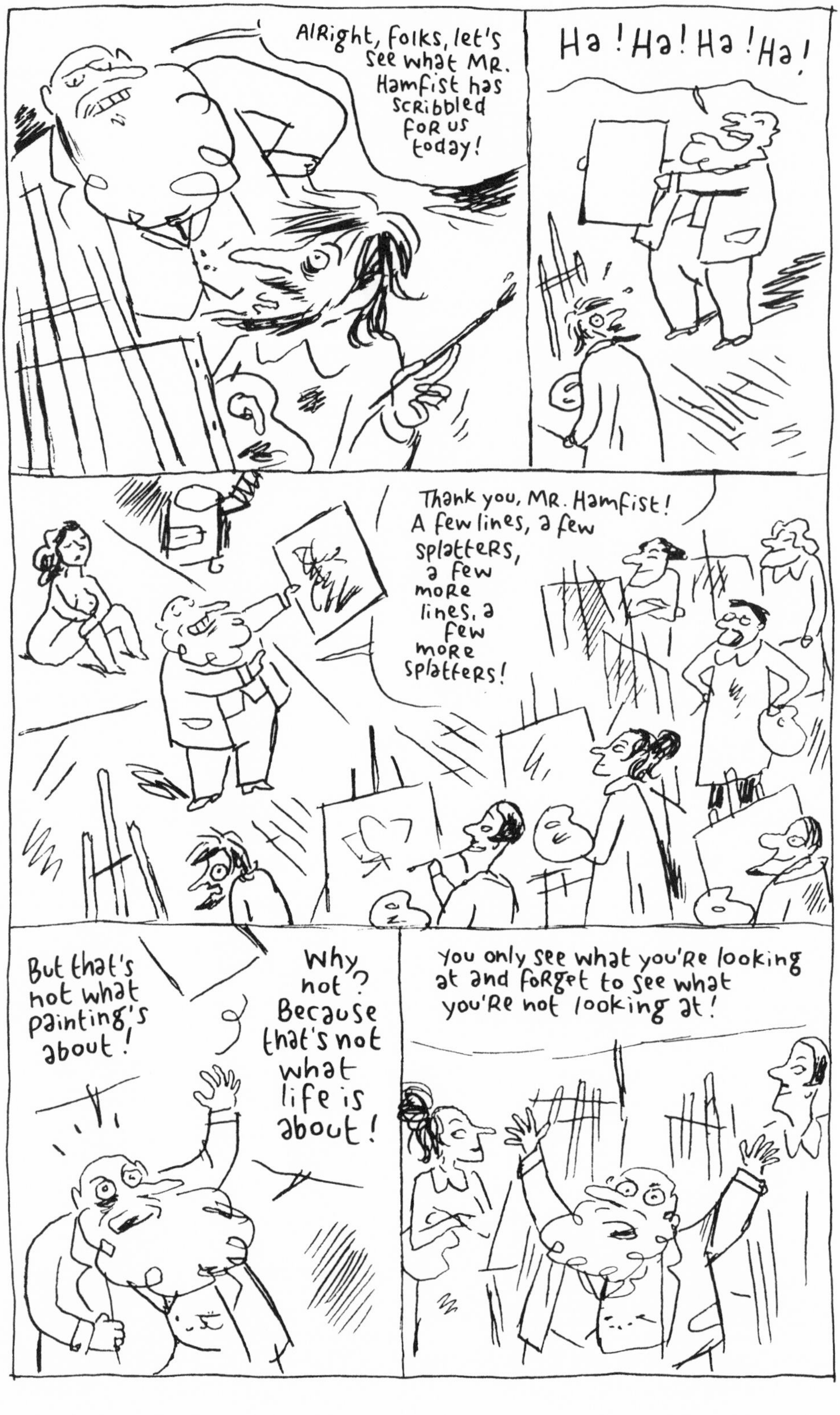

Alright, folks, let's see what Mr. Hamfist has scribbled for us today!
Ha! Ha! Ha! Ha!
Thank you, Mr. Hamfist! A few lines, a few splatters, a few more lines, a few more splatters!
But that's not what painting's about!
Why not? Because that's not what life is about!
You only see what you're looking at and forget to see what you're not looking at!

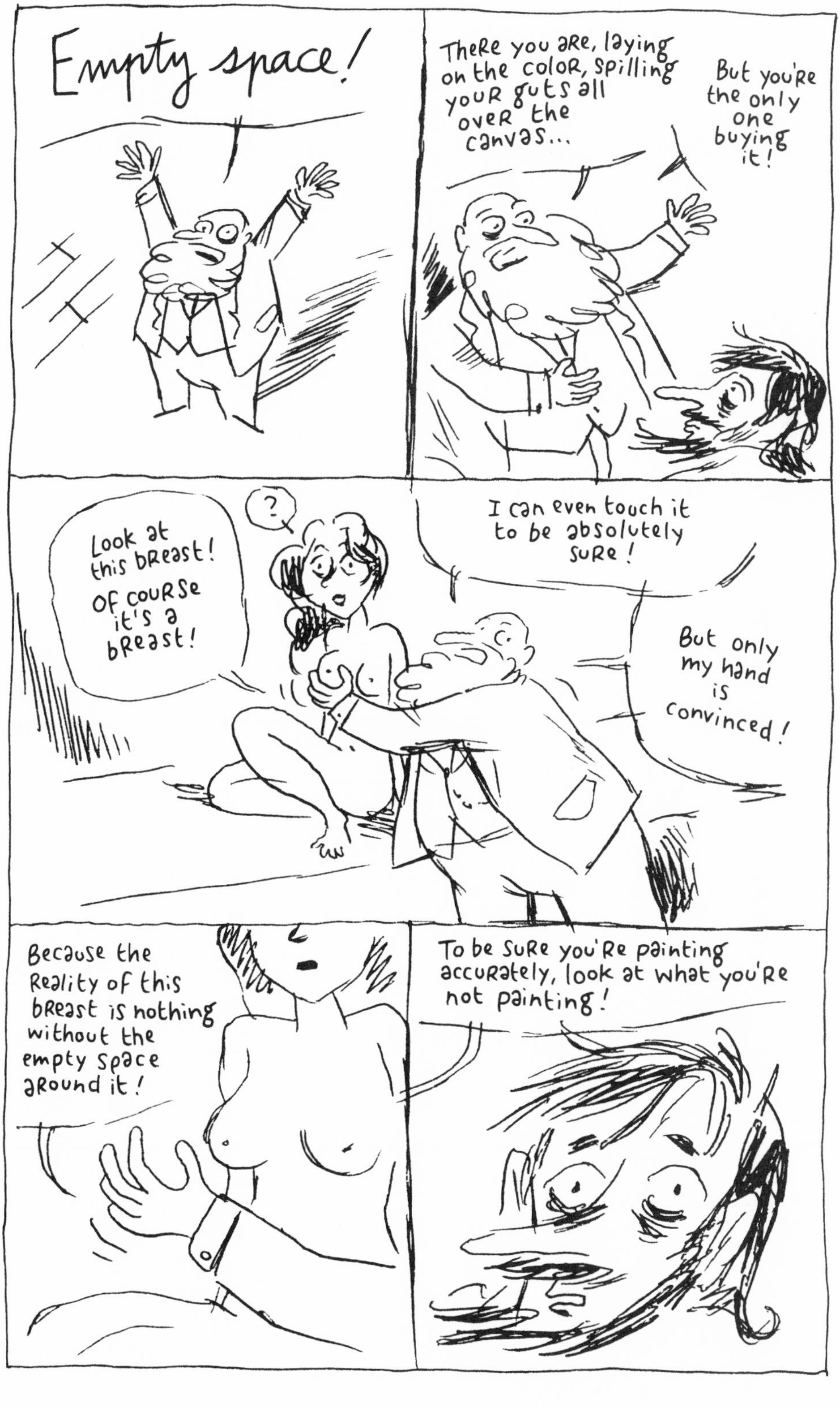
Empty space!
There you are, laying on the color, spilling your guts all over the canvas...
But you're the only one buying it!
Look at this breast! Of course it's a breast!
?
I can even touch it to be absolutely sure!
But only my hand is convinced!
Because the reality of this breast is nothing without the empty space around it!
To be sure you're painting accurately, look at what you're not painting!

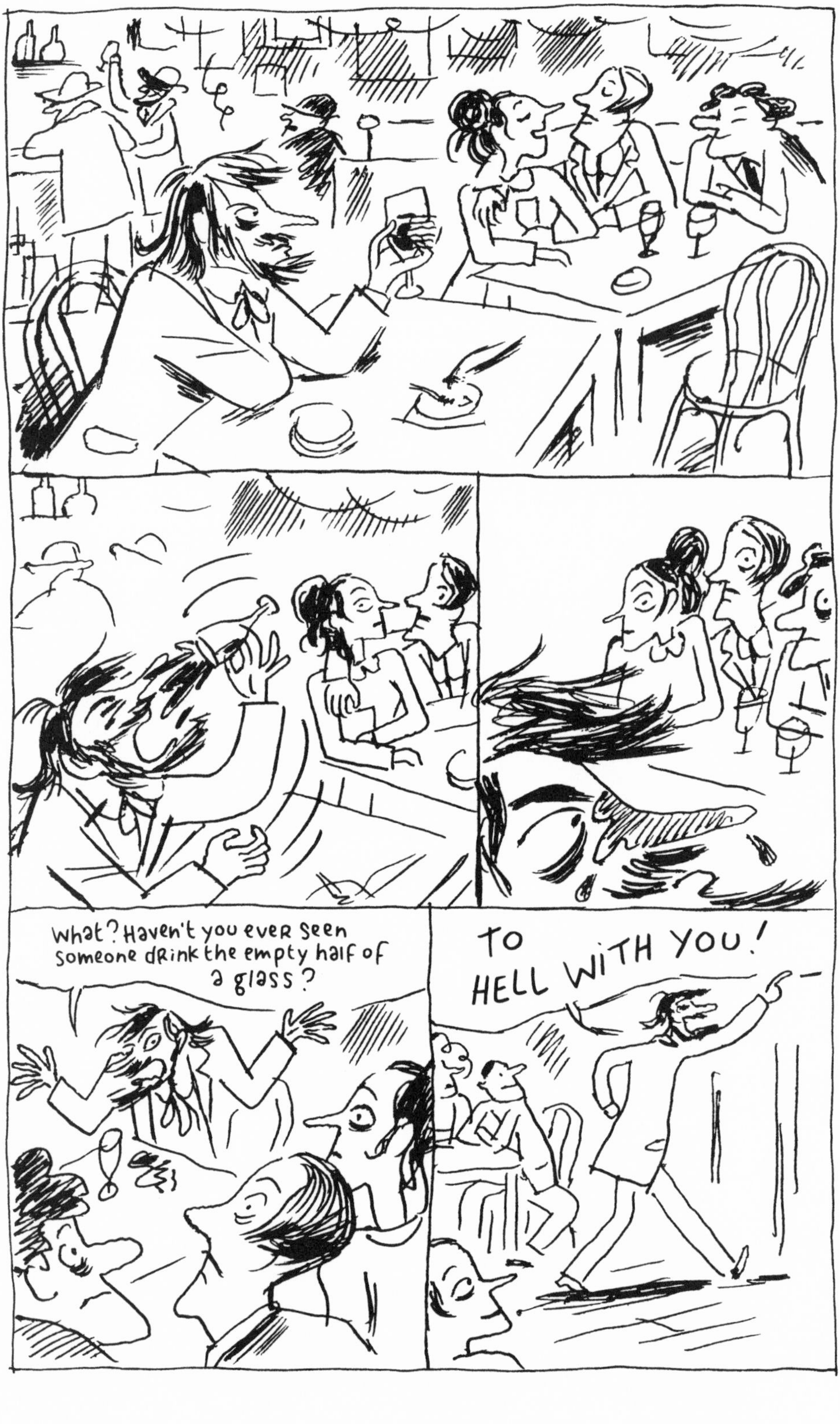
What? Haven't you ever seen someone drink the empty half of a glass?
TO HELL WITH YOU!

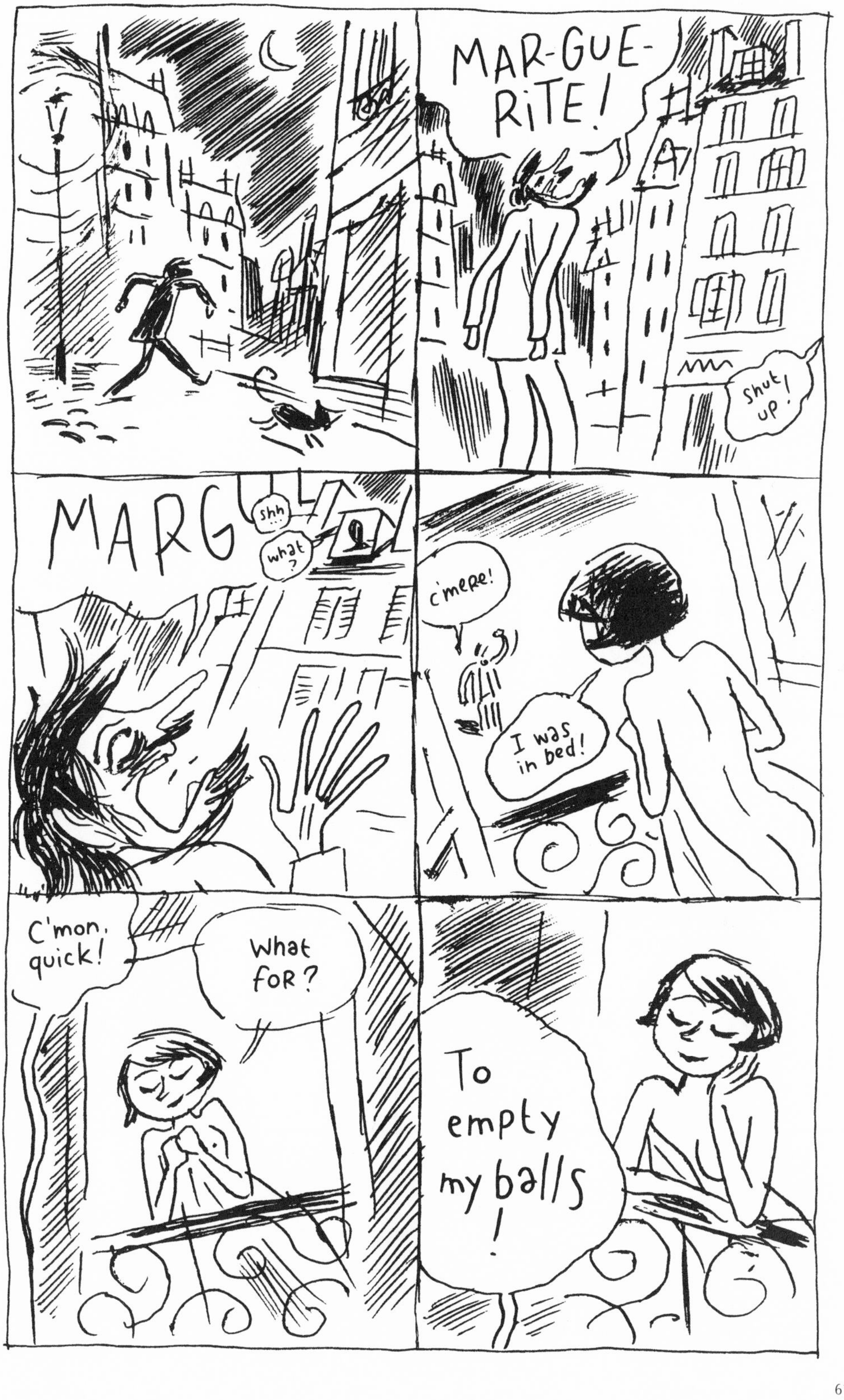
MAR-GUE-RITE!
Shut up!
MARG
shh...
what?
c'mere!
I was in bed!
C'mon, quick!
What for?
To empty my balls!

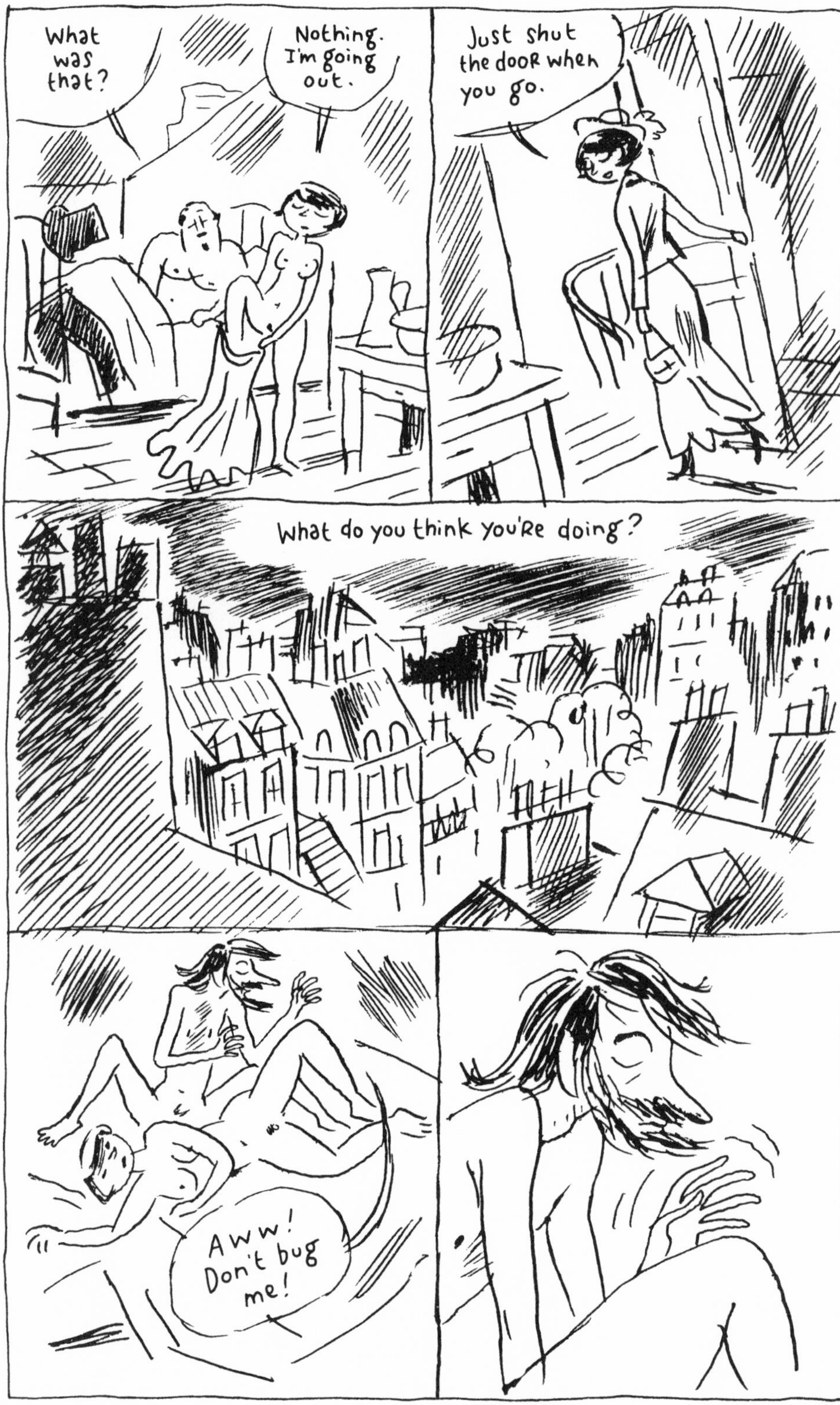
What was that?
Nothing. I'm going out.
Just shut the door when you go.
What do you think you're doing?
Aww! Don't bug me!

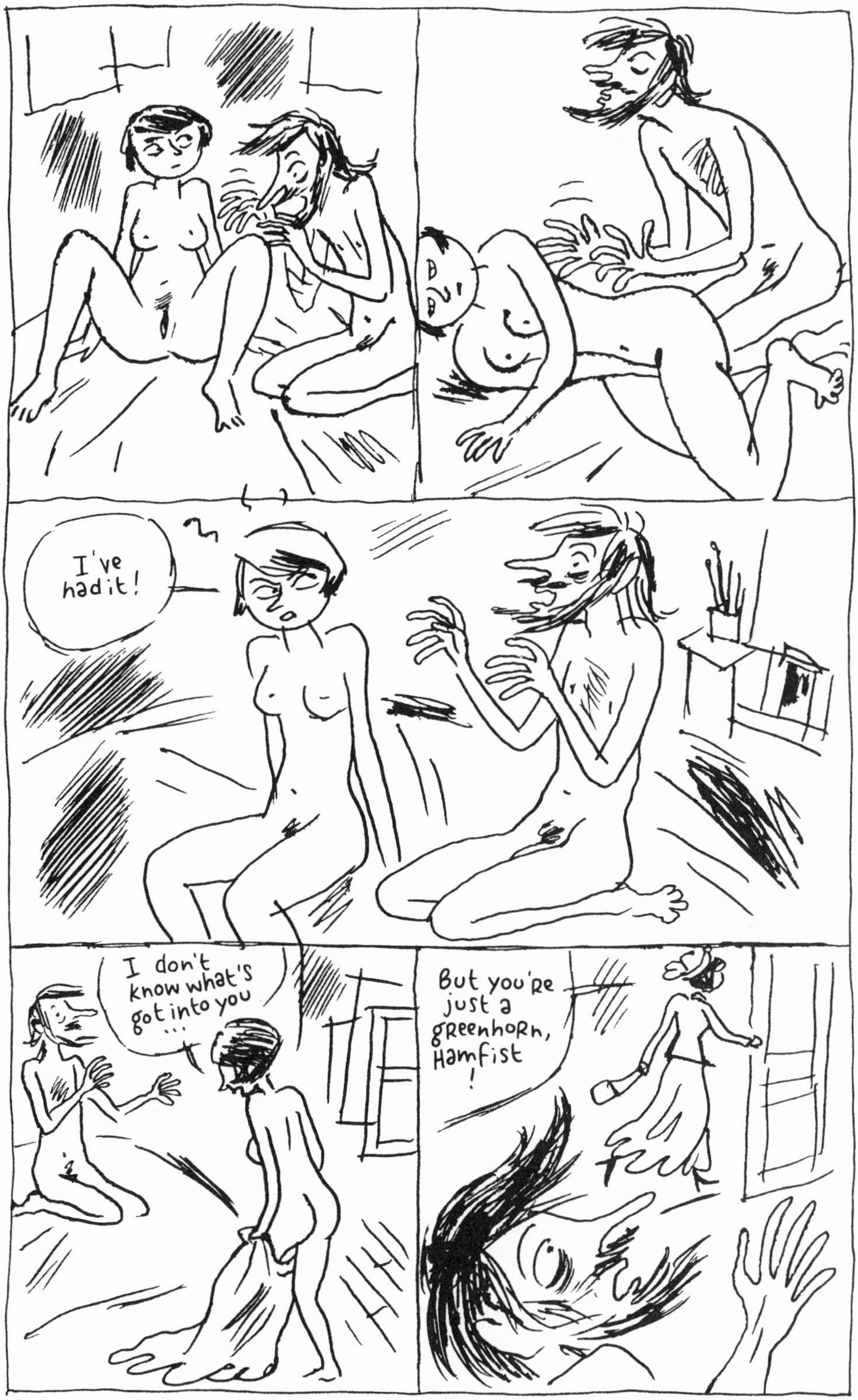
I've had it!
I don't know what's got into you ...
But you're just a greenhorn, Hamfist!

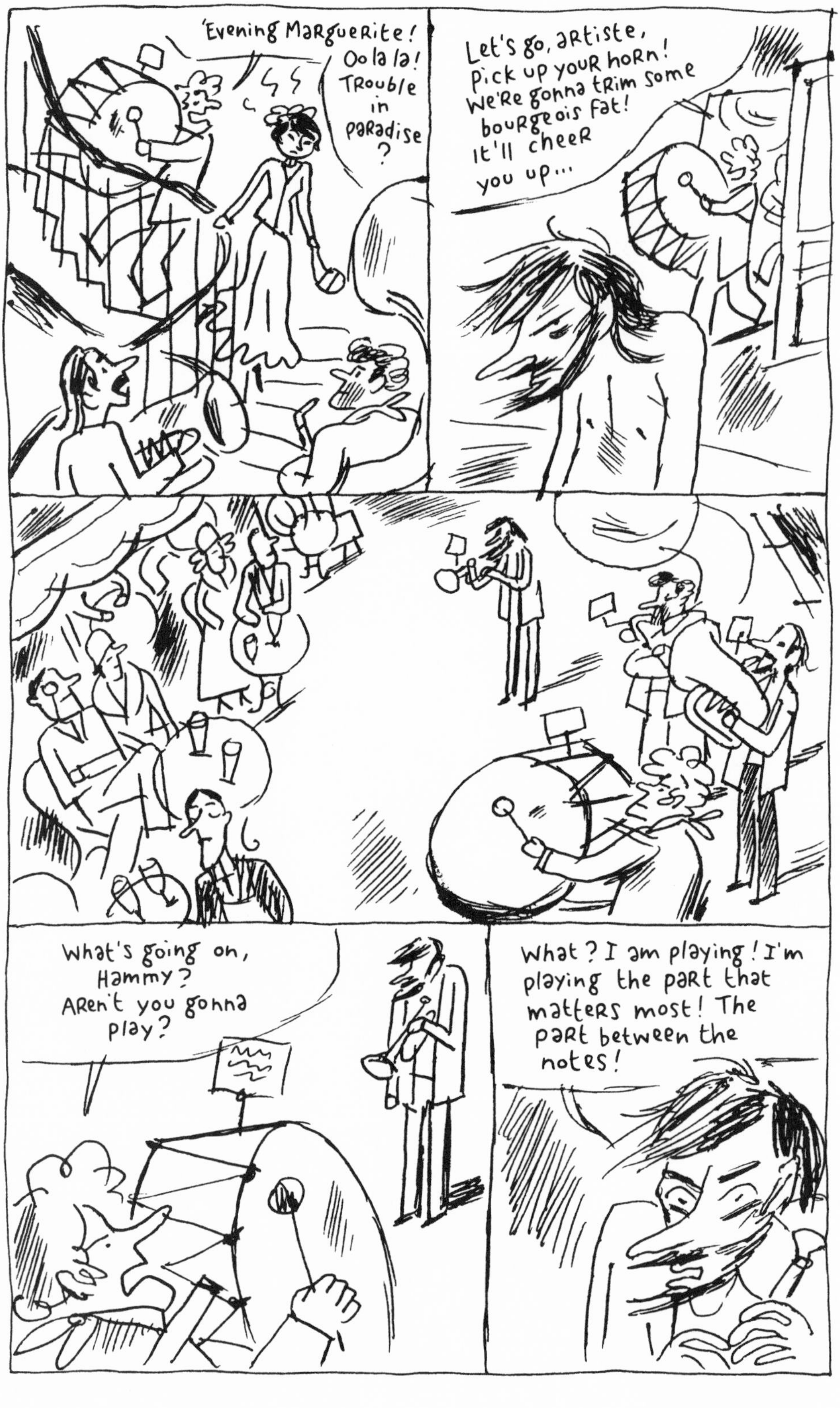
'Evening Marguerite!
Oo la la! Trouble in paradise?
Let's go, artiste, pick up your horn! We're gonna trim some bourgeois fat! It'll cheer you up...
What's going on, Hammy? Aren't you gonna play?
What? I am playing! I'm playing the part that matters most! The part between the notes!

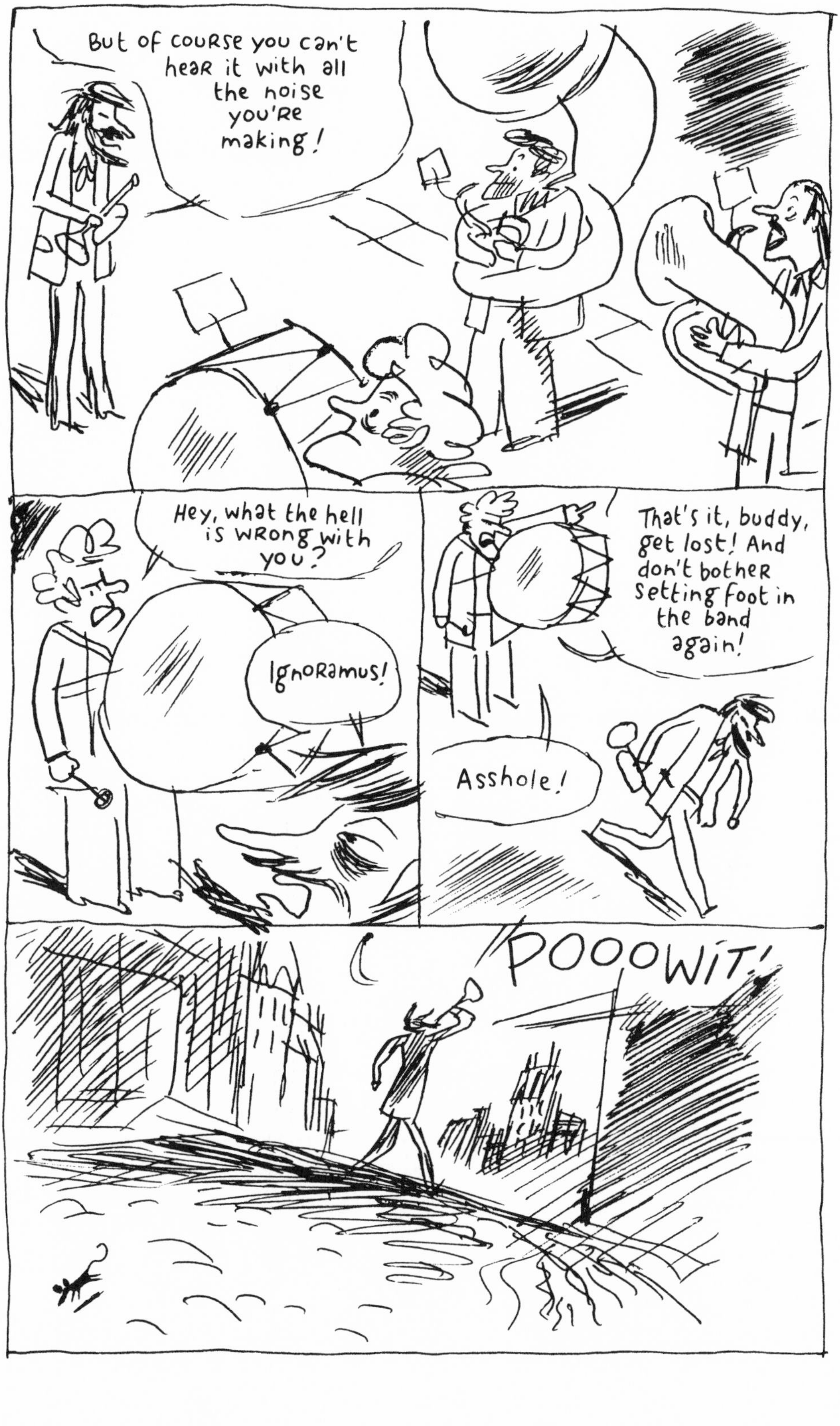
But of course you can't hear it with all the noise you're making!
Hey, what the hell is wrong with you?
Ignoramus!
That's it, buddy, get lost! And don't bother setting foot in the band again!
Asshole!
POOOWIT!

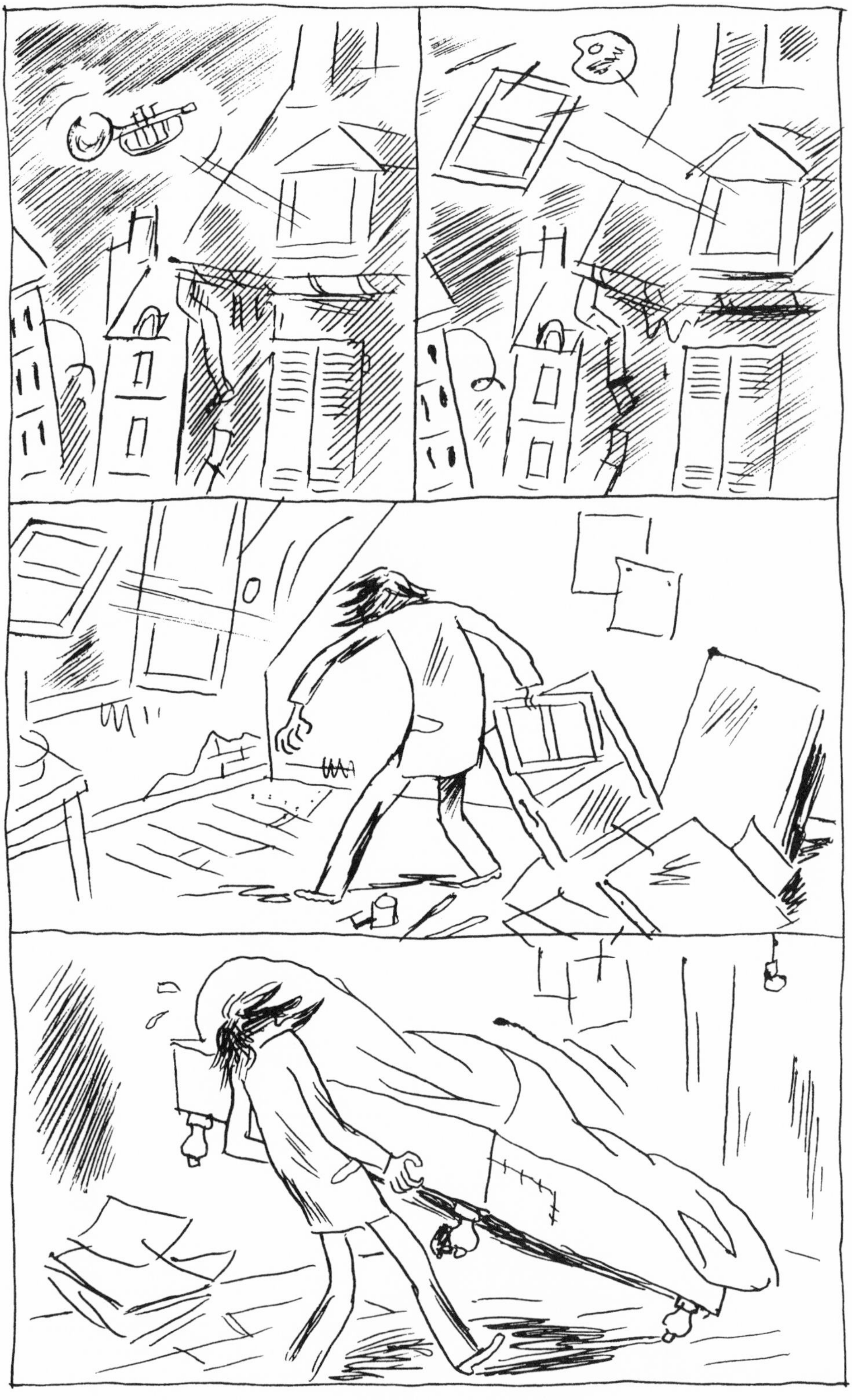

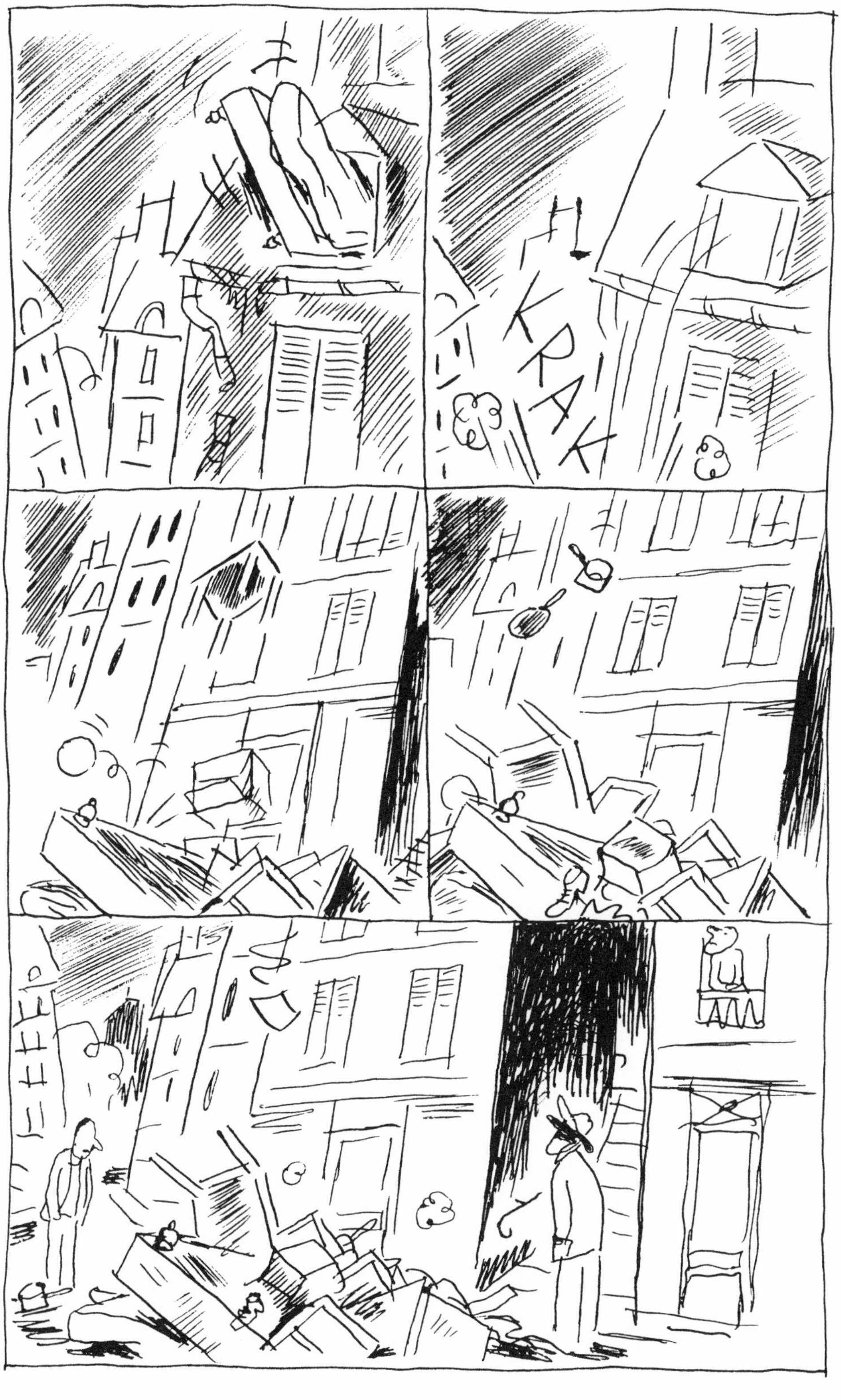
KRAK

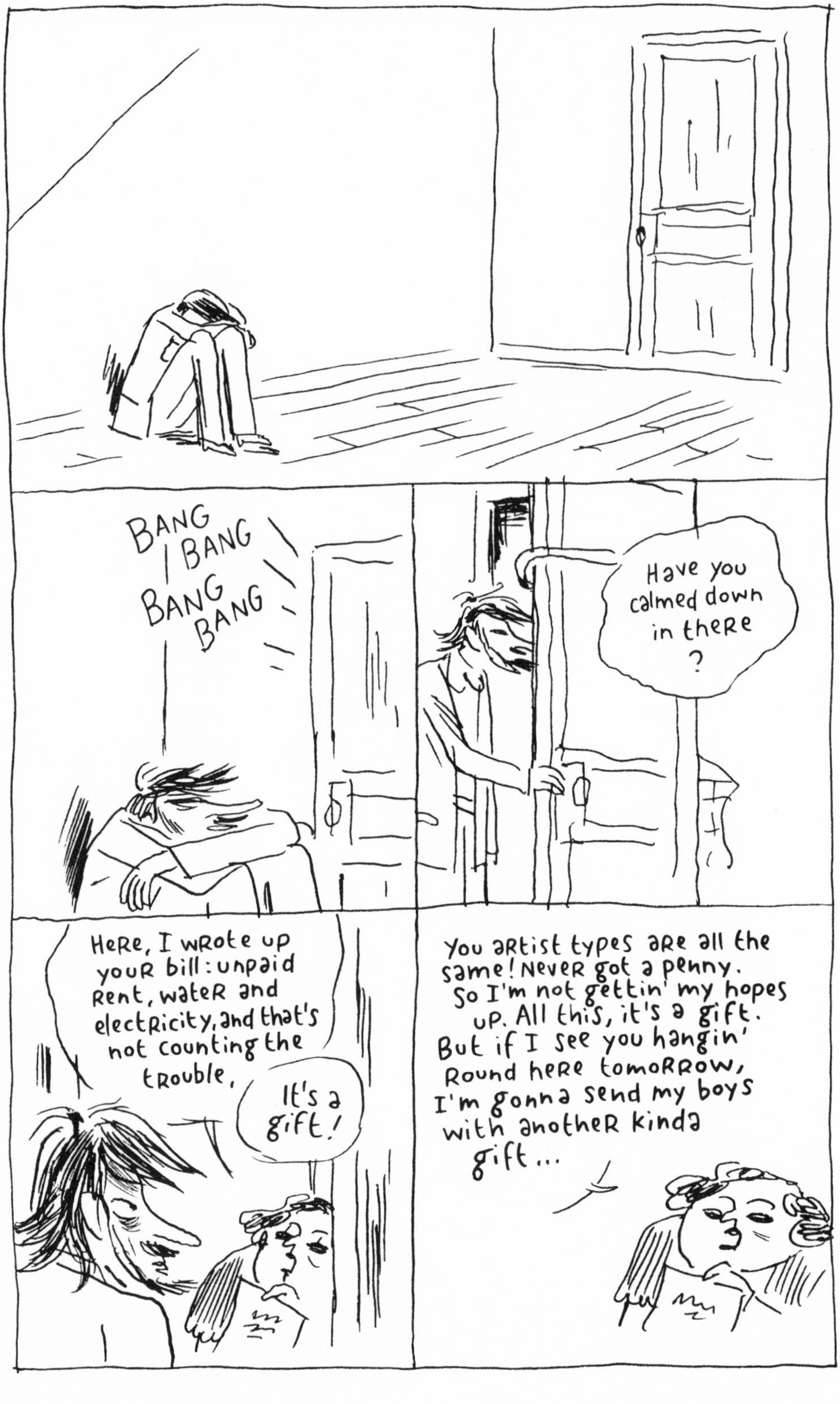
BANG BANG BANG BANG
Have you calmed down in there?
Here, I wrote up your bill: unpaid rent, water and electricity, and that's not counting the trouble,
It's a gift!
You artist types are all the same! Never got a penny. So I'm not gettin' my hopes up. All this, it's a gift. But if I see you hangin' round here tomorrow, I'm gonna send my boys with another kinda gift...

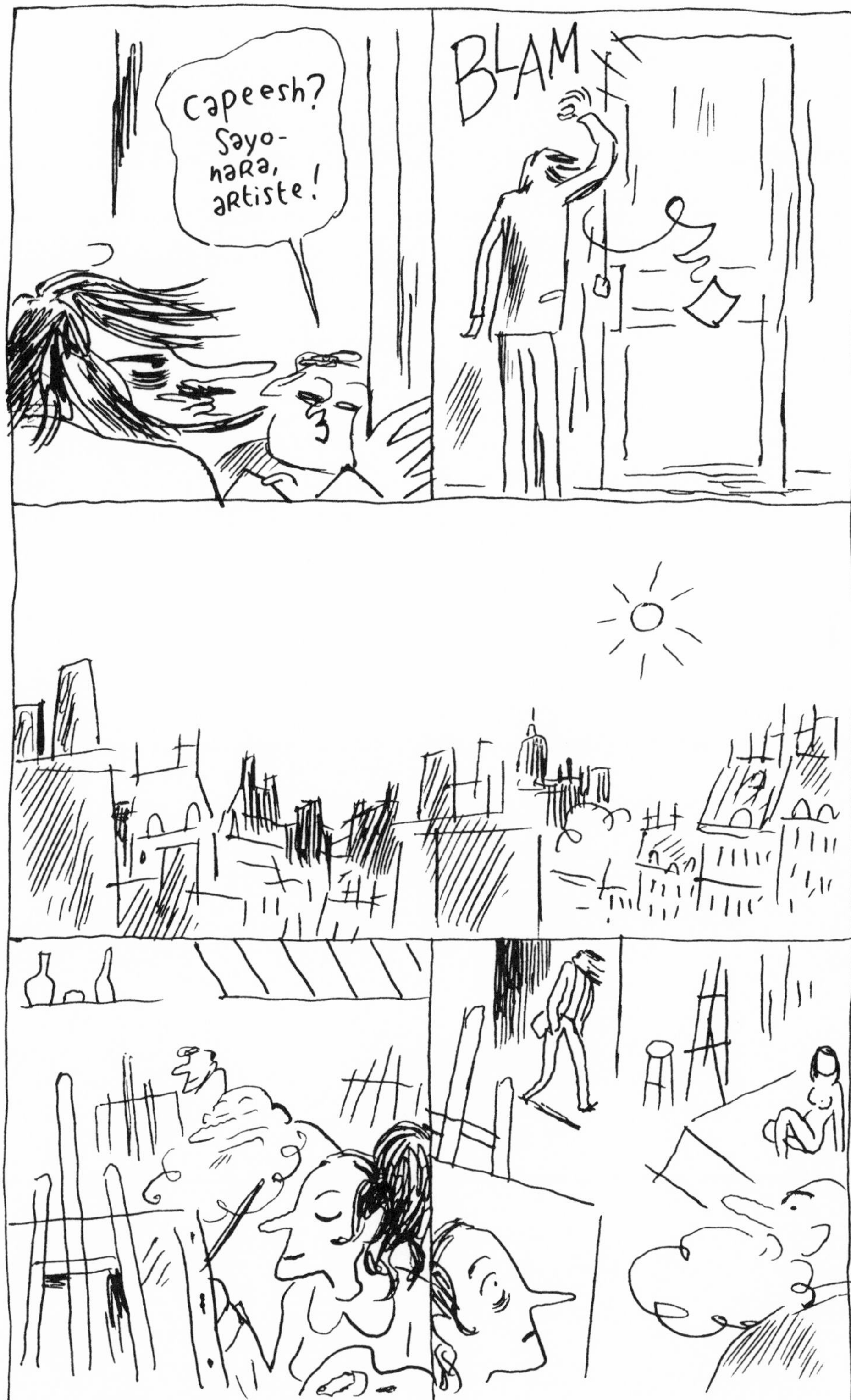
Capeesh? Sayo-nara, artiste!
BLAM

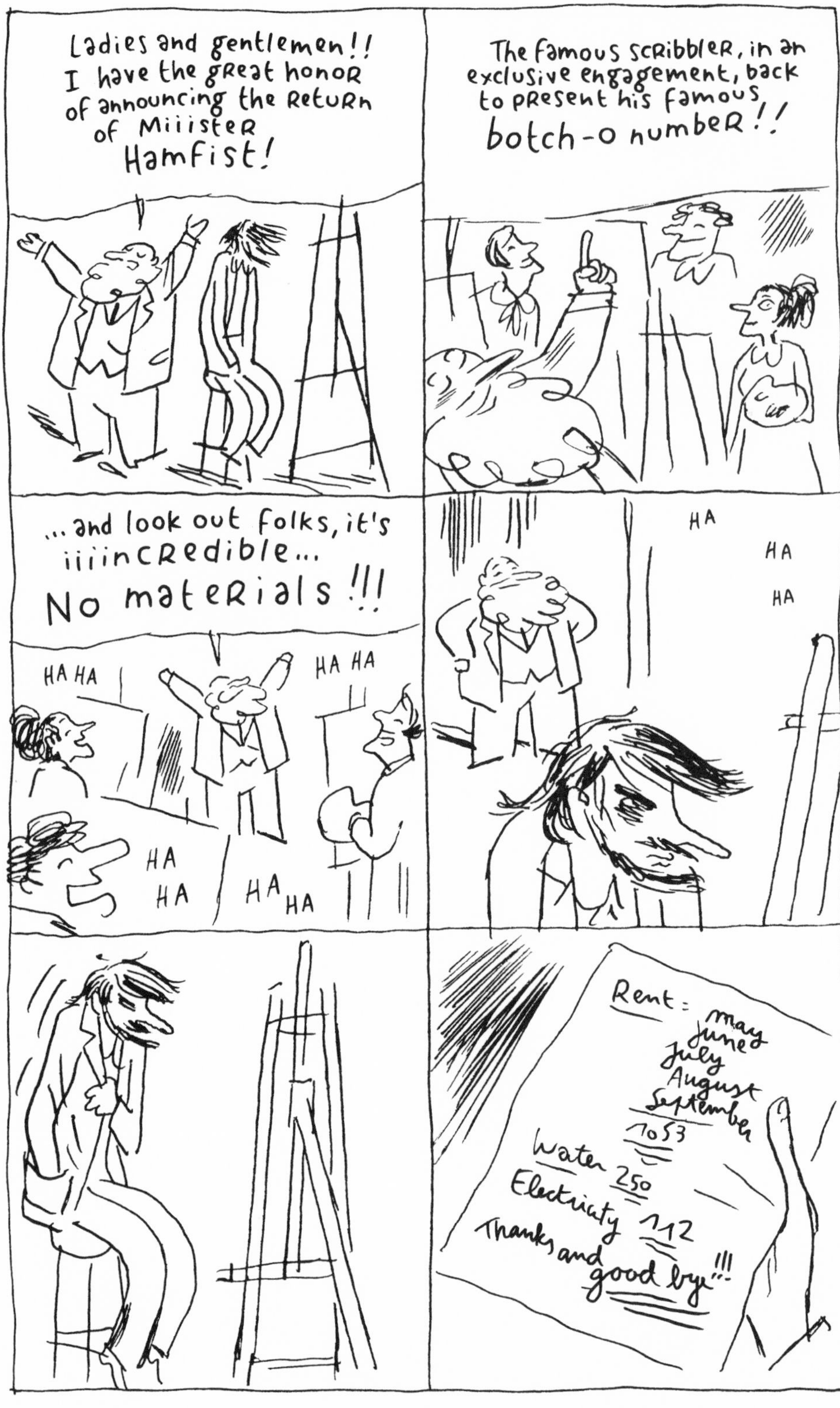
Ladies and gentlemen!! I have the great honor of announcing the Return of Miiister Hamfist!
The famous scribbler, in an exclusive engagement, back to present his famous botch-o number!!
...and look out folks, it's iiiincredible... No materials!!!
HA HA
HA HA
HA HA
HA HA
HA HA HA
Rent: may June July August September
1053
Water 250
Electricity 112
Thanks and good bye!!!

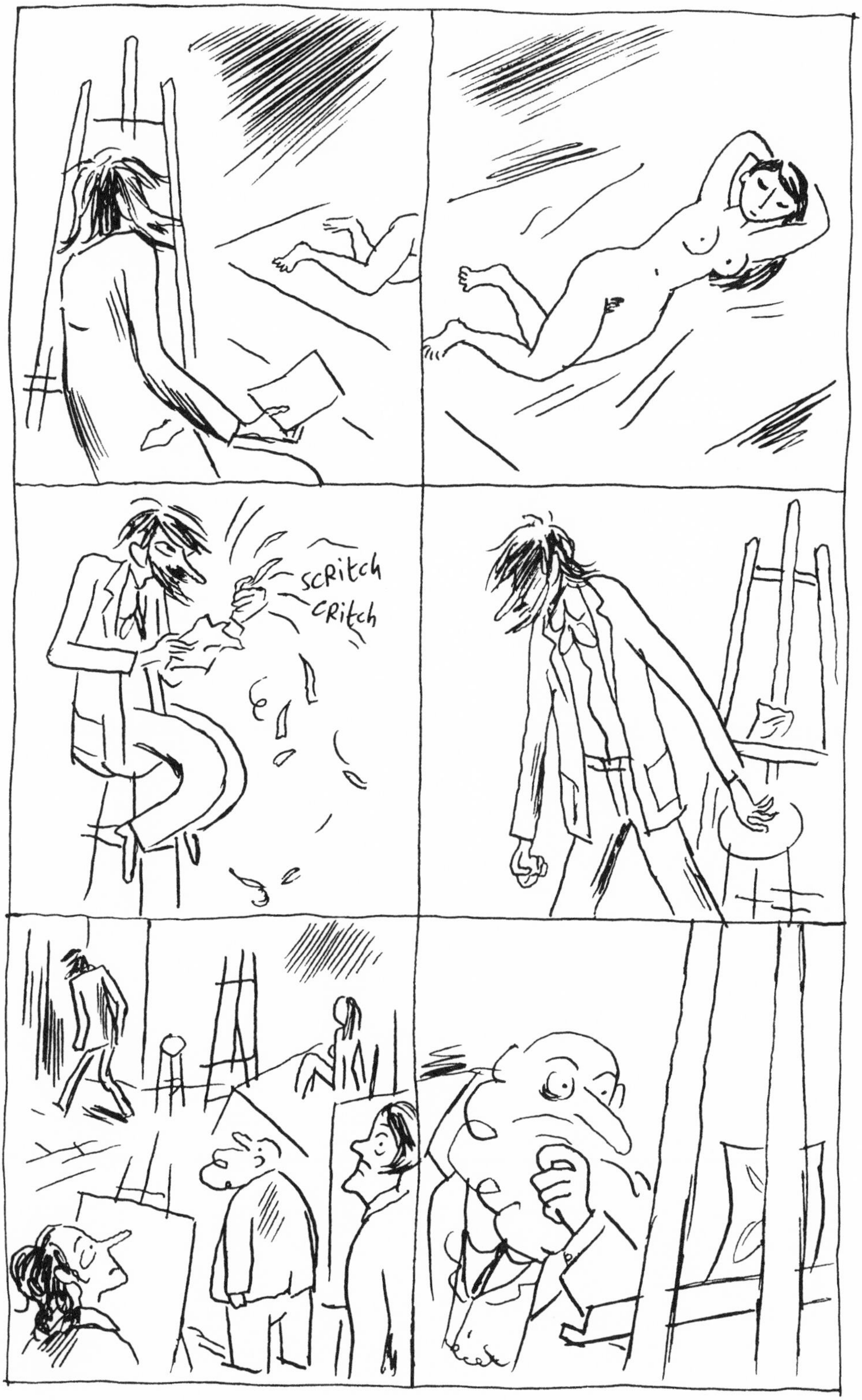
SCRITCH
CRITCH

Run Movie 4 The old lady and the turtle

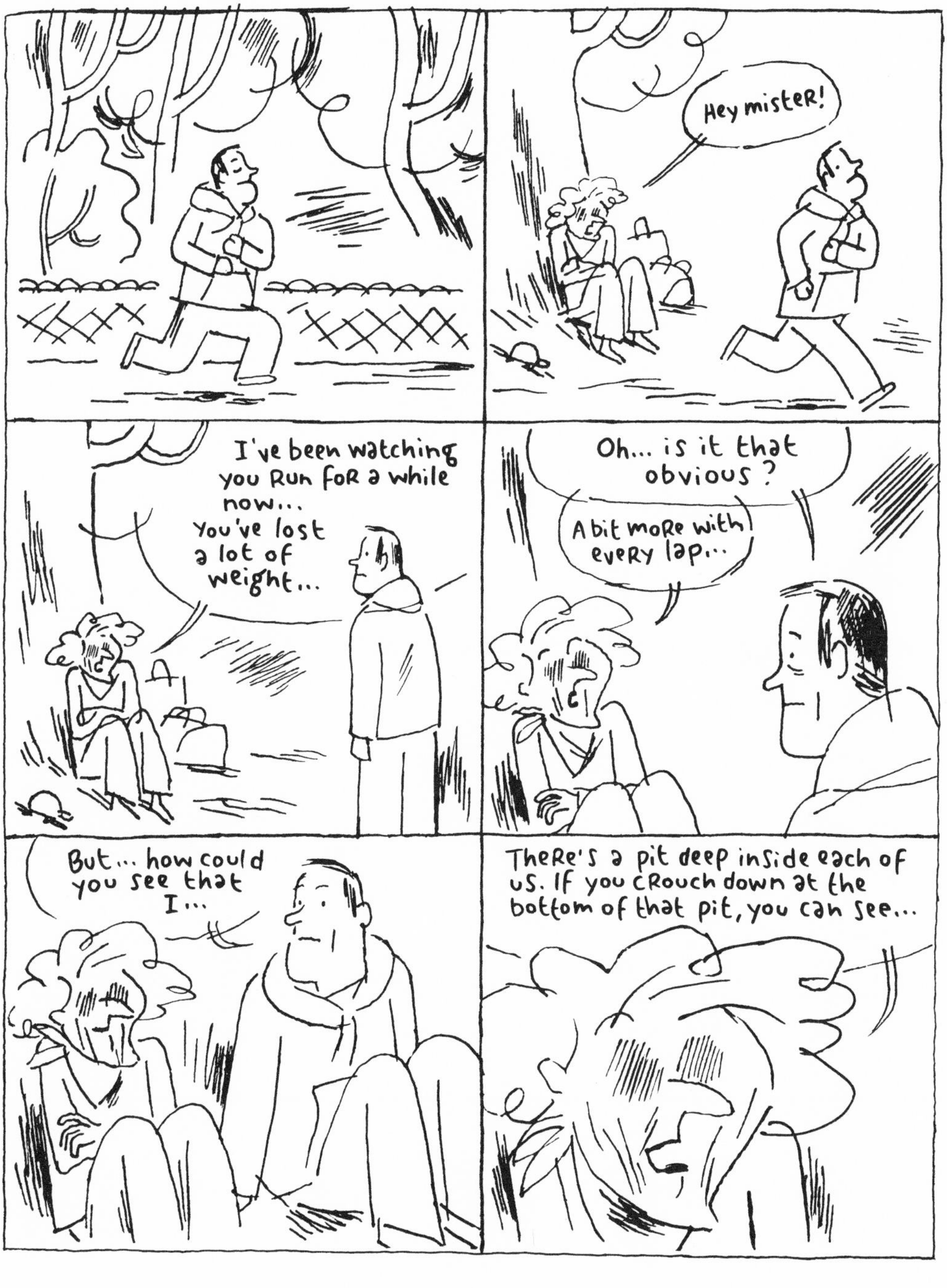
Hey mister!
I've been watching you run for a while now... You've lost a lot of weight...
Oh... is it that obvious?
A bit more with every lap...
But... how could you see that I...
There's a pit deep inside each of us. If you crouch down at the bottom of that pit, you can see...

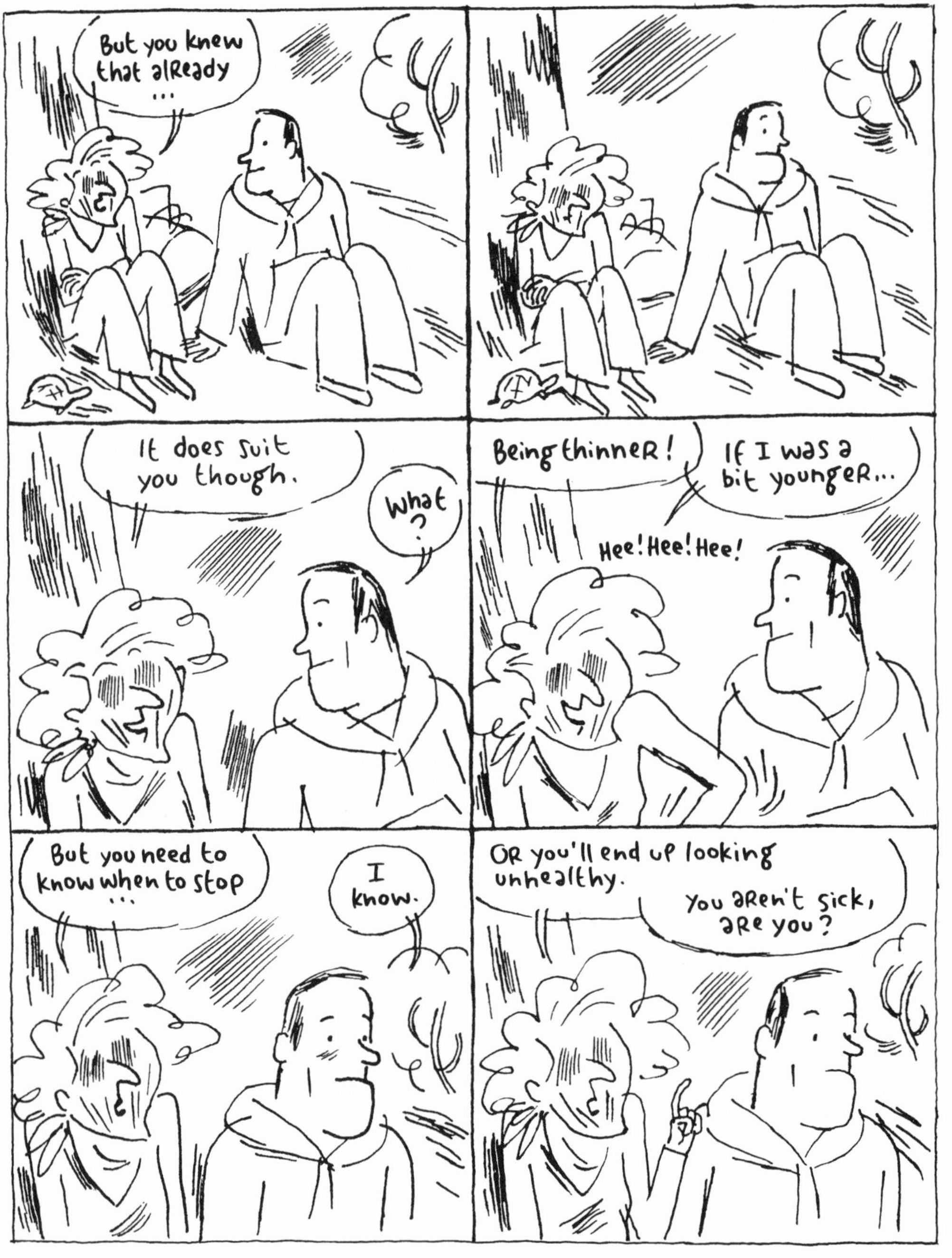
But you knew that already ...
It does suit you though.
What ?
Being thinner !
If I was a bit younger...
Hee! Hee! Hee!
But you need to know when to stop ...
I know.
Or you'll end up looking unhealthy.
You aren't sick, are you ?

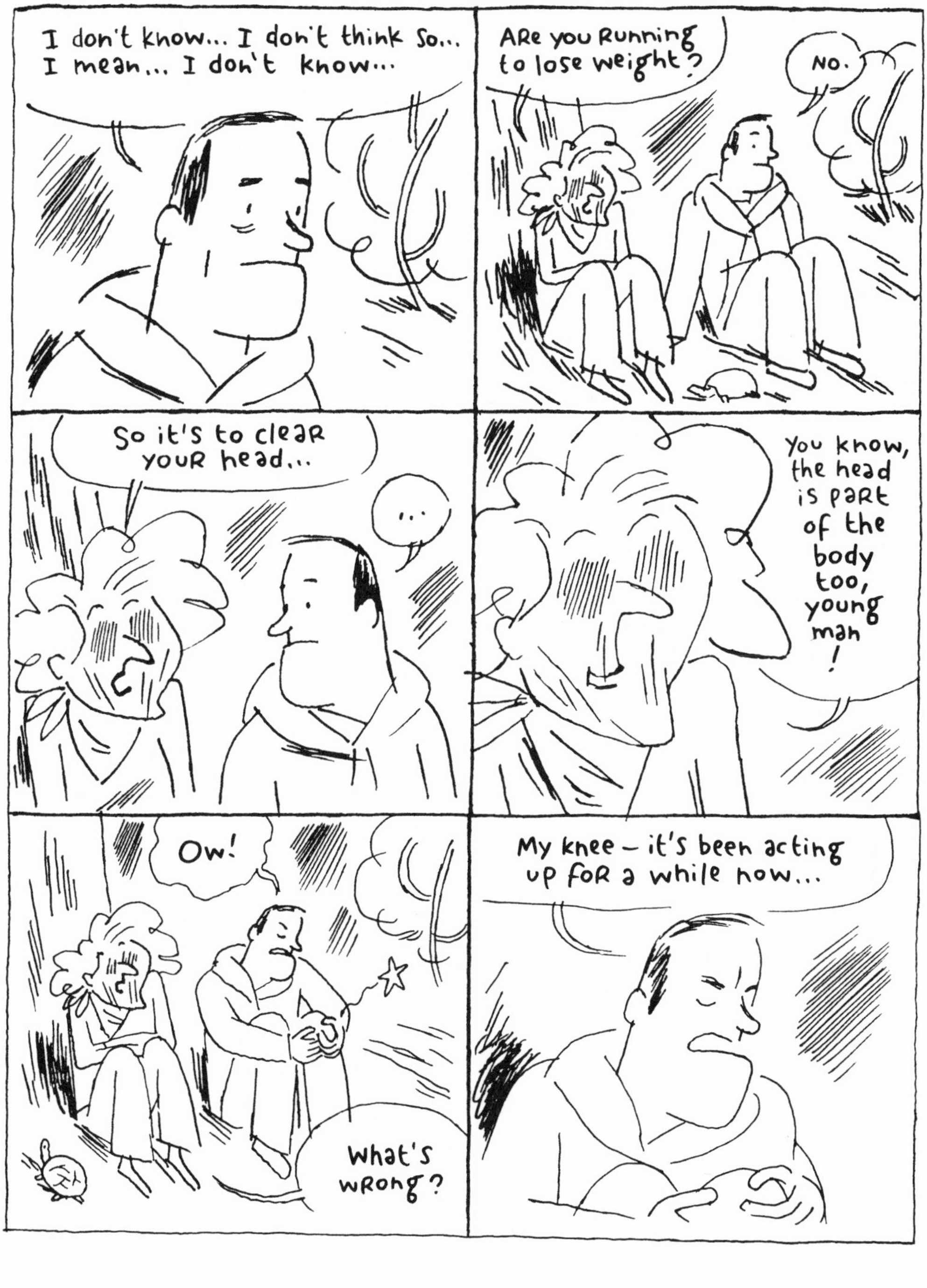
I don't know... I don't think so... I mean... I don't know...
Are you running to lose weight?
No.
So it's to clear your head...
...
You know, the head is part of the body too, young man!
Ow!
What's wrong?
My knee – it's been acting up for a while now...

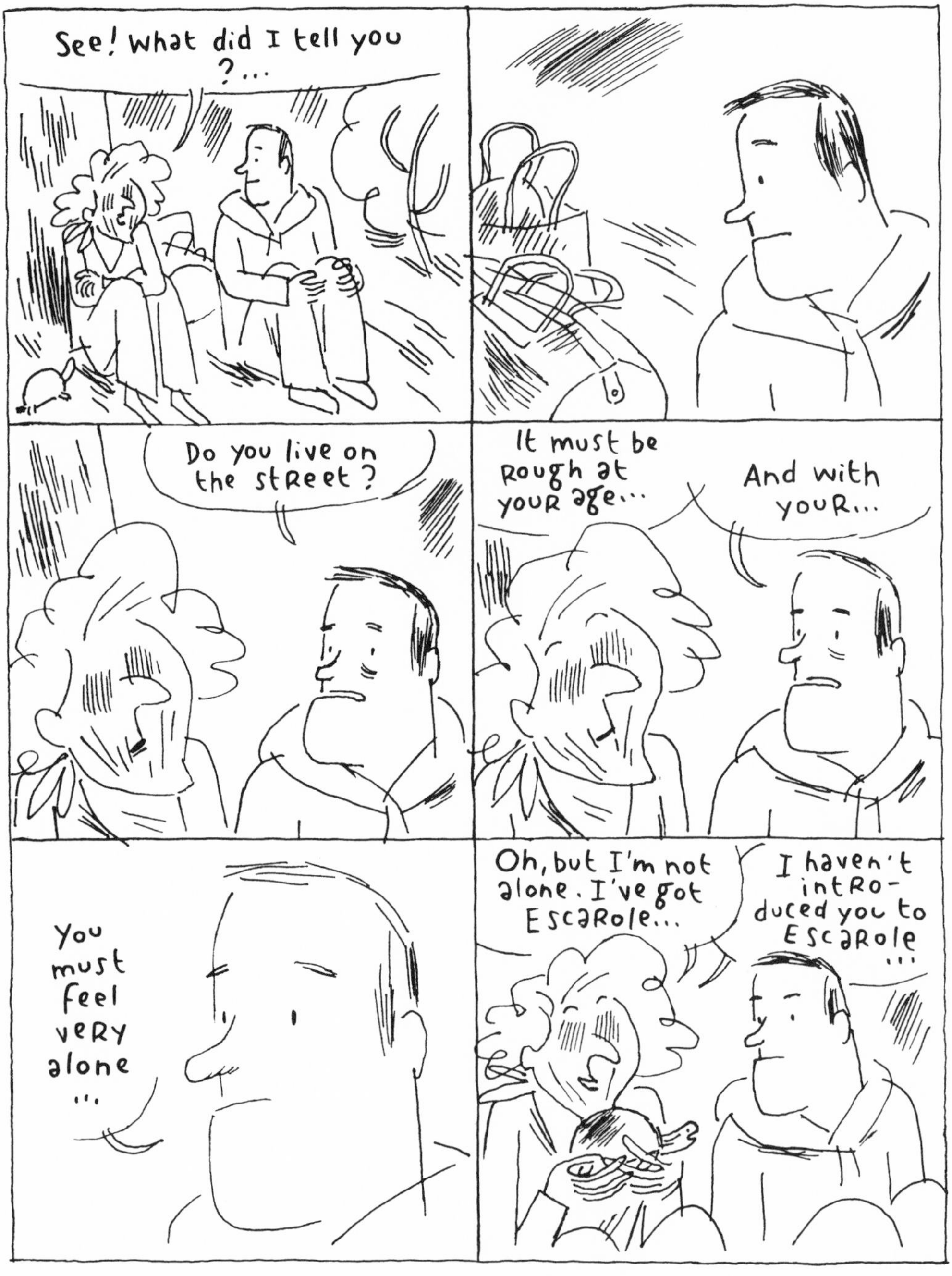
See! What did I tell you ?...
Do you live on the street ?
It must be rough at your age...
And with your...
You must feel very alone ...
Oh, but I'm not alone. I've got Escarole...
I haven't introduced you to Escarole ...

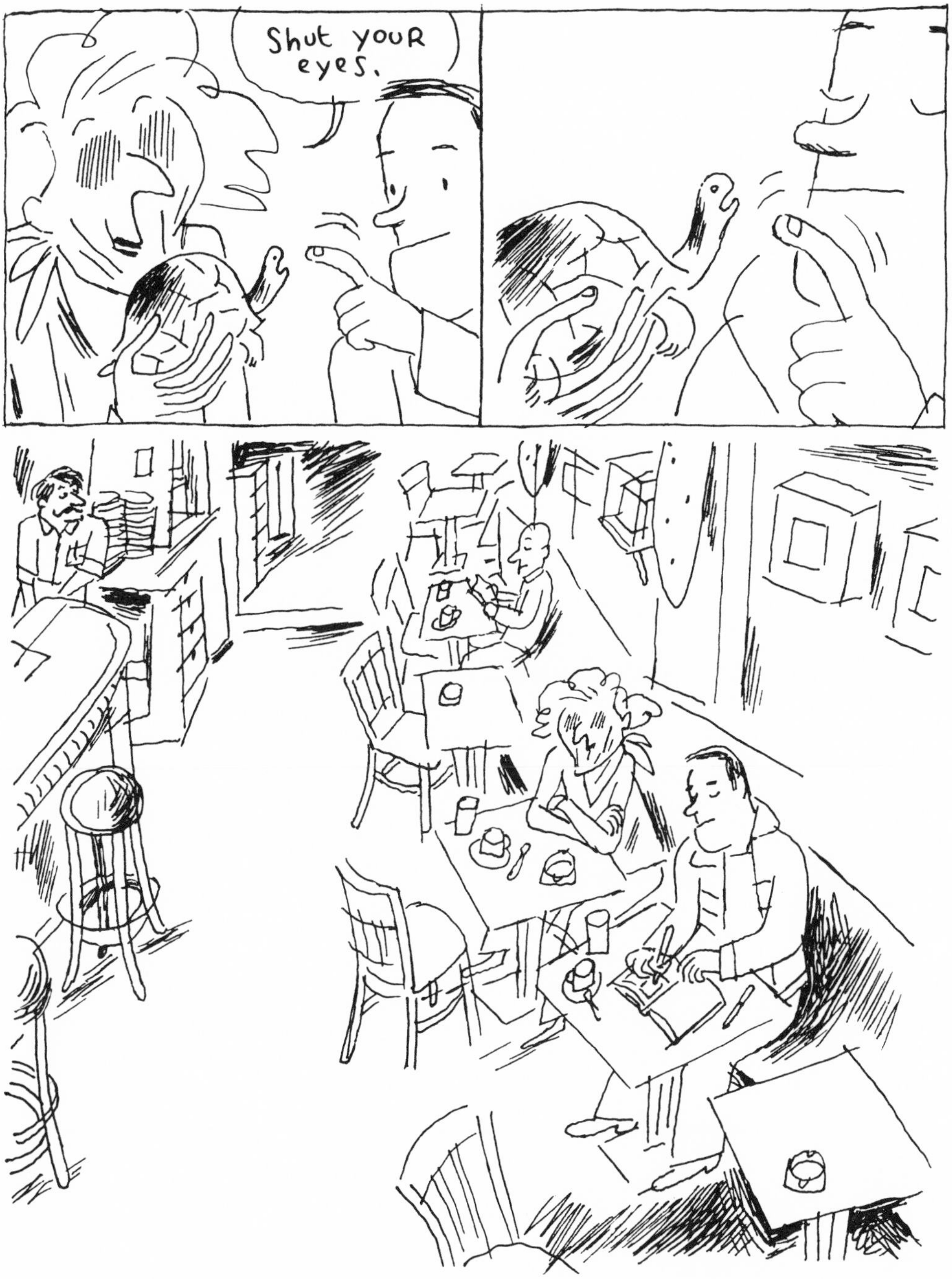
Shut your eyes.

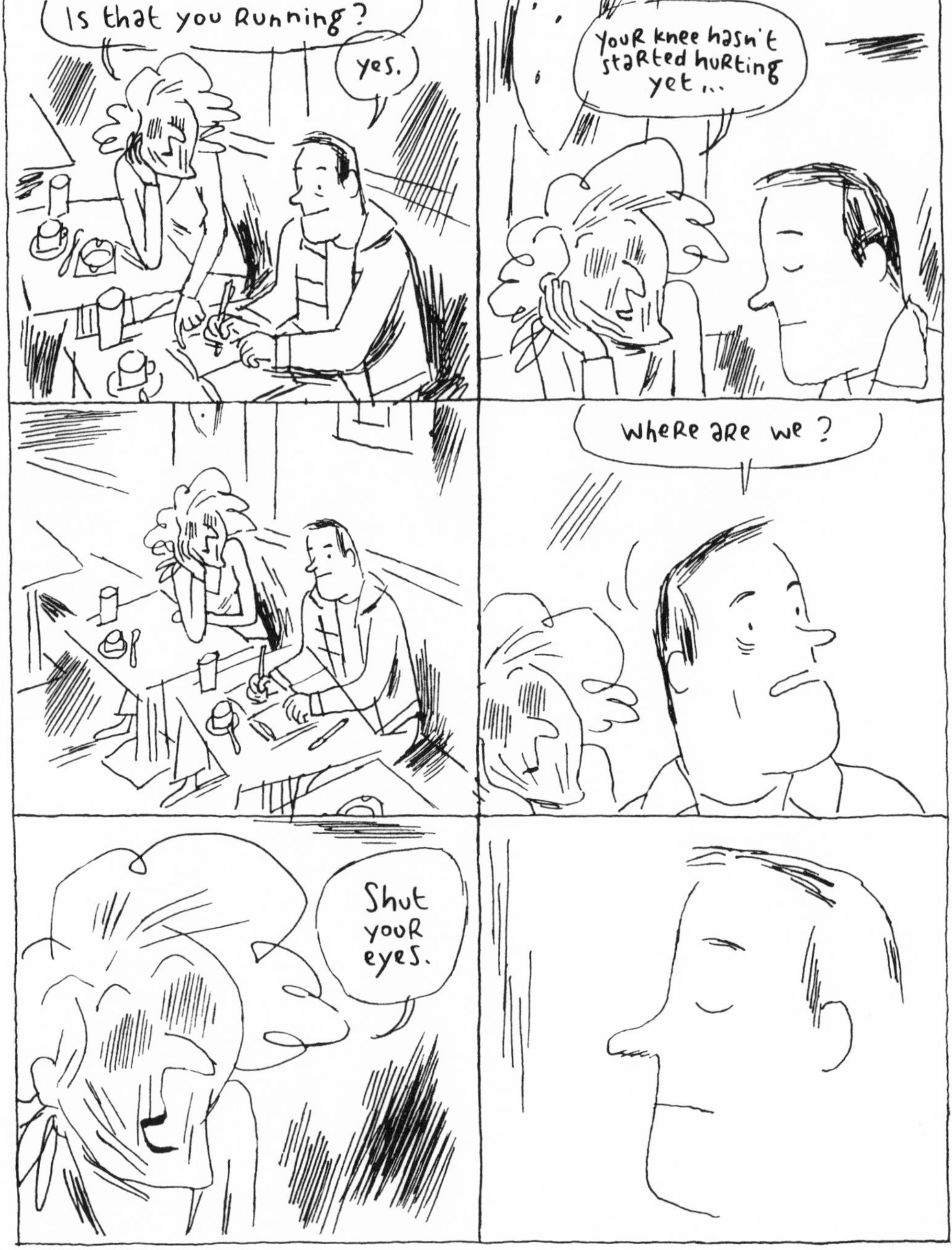
Is that you Running?
yes.
Your knee hasn't started hurting yet...
Where are we?
Shut your eyes.

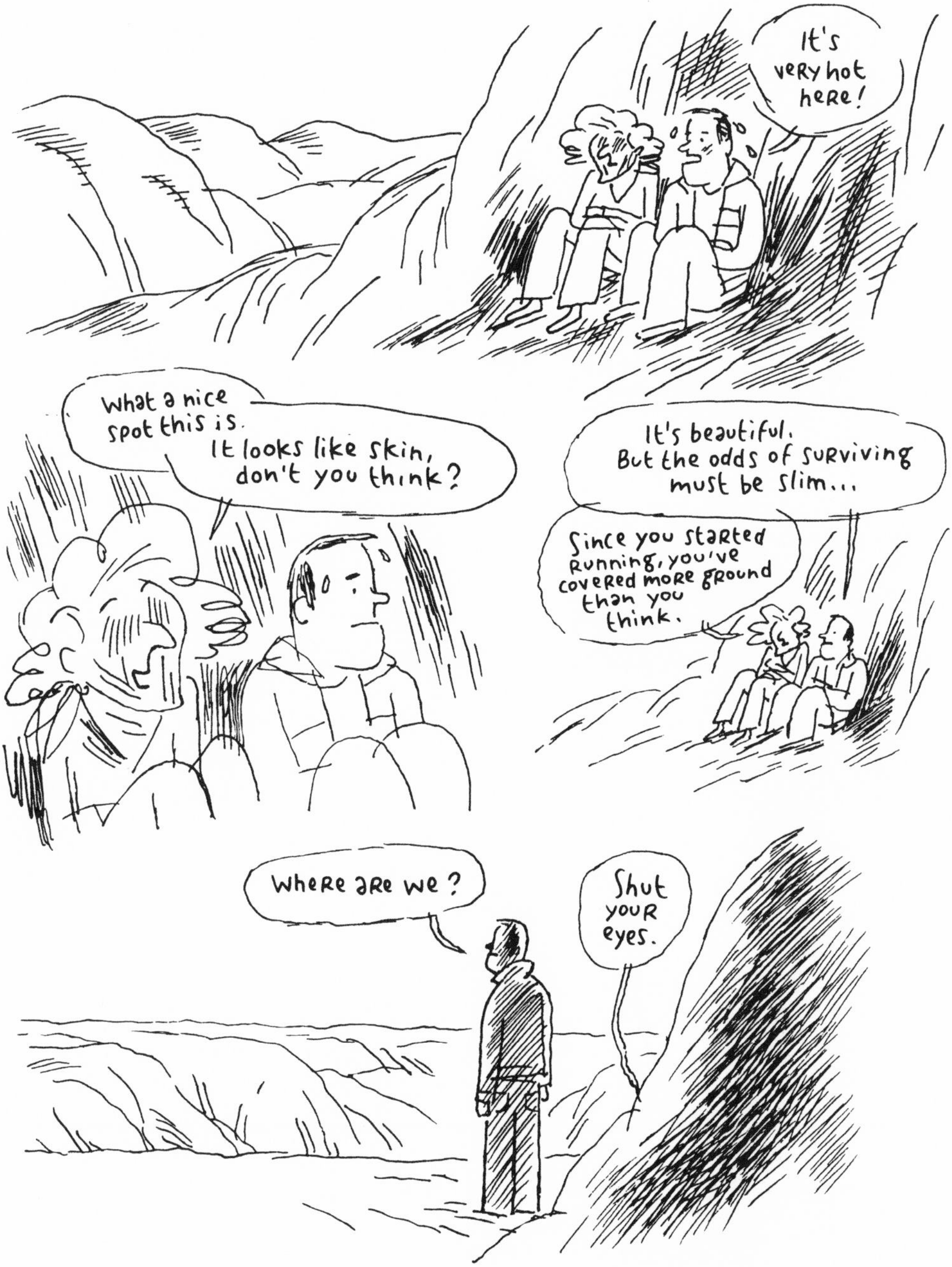
It's very hot here!
What a nice spot this is.
It looks like skin, don't you think?
It's beautiful. But the odds of surviving must be slim...
Since you started running, you've covered more ground than you think.
Where are we?
Shut your eyes.

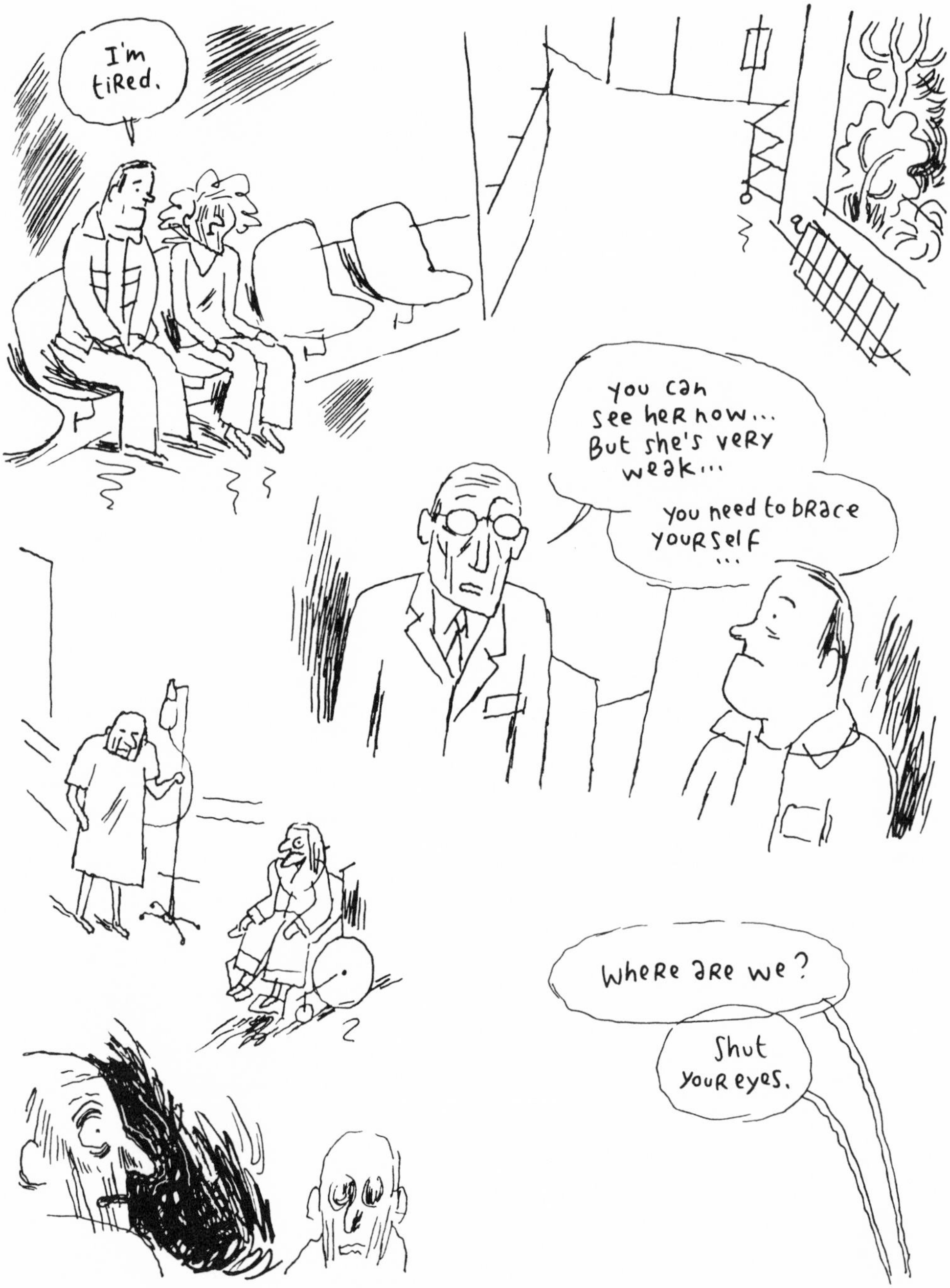
I'm tired.
you can see her now... But she's very weak...
you need to brace yourself ...
Where are we?
Shut your eyes.

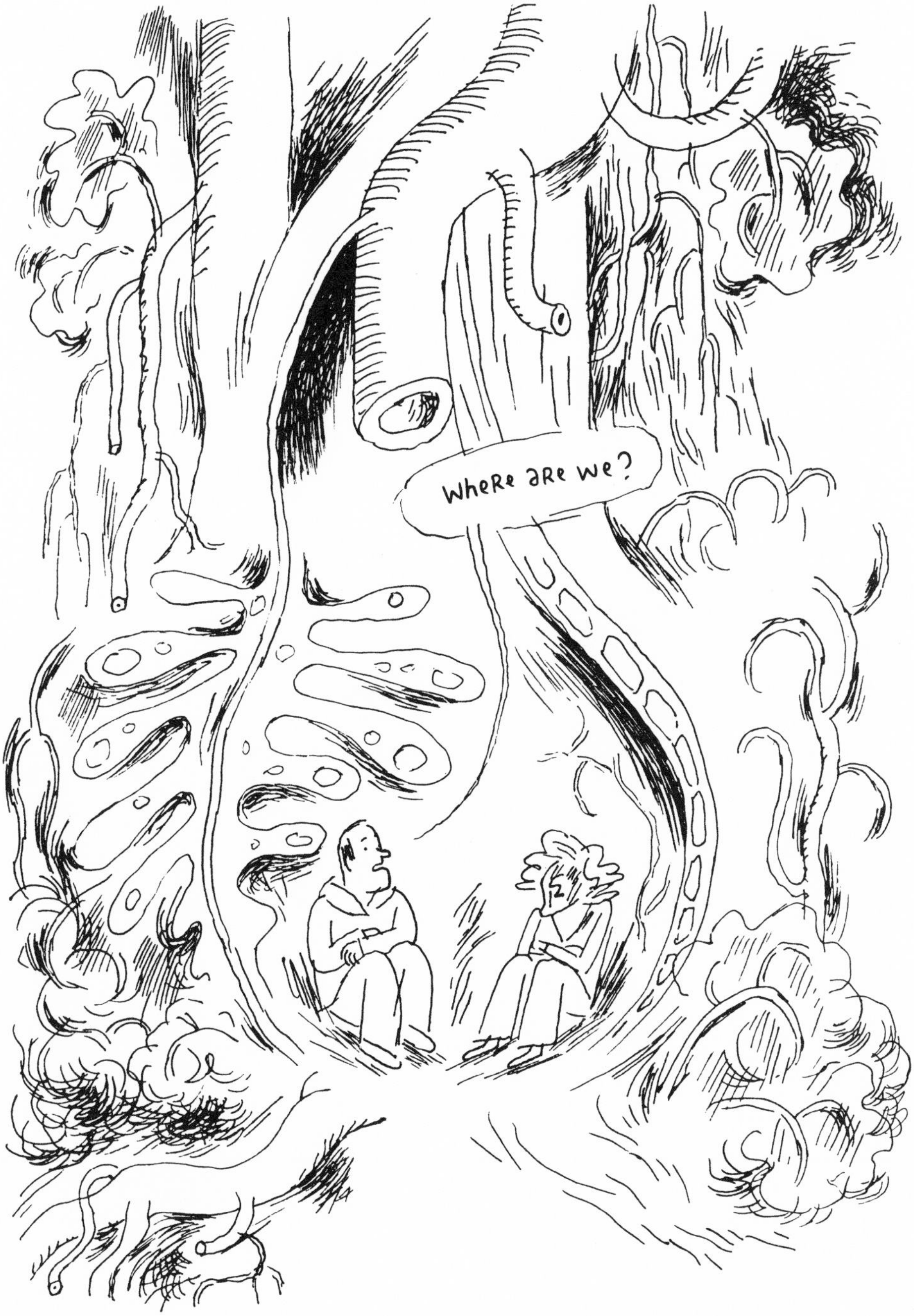
Where are we?

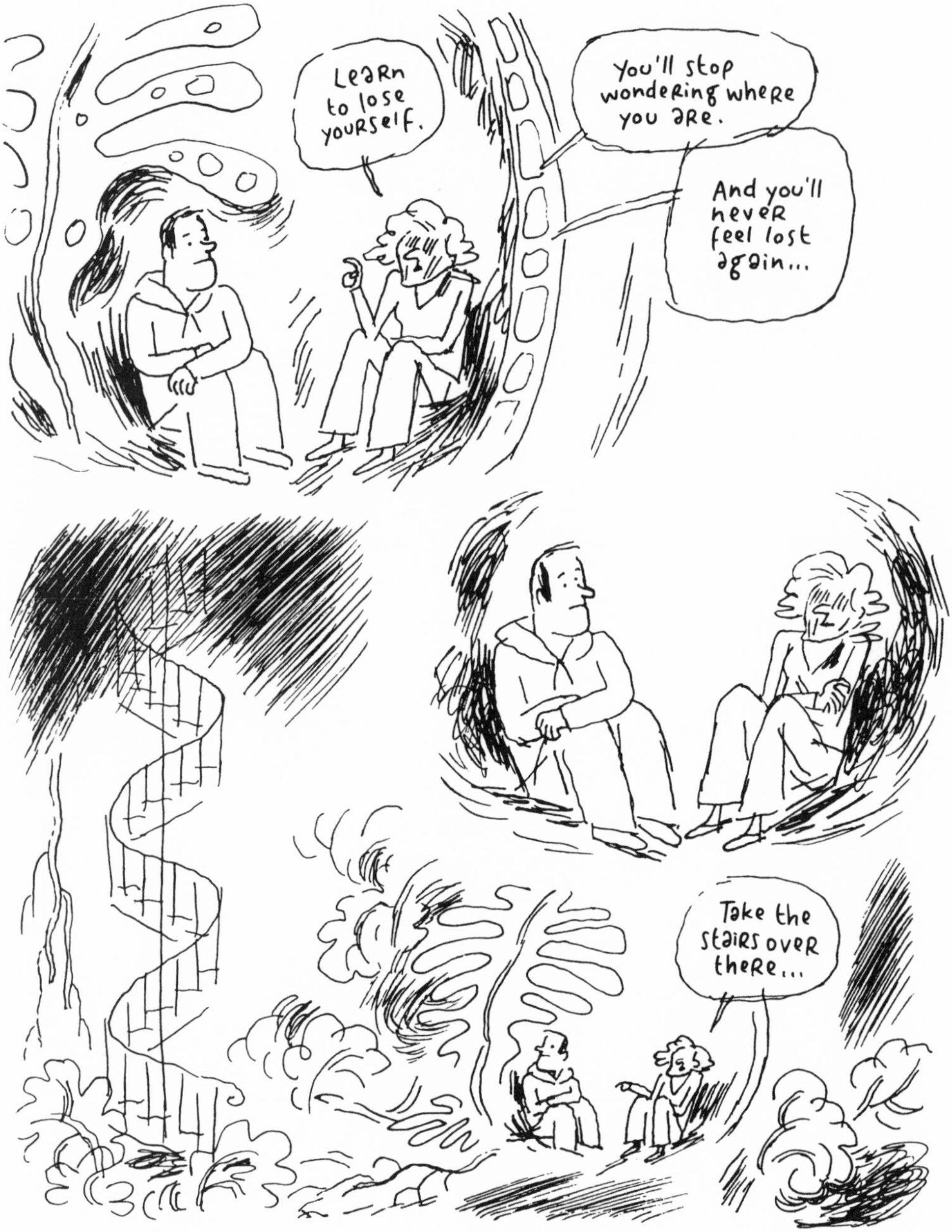
Learn to lose yourself.
You'll stop wondering where you are.
And you'll never feel lost again...
Take the stairs over there...

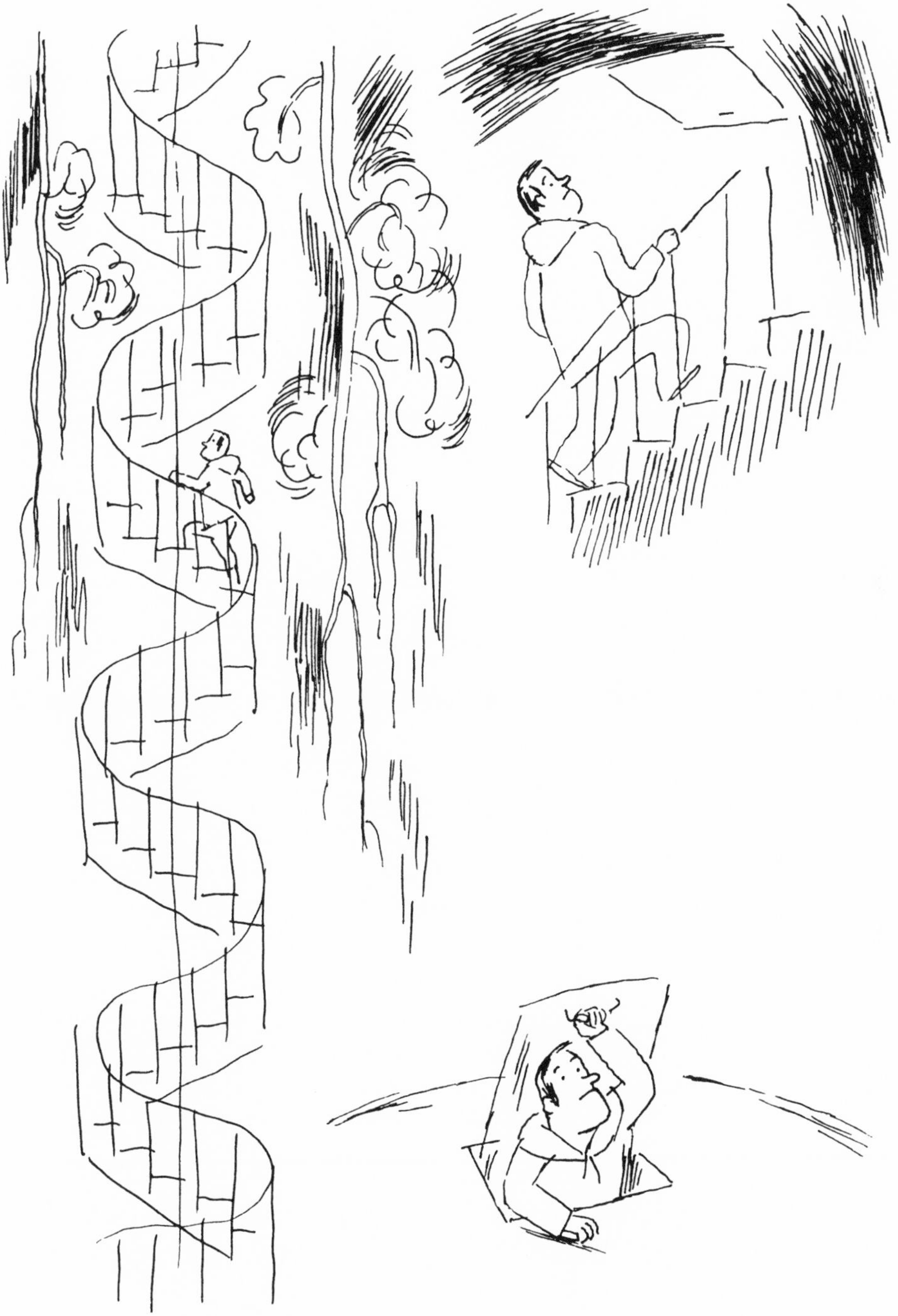

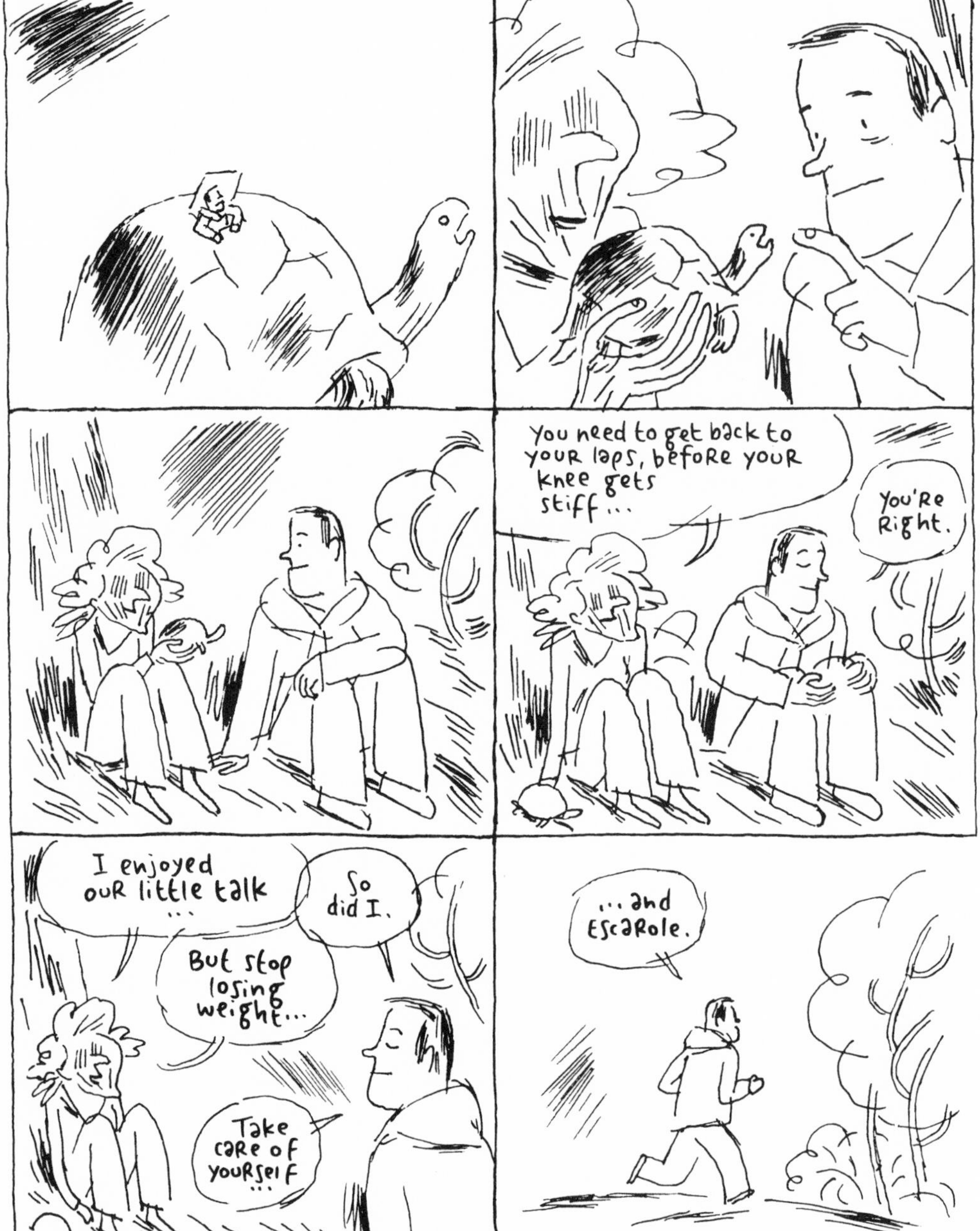
You need to get back to your laps, before your knee gets stiff...
You're Right.
I enjoyed our little talk ...
So did I.
But stop losing weight...
Take care of yourself ...
...and Escarole.

the rats

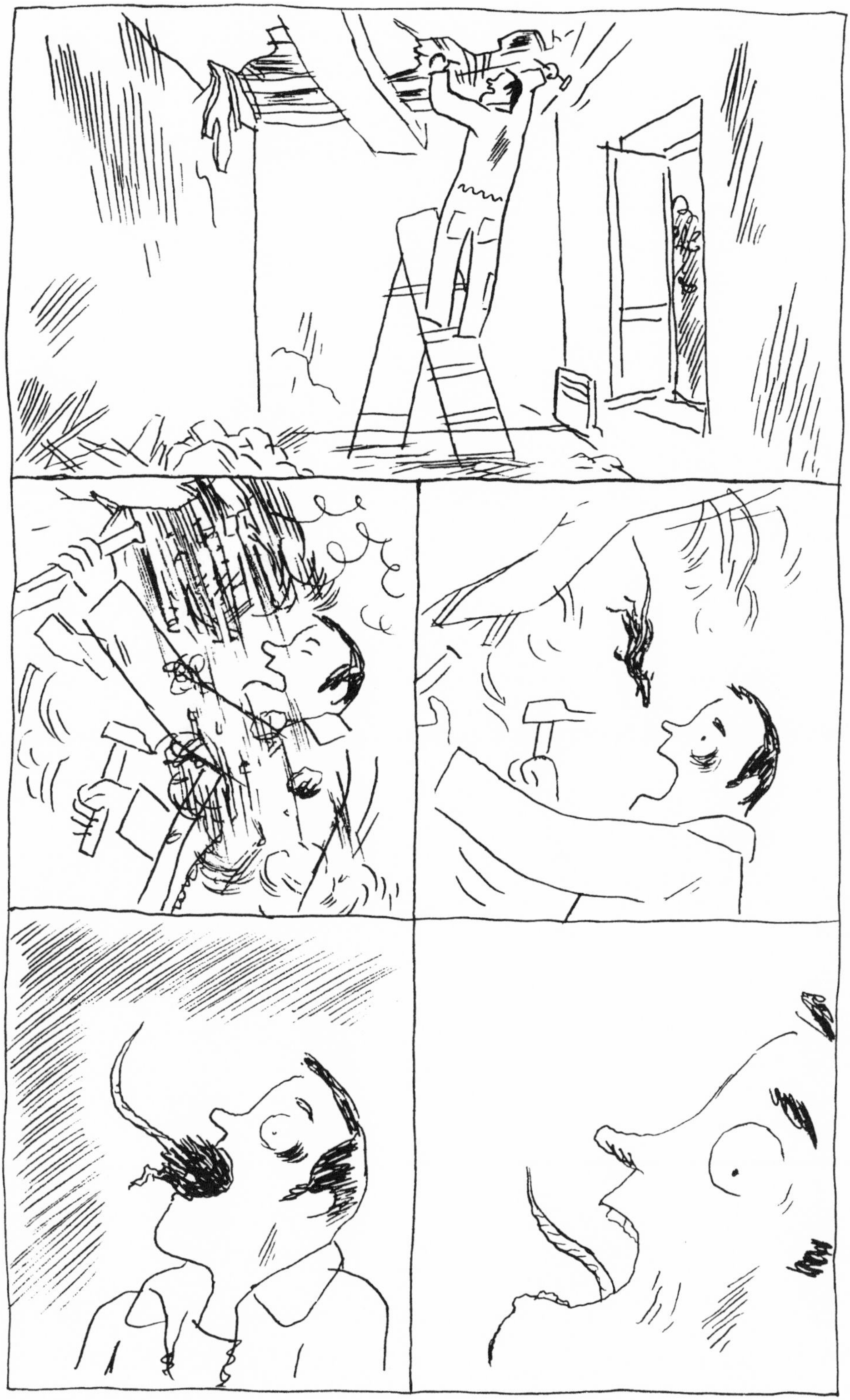

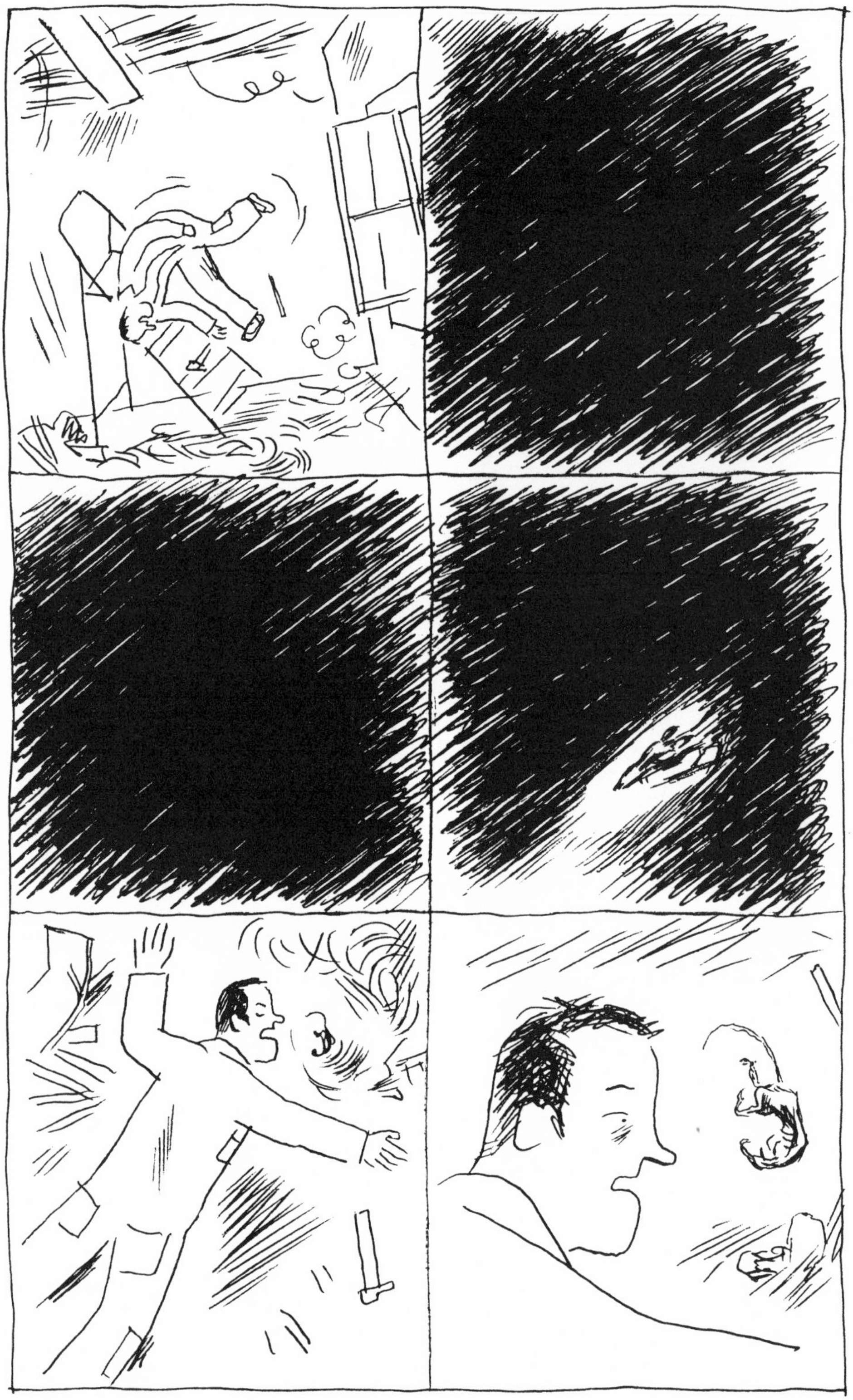

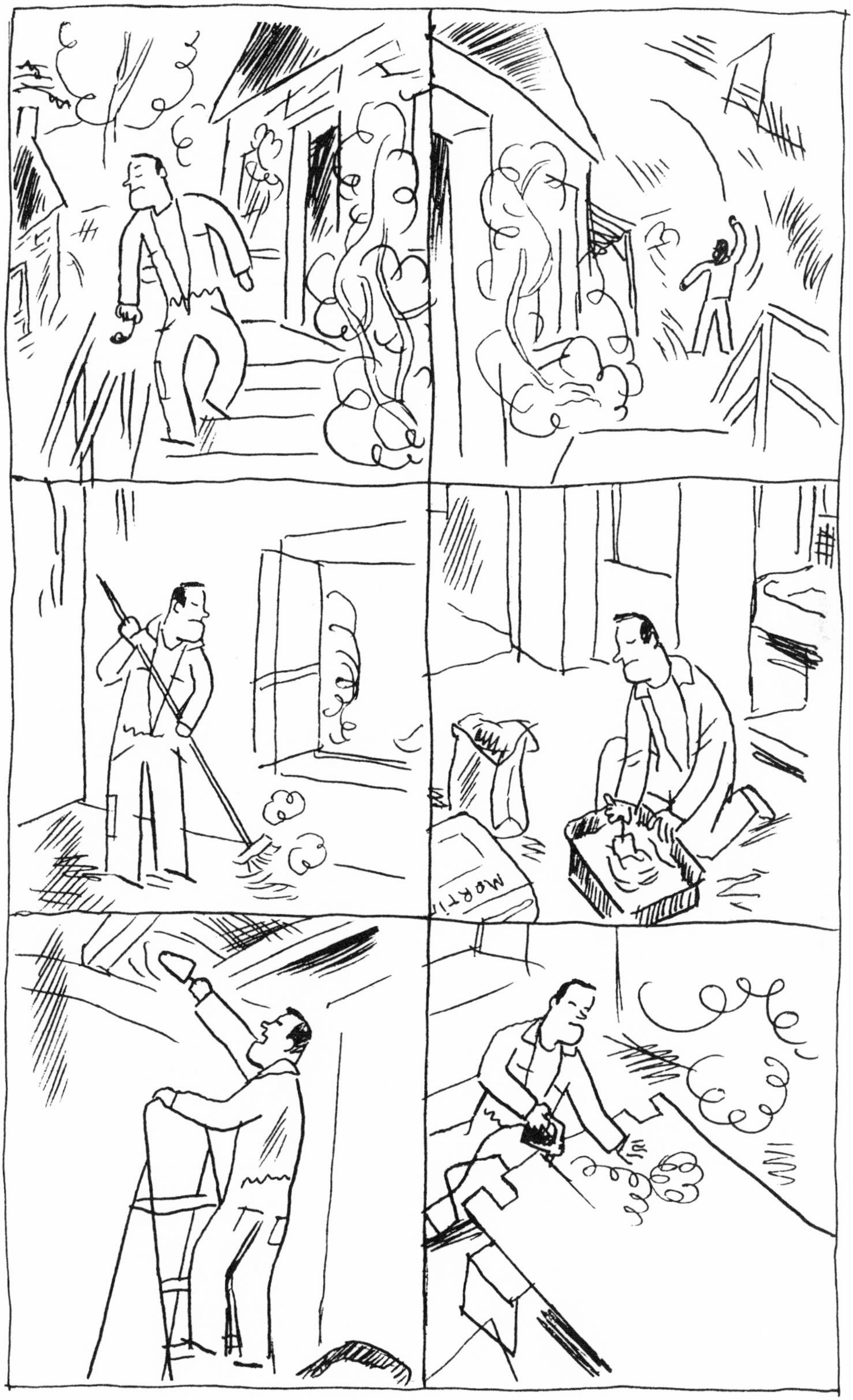
MORTI

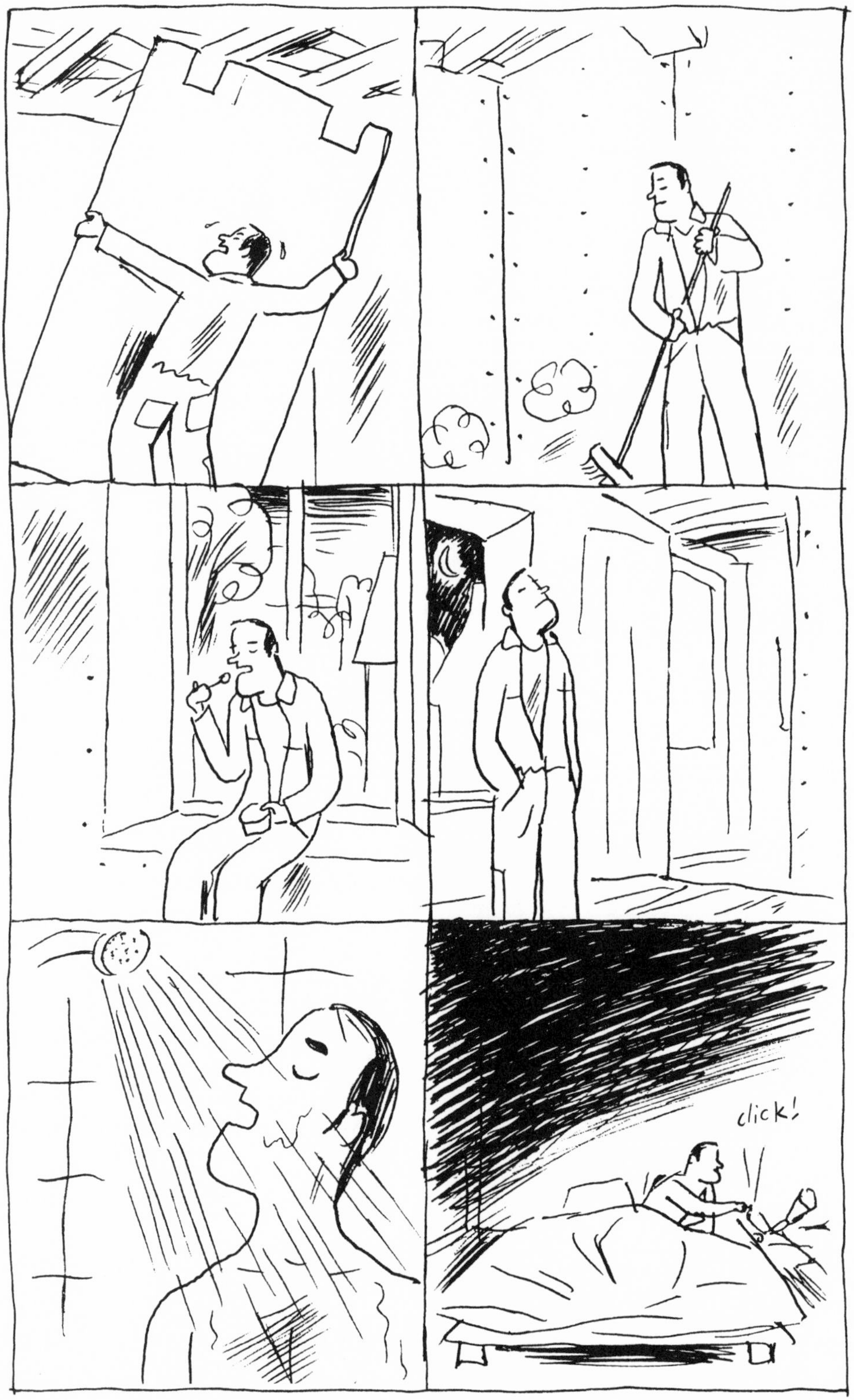
click!

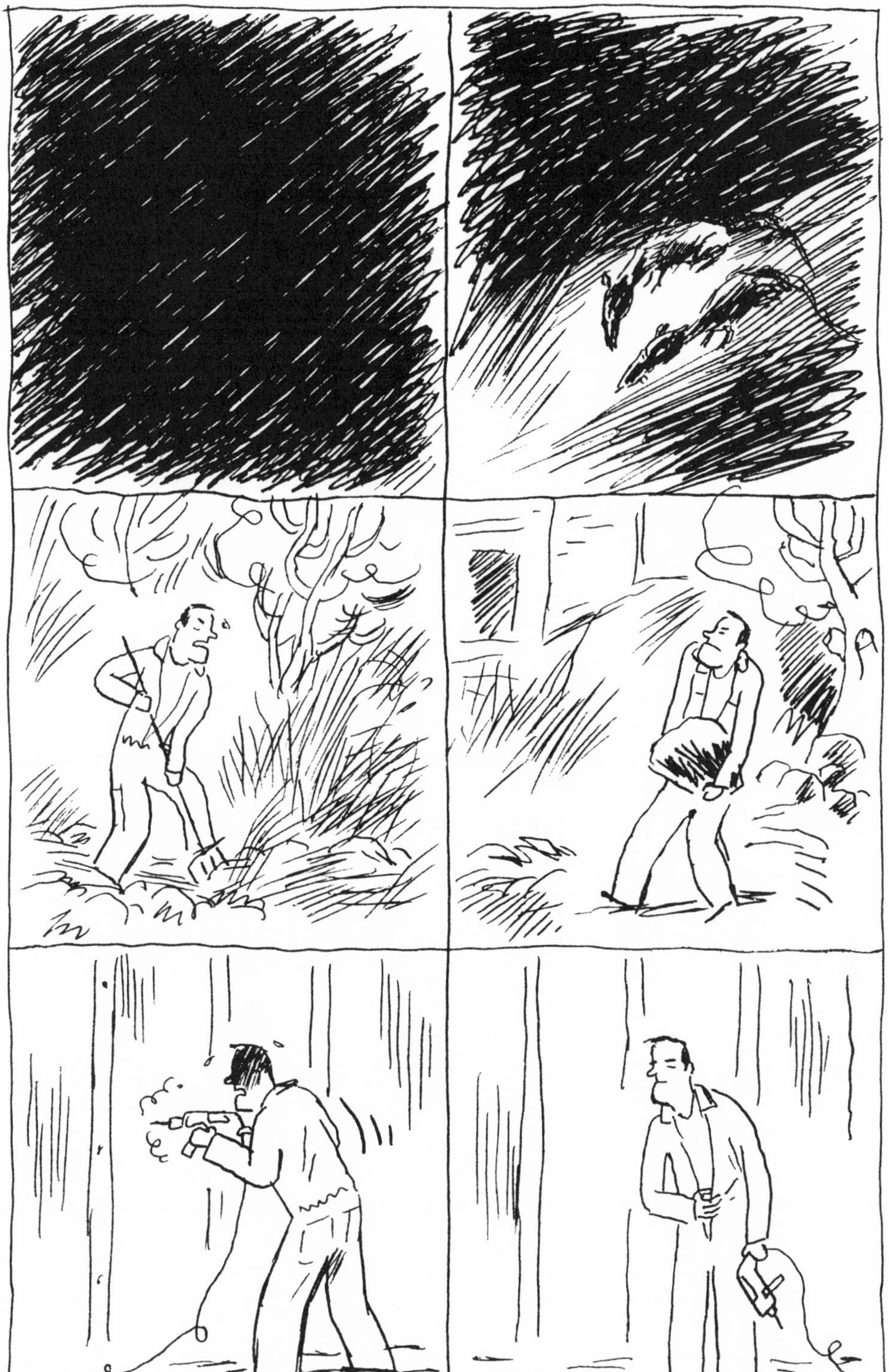

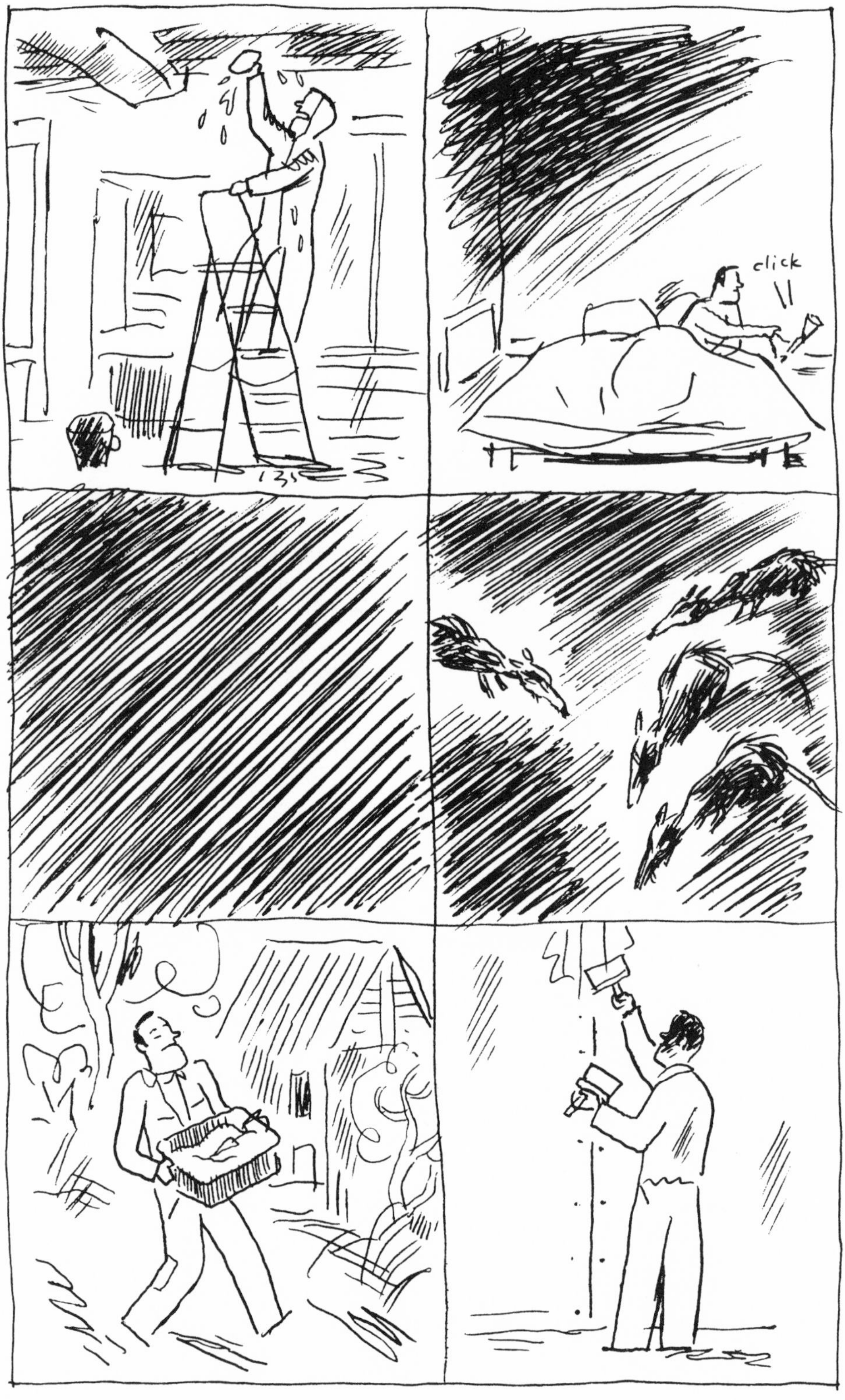
click

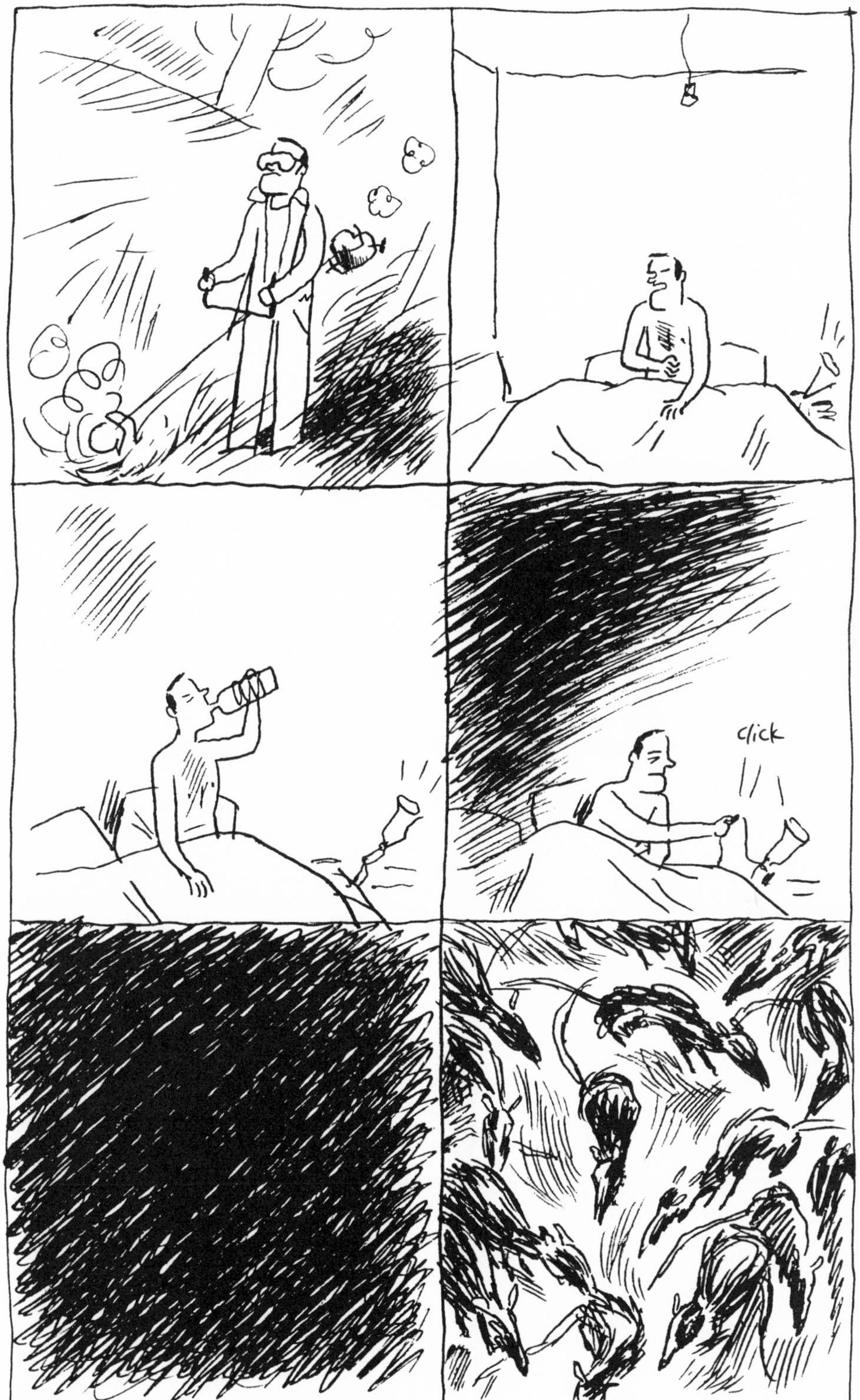
click

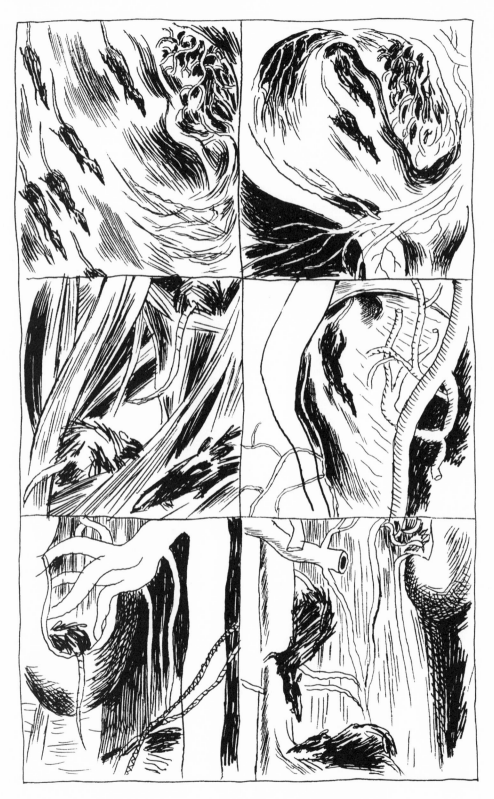

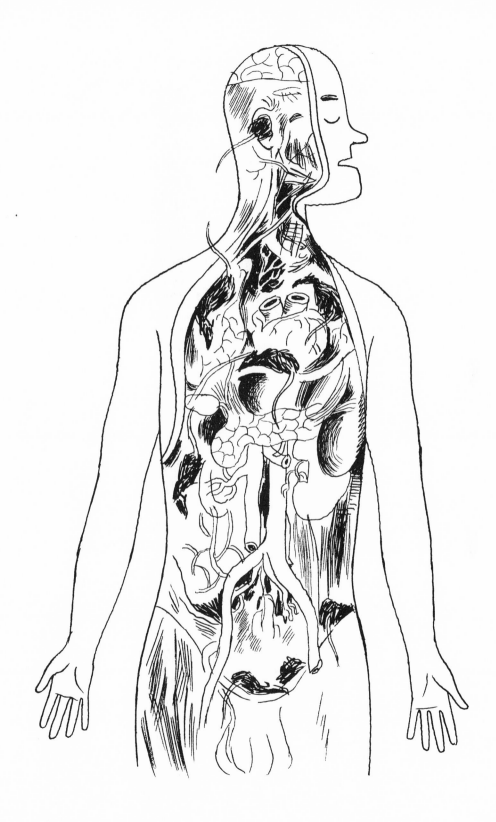

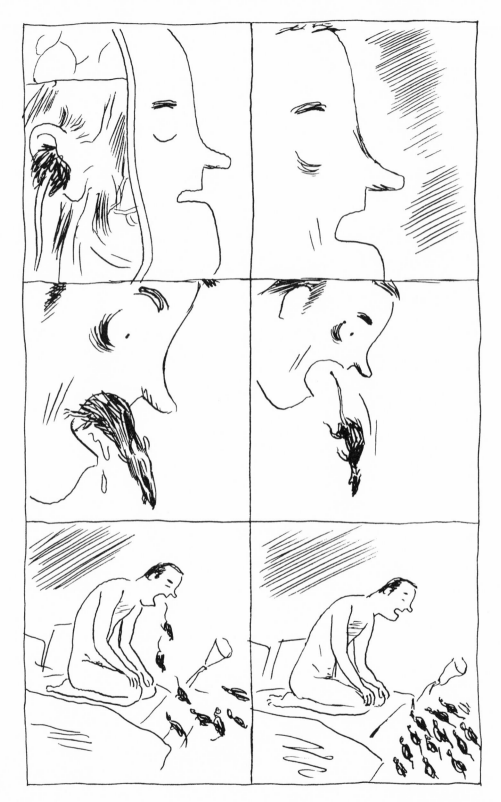

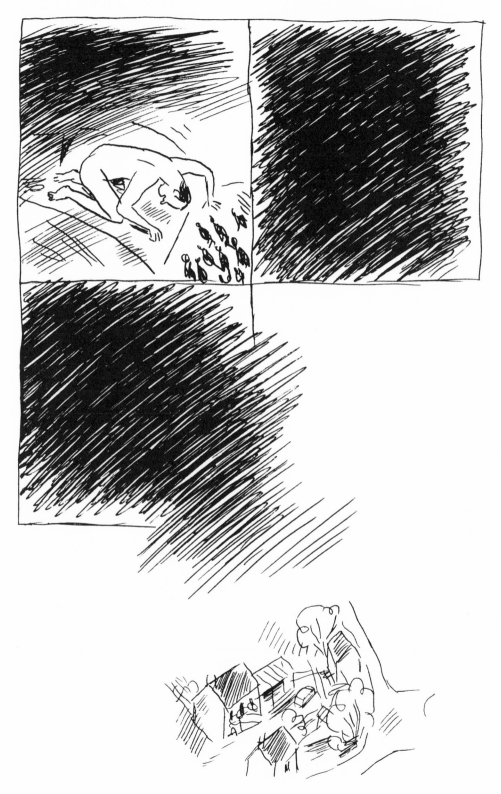

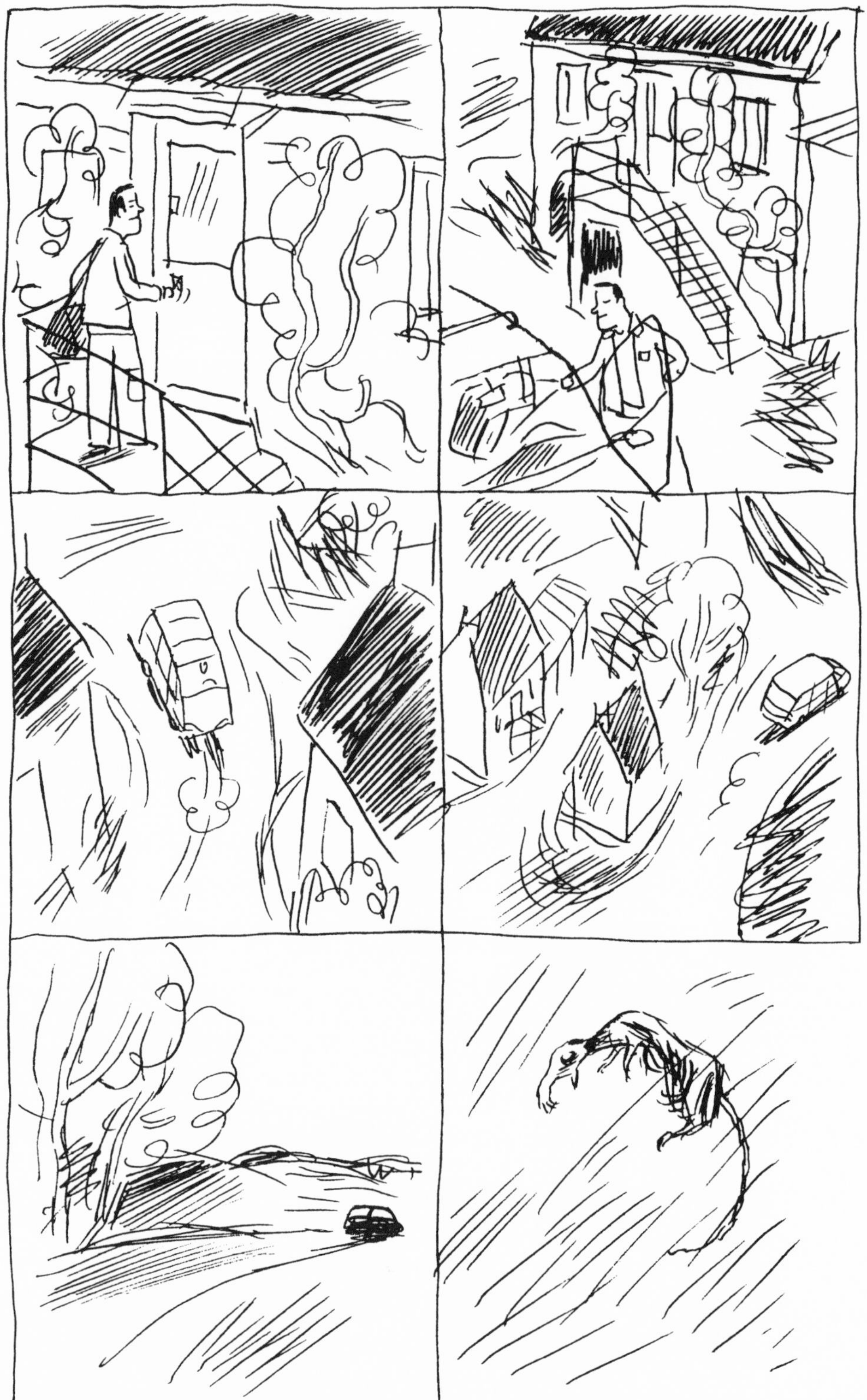

Labyrinth

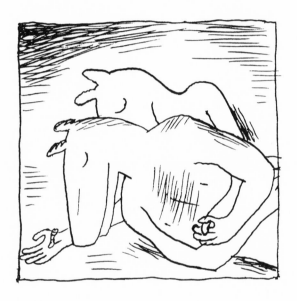

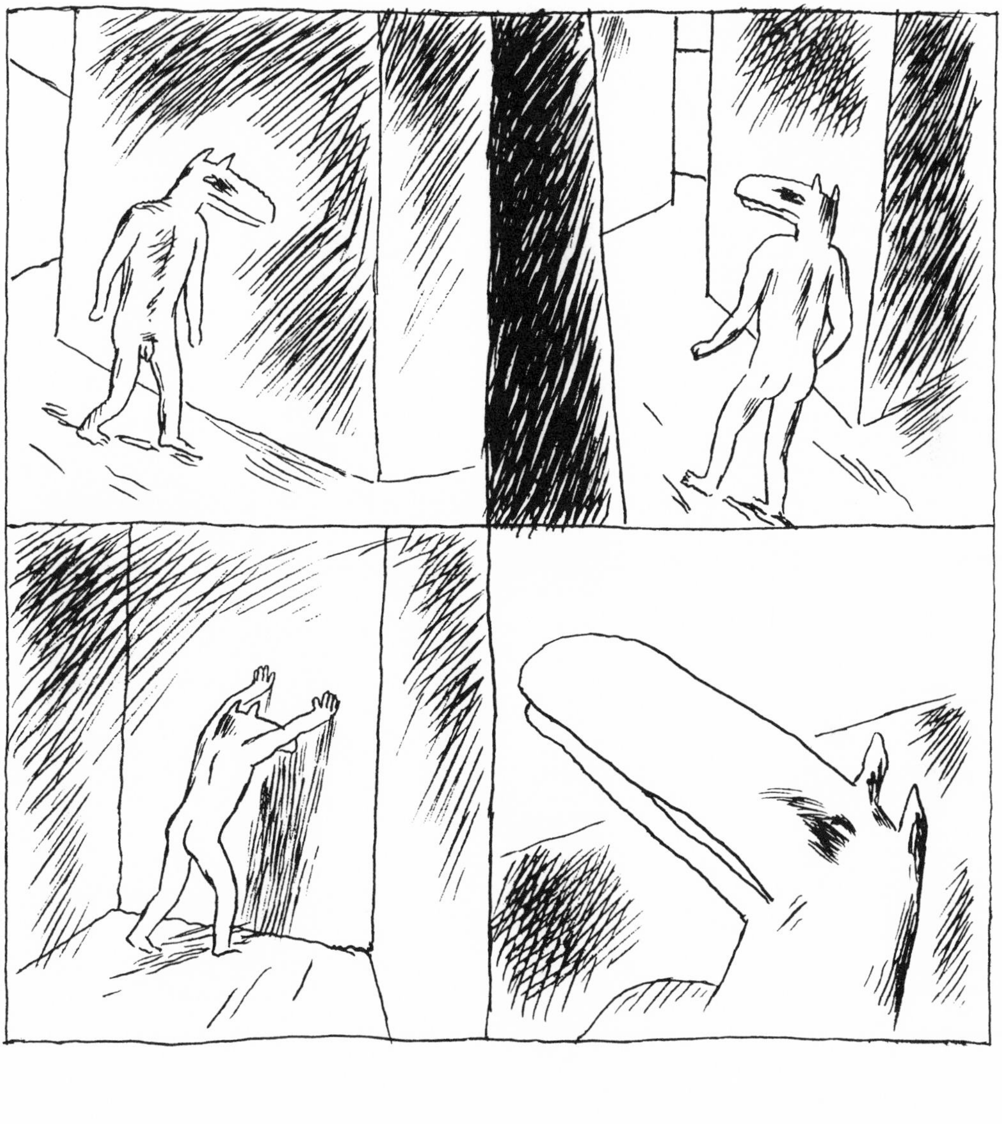

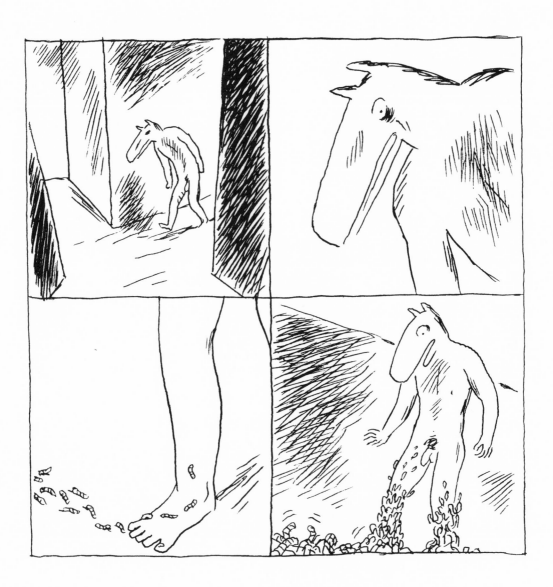

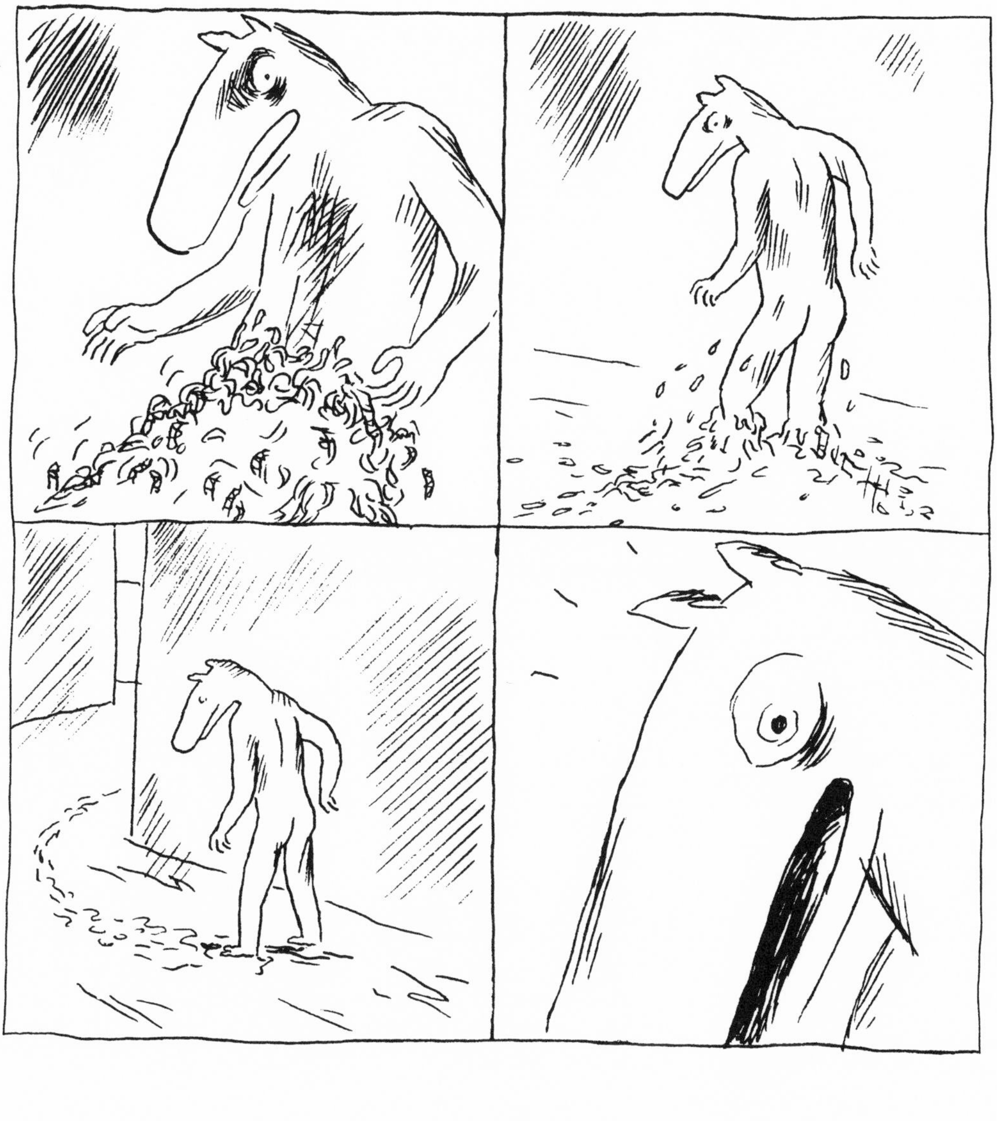

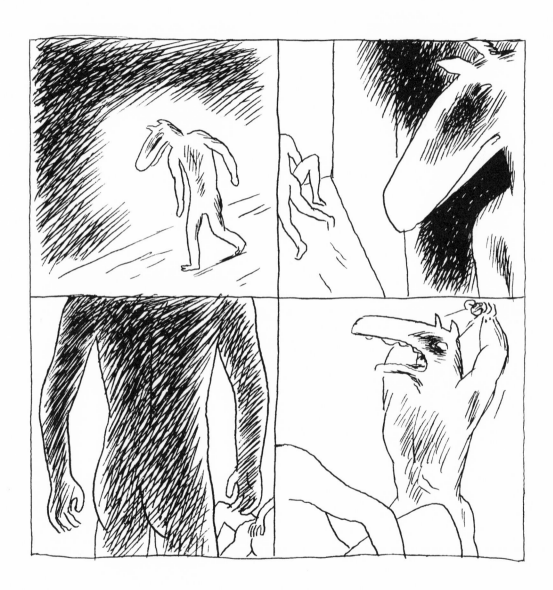

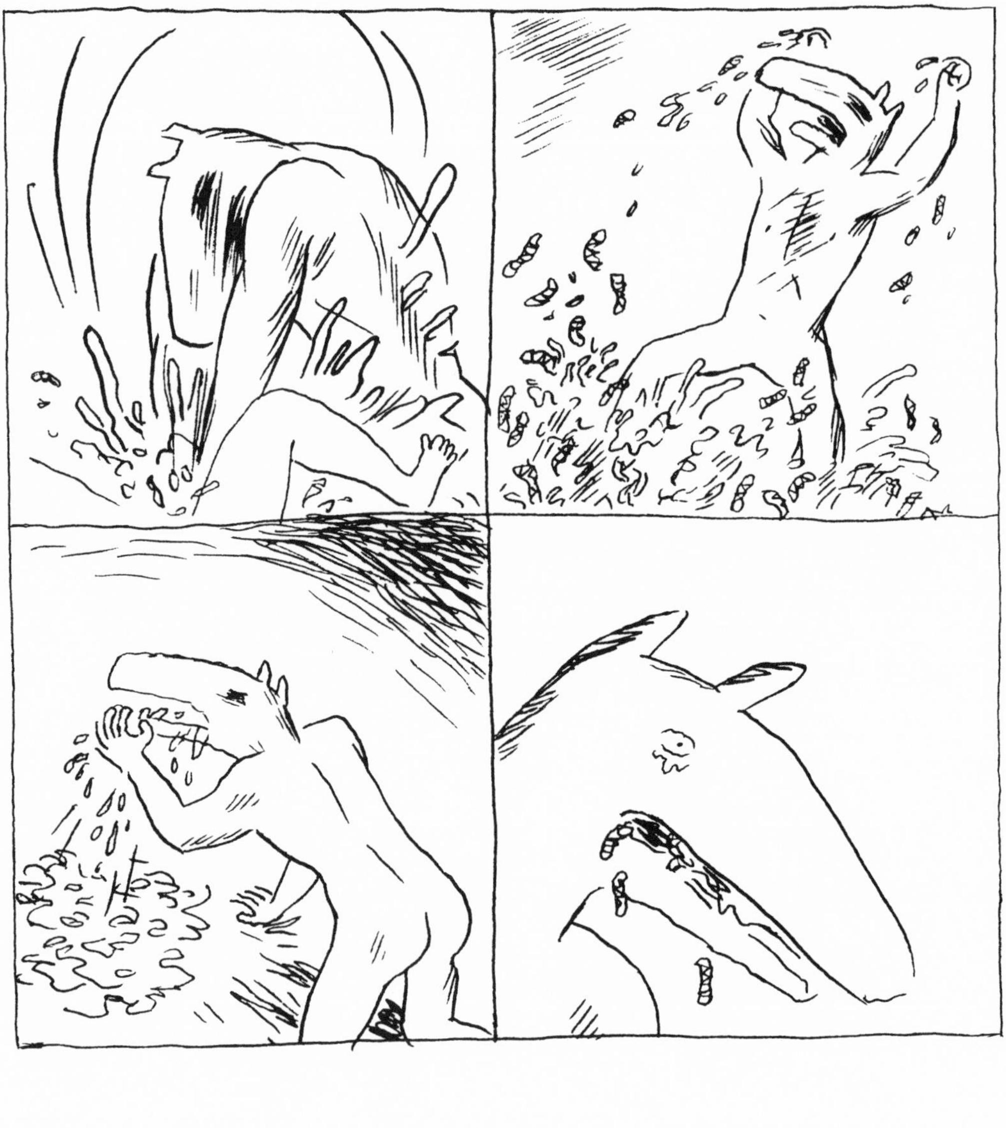

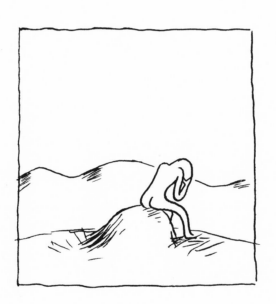

Run Movie 5 Mom

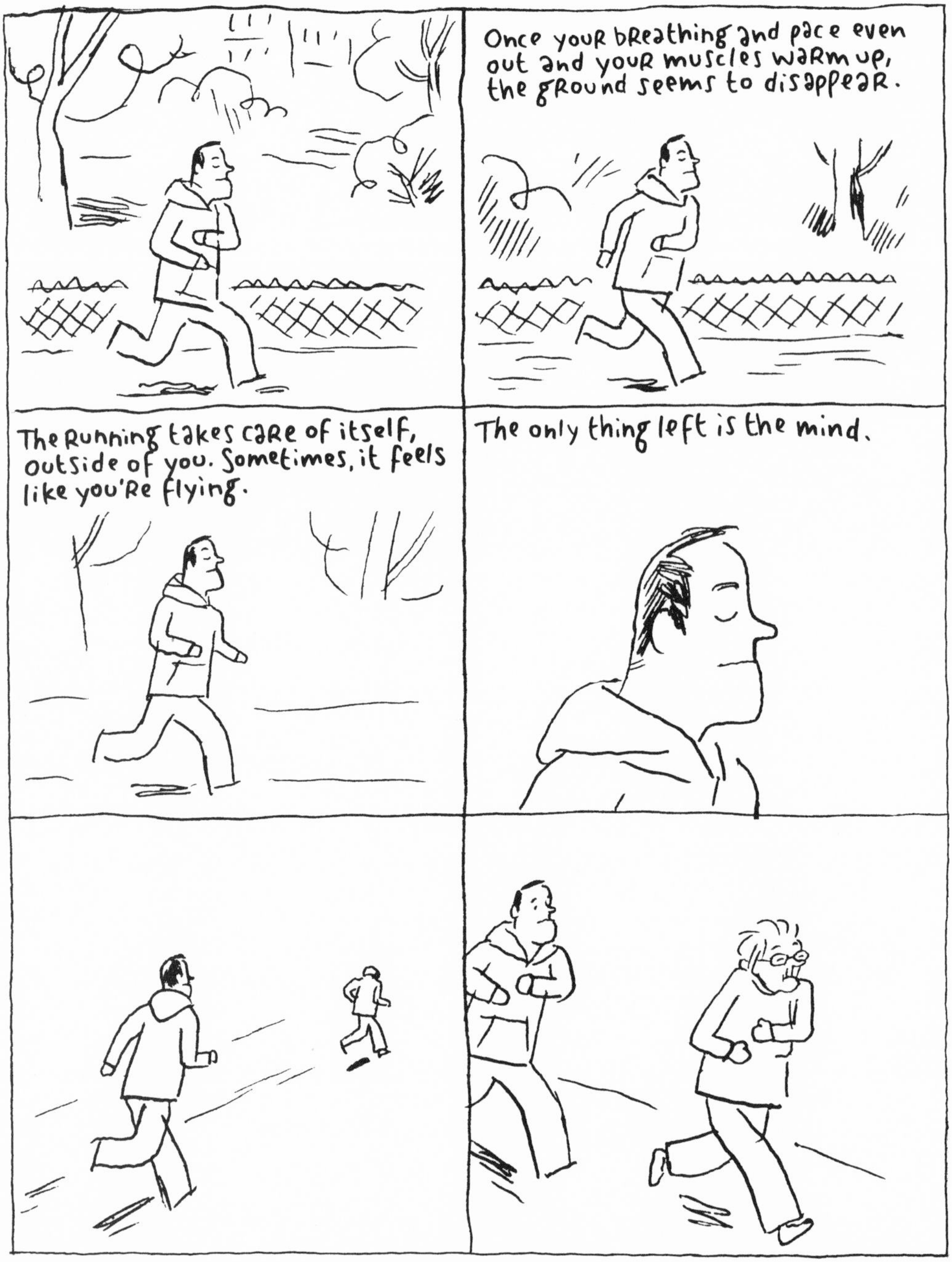
Once your breathing and pace even out and your muscles warm up, the ground seems to disappear.
The running takes care of itself, outside of you. Sometimes, it feels like you're flying.
The only thing left is the mind.

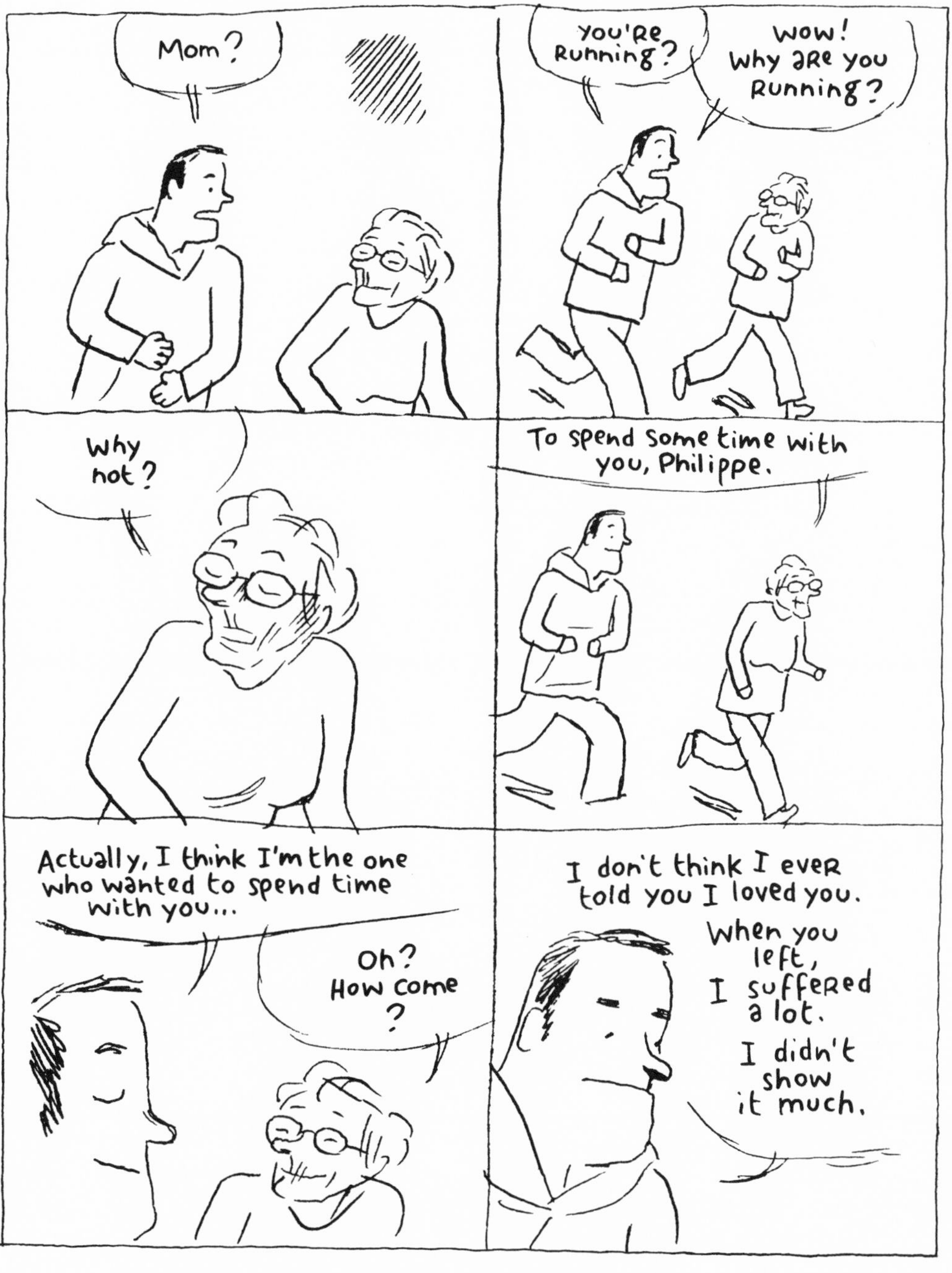
Mom?
You're Running?
Wow! Why are you Running?
Why not?
To spend some time with you, Philippe.
Actually, I think I'm the one who wanted to spend time with you...
Oh? How come?
I don't think I ever told you I loved you.
When you left, I suffered a lot.
I didn't show it much.

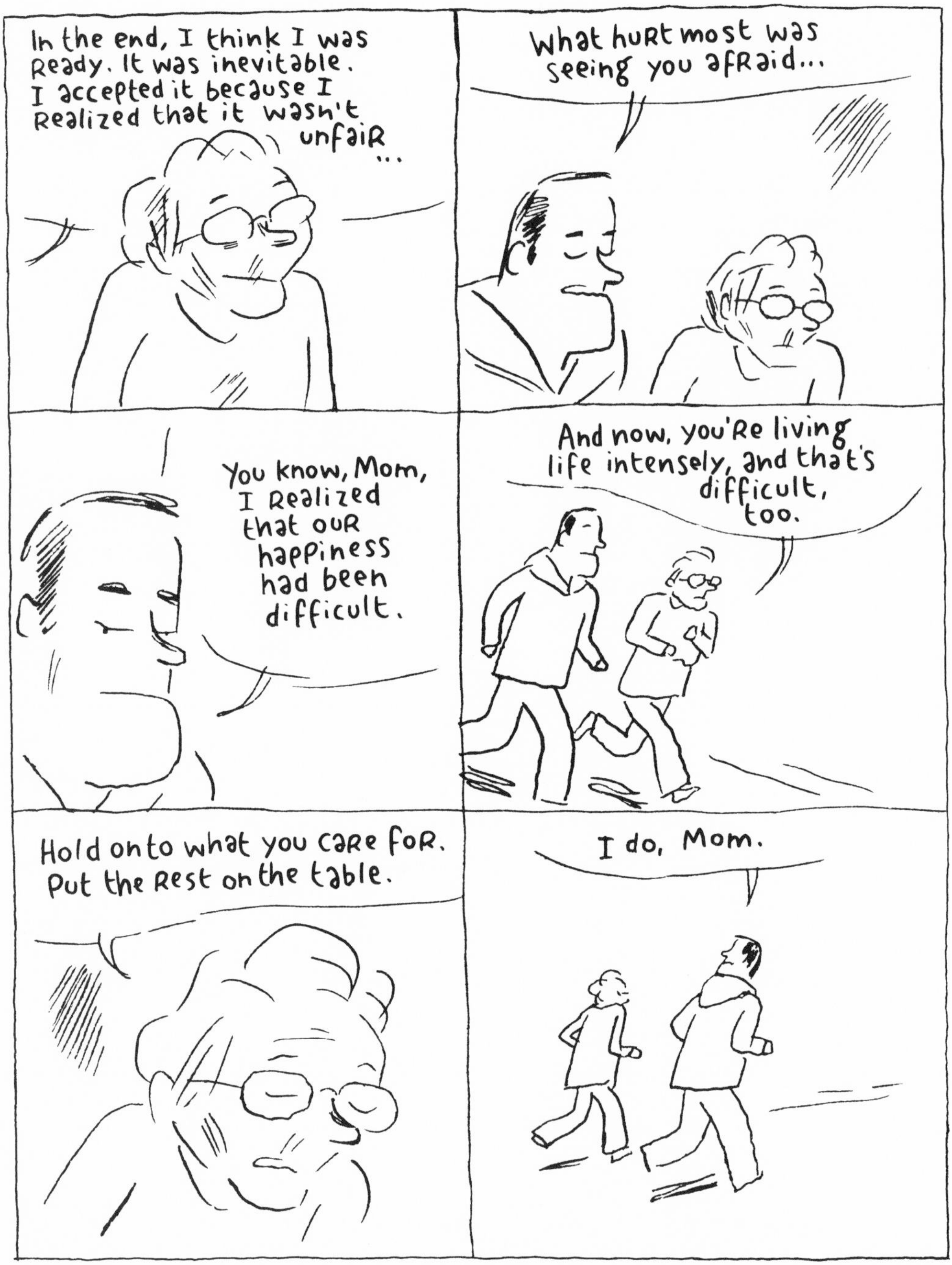

In the end, I think I was Ready. It was inevitable. I accepted it because I Realized that it wasn't unfaiR...
What hurt most was seeing you afRaid...
You know, Mom, I Realized that our happiness had been difficult.
And now, you're living life intensely, and that's difficult, too.
Hold onto what you care for. Put the Rest on the table.
I do, Mom.

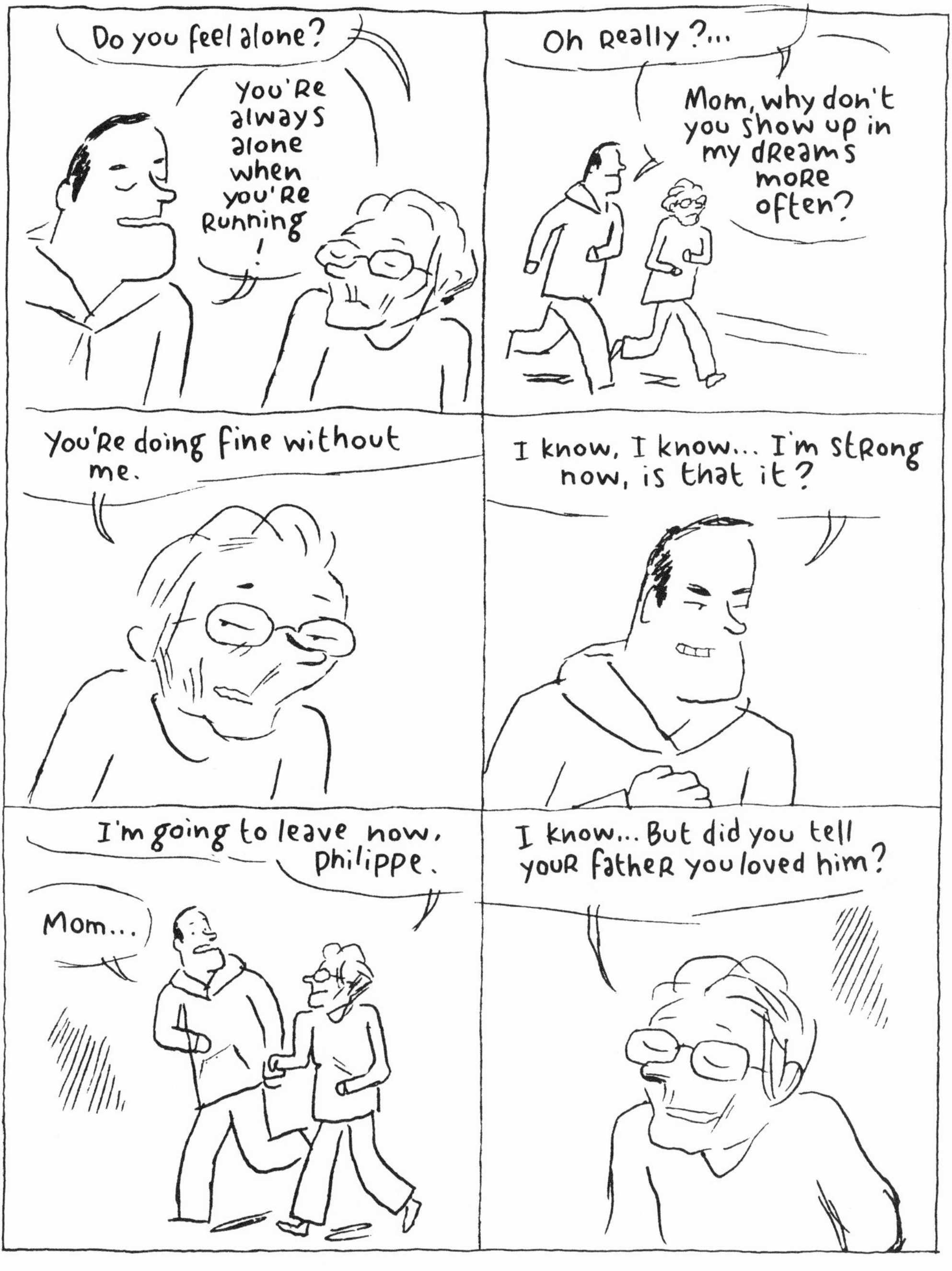
Do you feel alone?
You're always alone when you're Running!
Oh Really?...
Mom, why don't you show up in my dreams more often?
You're doing fine without me.
I know, I know... I'm strong now, is that it?
I'm going to leave now, Philippe.
Mom...
I know... But did you tell your father you loved him?

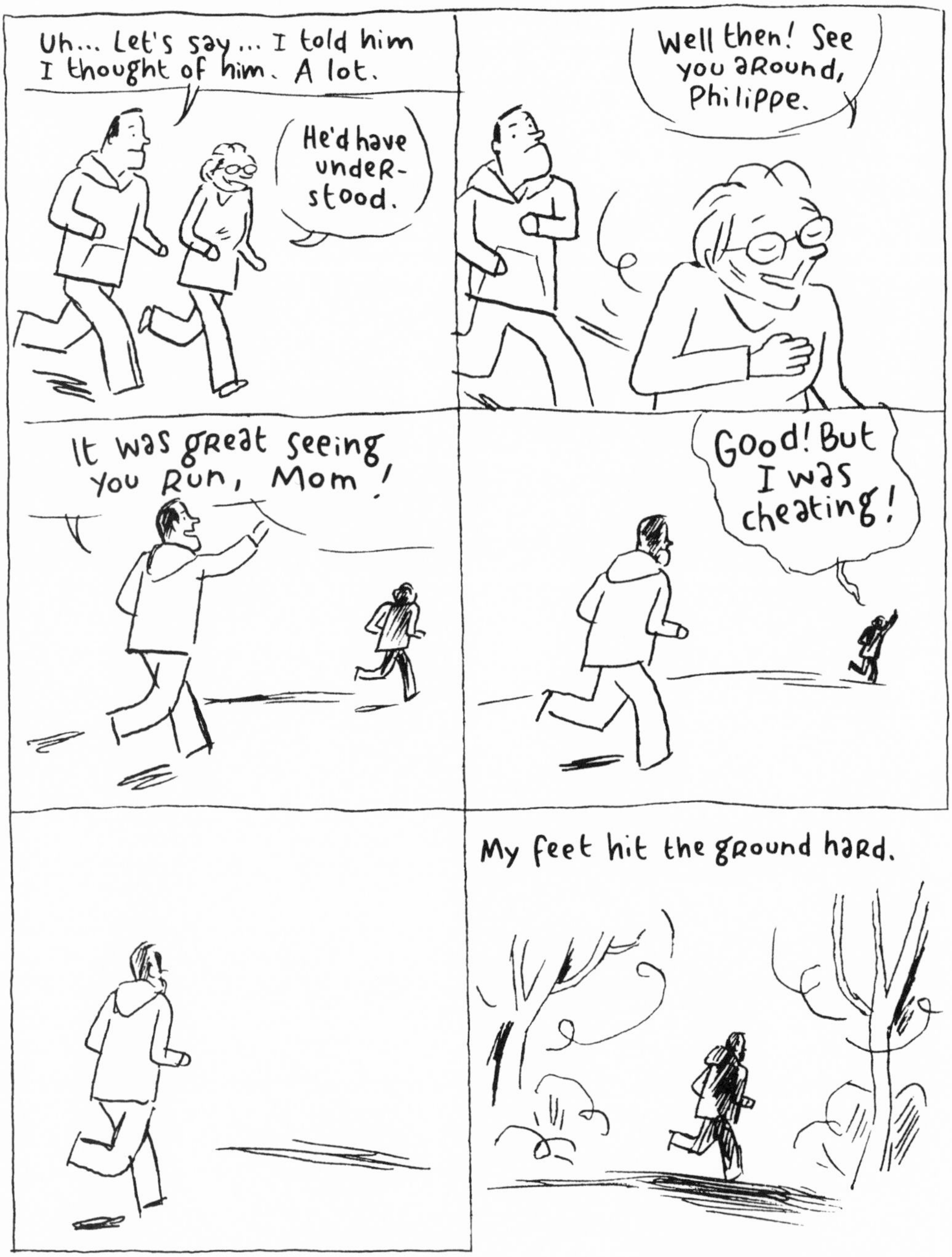
Uh... Let's say... I told him I thought of him. A lot.
He'd have understood.
Well then! See you around, Philippe.
It was great seeing you run, Mom!
Good! But I was cheating!
My feet hit the ground hard.

Run Movie 6 The duck

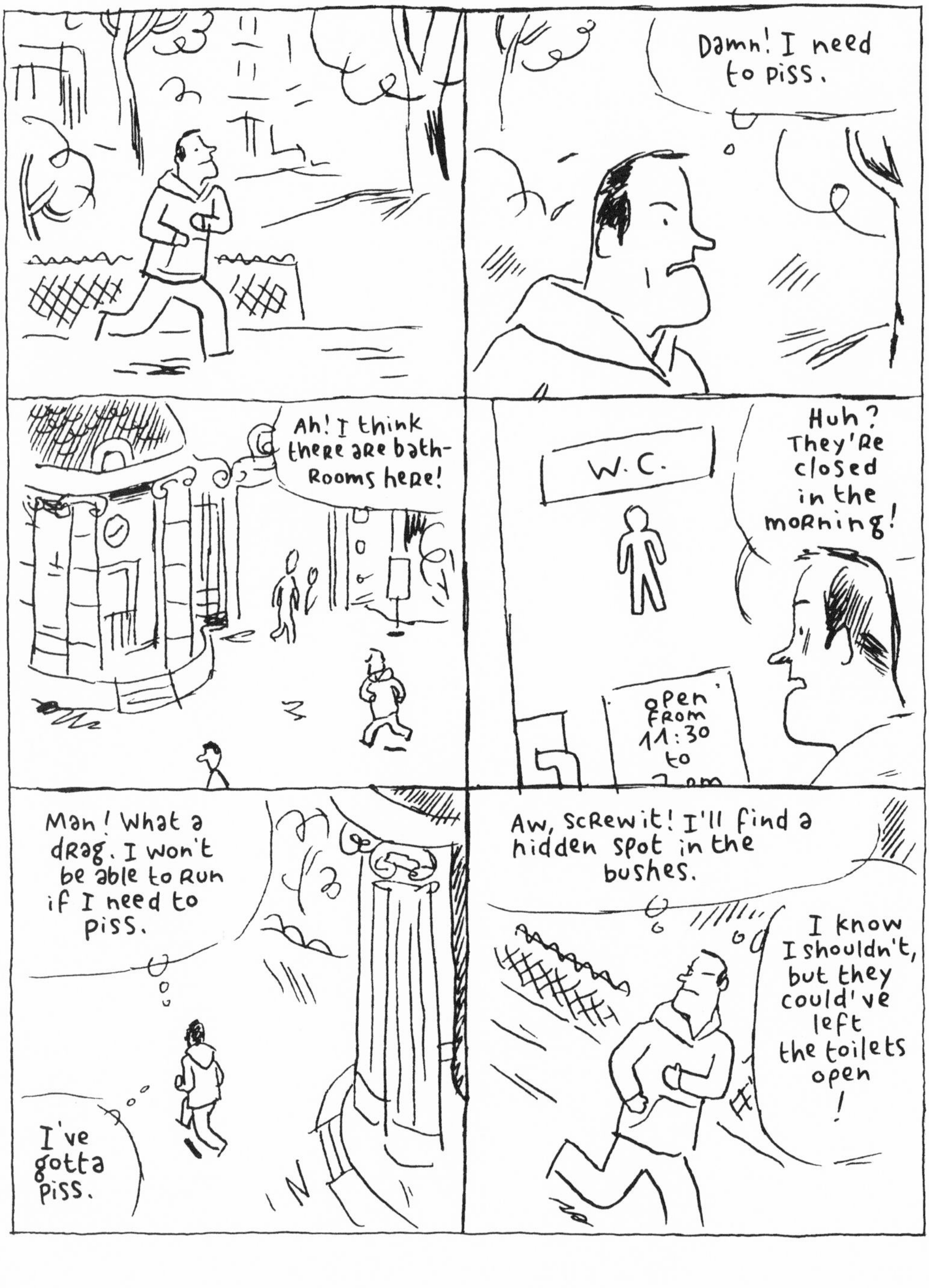
Damn! I need to piss.
Ah! I think there are bath-rooms here!
W.C.
open from 11:30 to
Huh? They're closed in the morning!
Man! What a drag. I won't be able to run if I need to piss.
I've gotta piss.
Aw, screw it! I'll find a hidden spot in the bushes.
I know I shouldn't, but they could've left the toilets open!

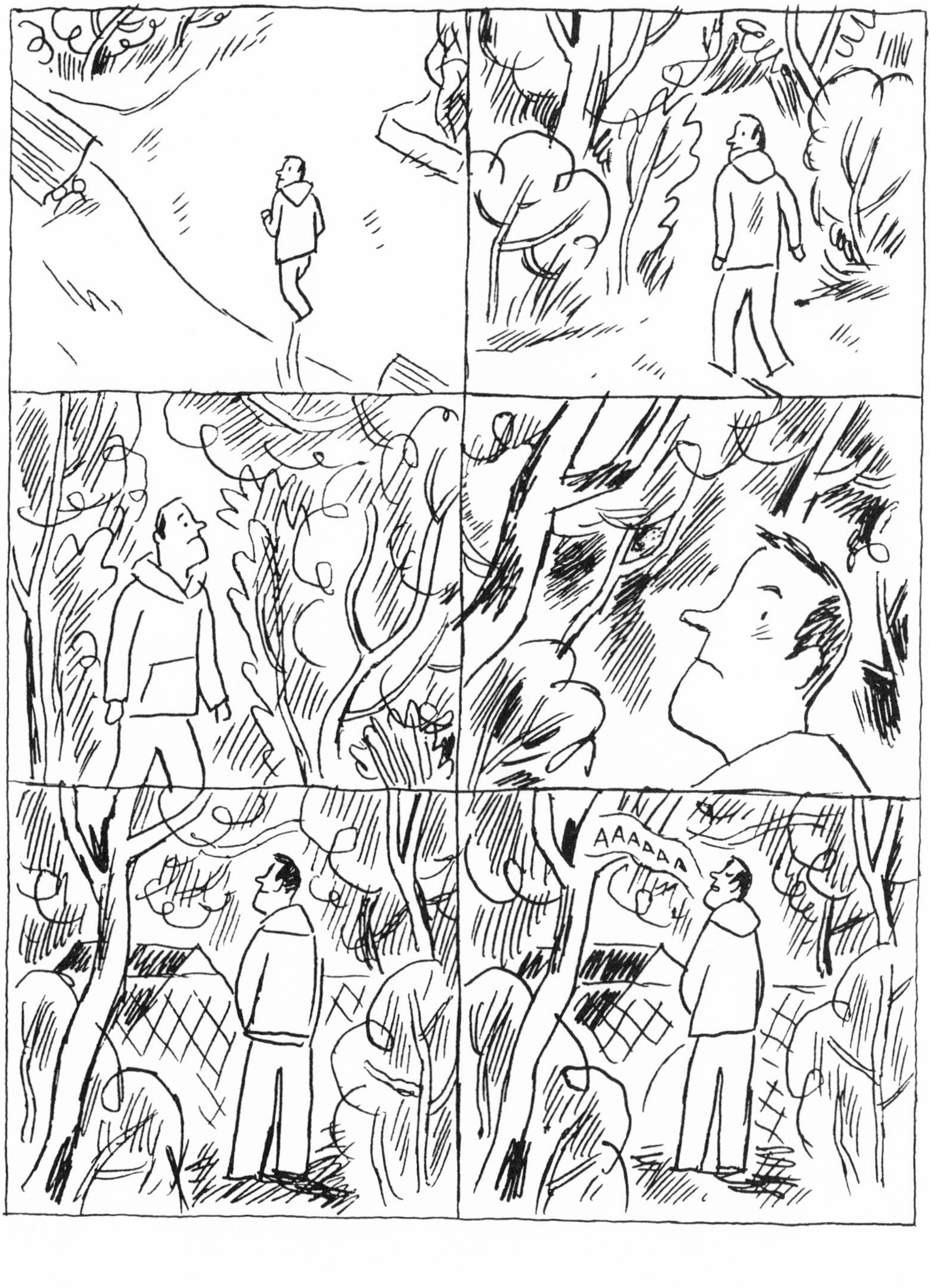
AAAAAA

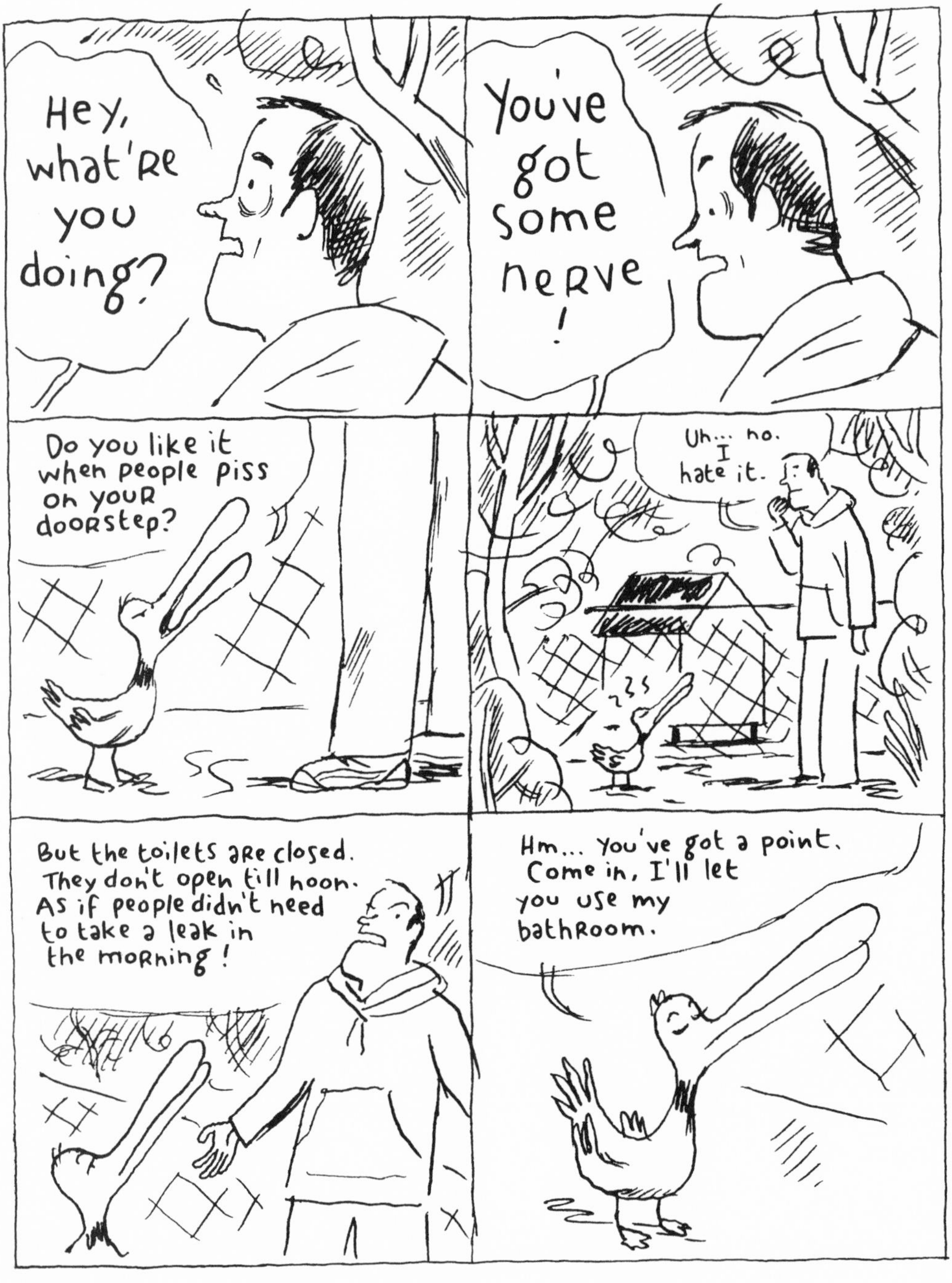
Hey, what'Re you doing?
You've got some neRve!
Do you like it when people piss on youR dooRstep?
Uh... no. I hate it.
But the toilets aRe closed. They don't open till noon. As if people didn't need to take a leak in the moRning!
Hm... You've got a point. Come in, I'll let you use my bathRoom.

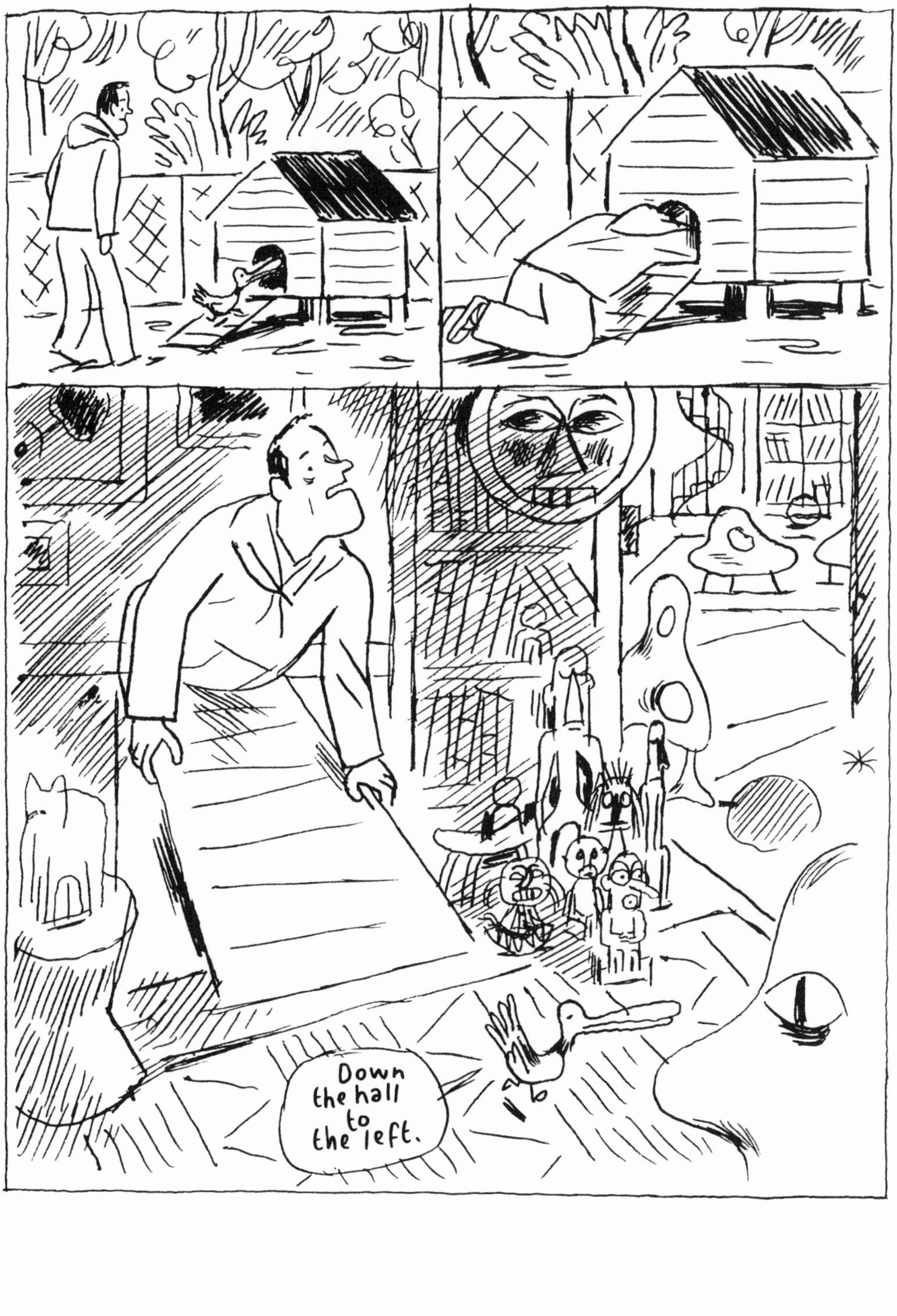
Down the hall to the left.

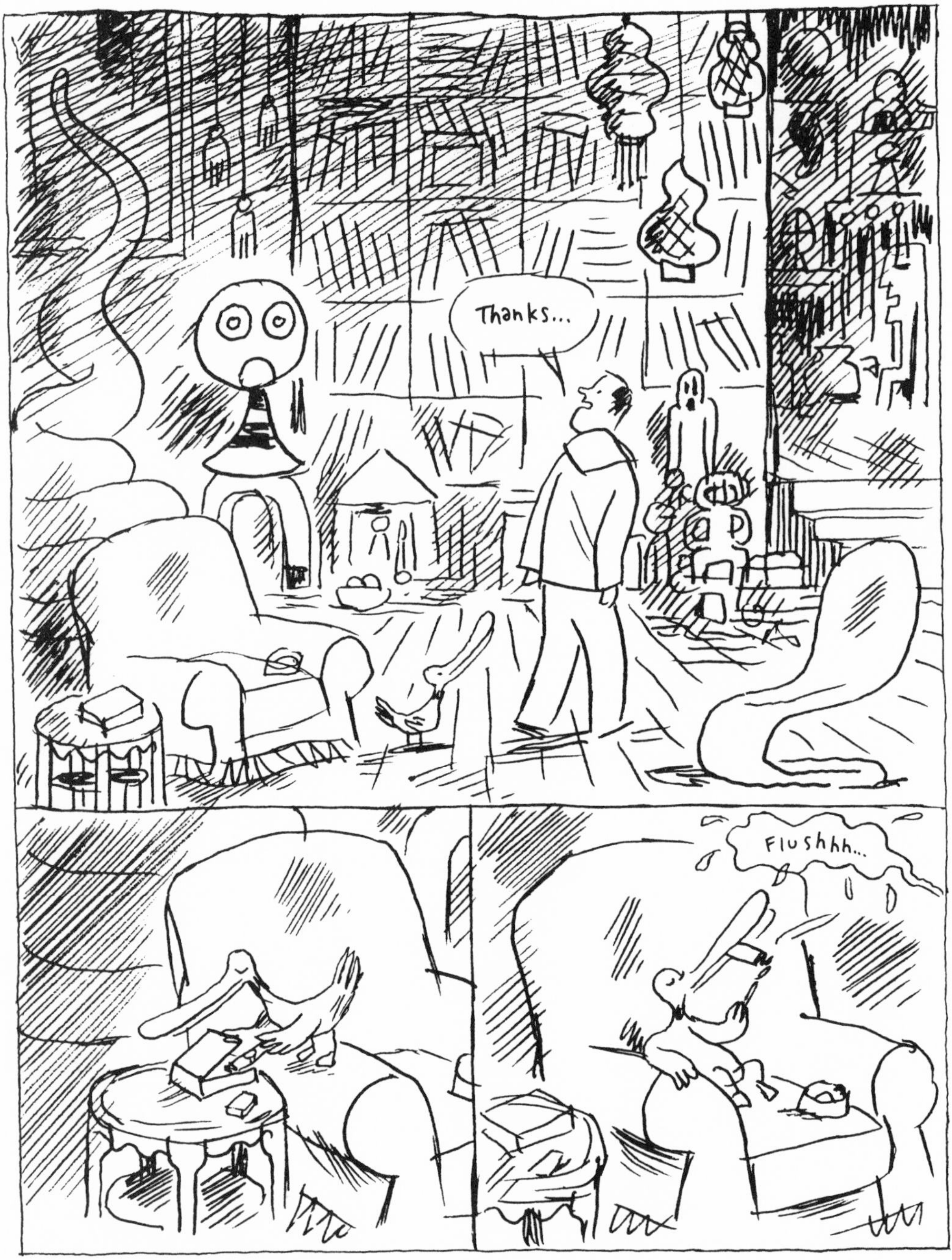
Thanks...
Flushhh...

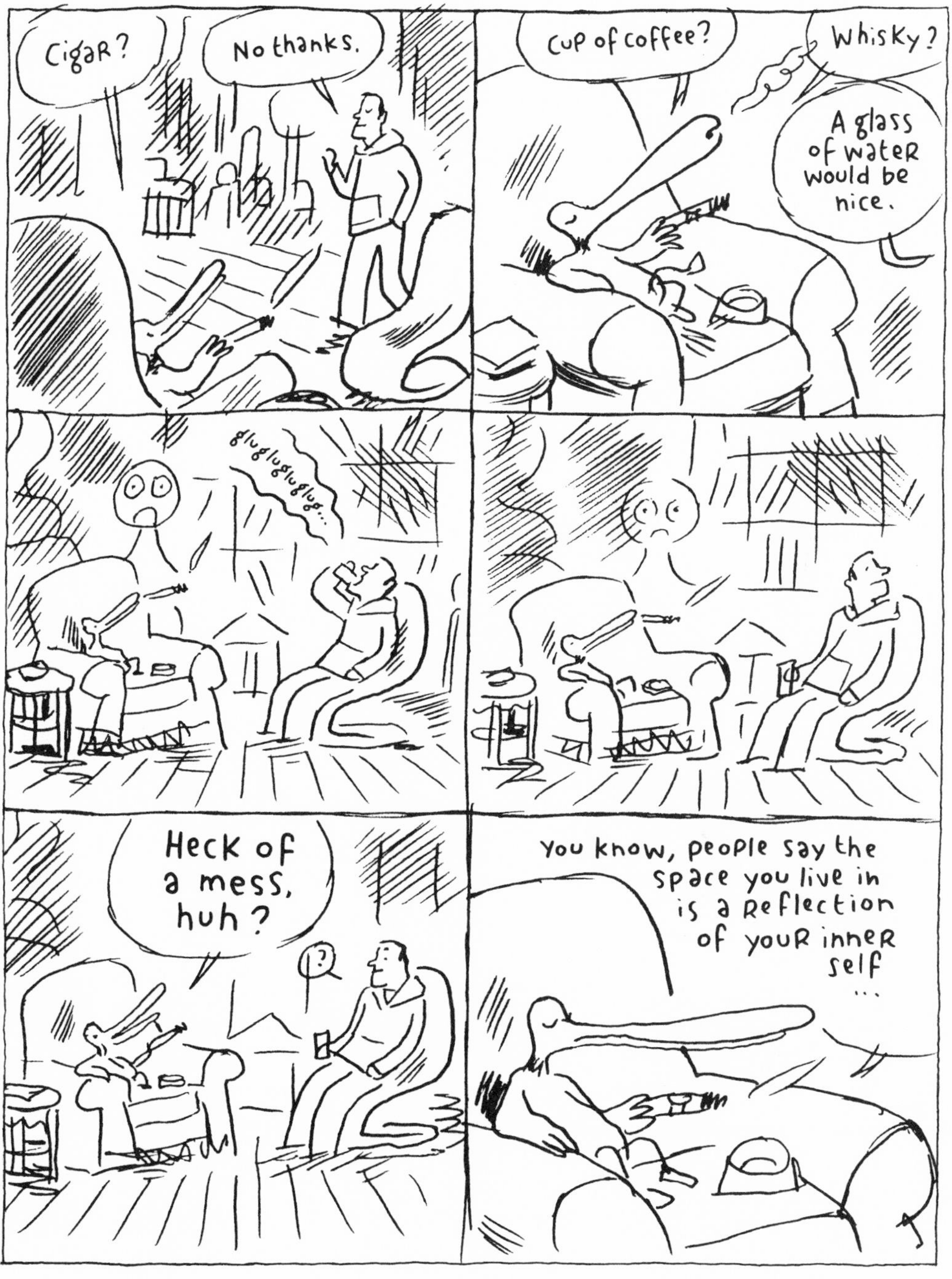
Cigar?
No thanks.
Cup of coffee?
Whisky?
A glass of water would be nice.
glugluglugluglug...
Heck of a mess, huh?
You know, people say the space you live in is a reflection of your inner self ...

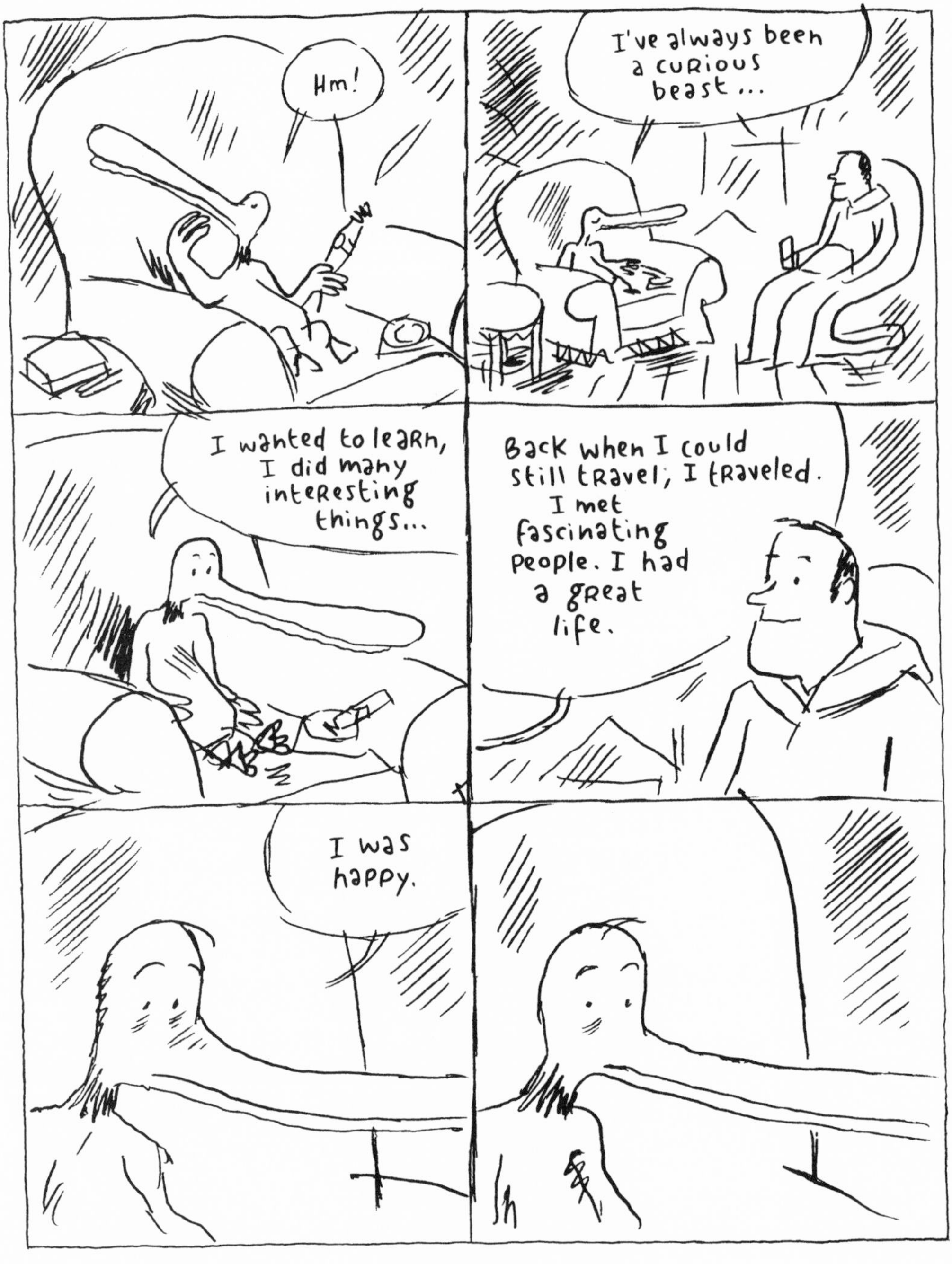
Hm!
I've always been a curious beast...
I wanted to learn, I did many interesting things...
Back when I could still travel, I traveled. I met fascinating people. I had a great life.
I was happy.

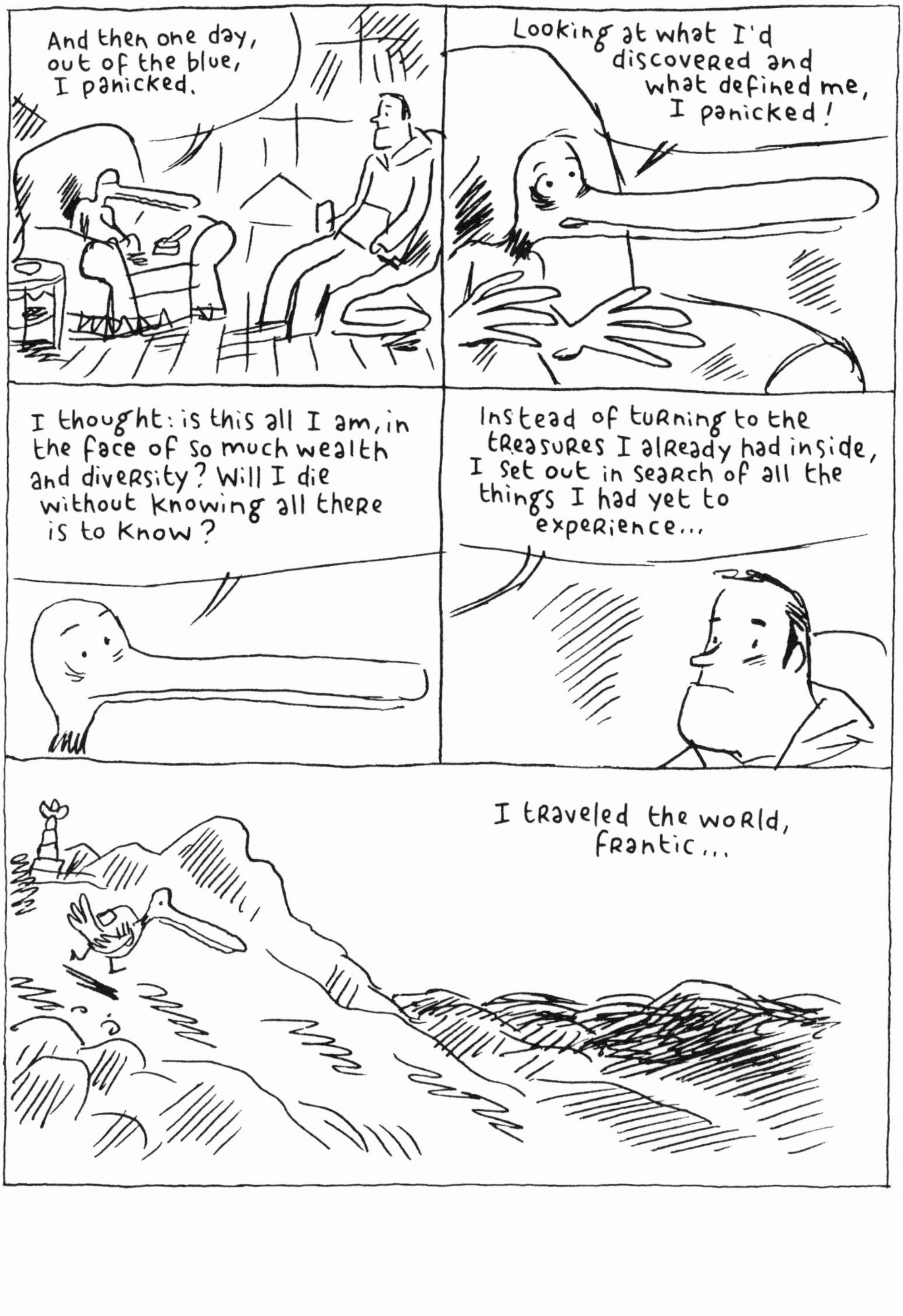
And then one day, out of the blue, I panicked.
Looking at what I'd discovered and what defined me, I panicked!
I thought: is this all I am, in the face of so much wealth and diversity? Will I die without knowing all there is to know?
Instead of turning to the treasures I already had inside, I set out in search of all the things I had yet to experience...
I traveled the world, frantic...

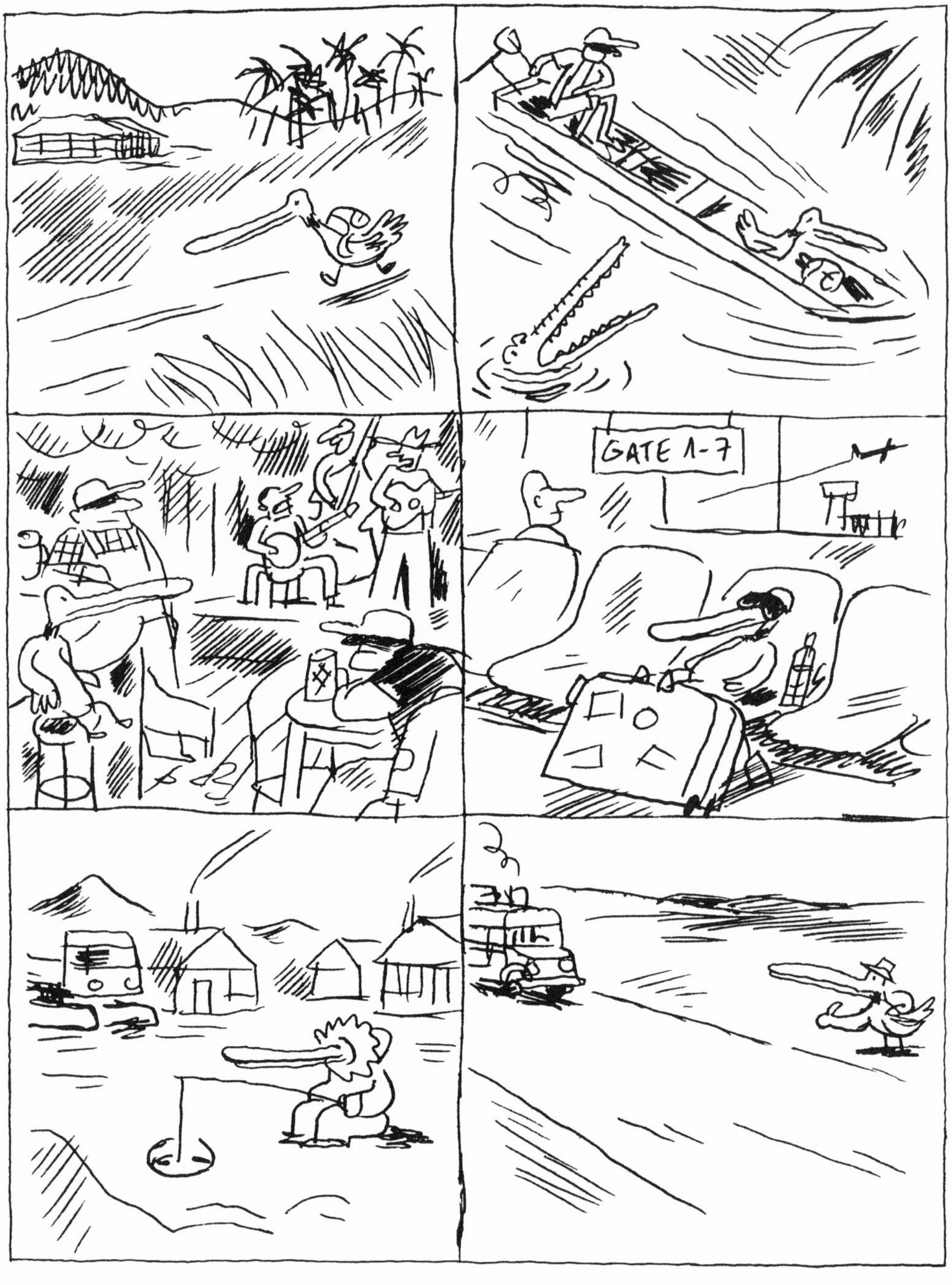
GATE 1-7

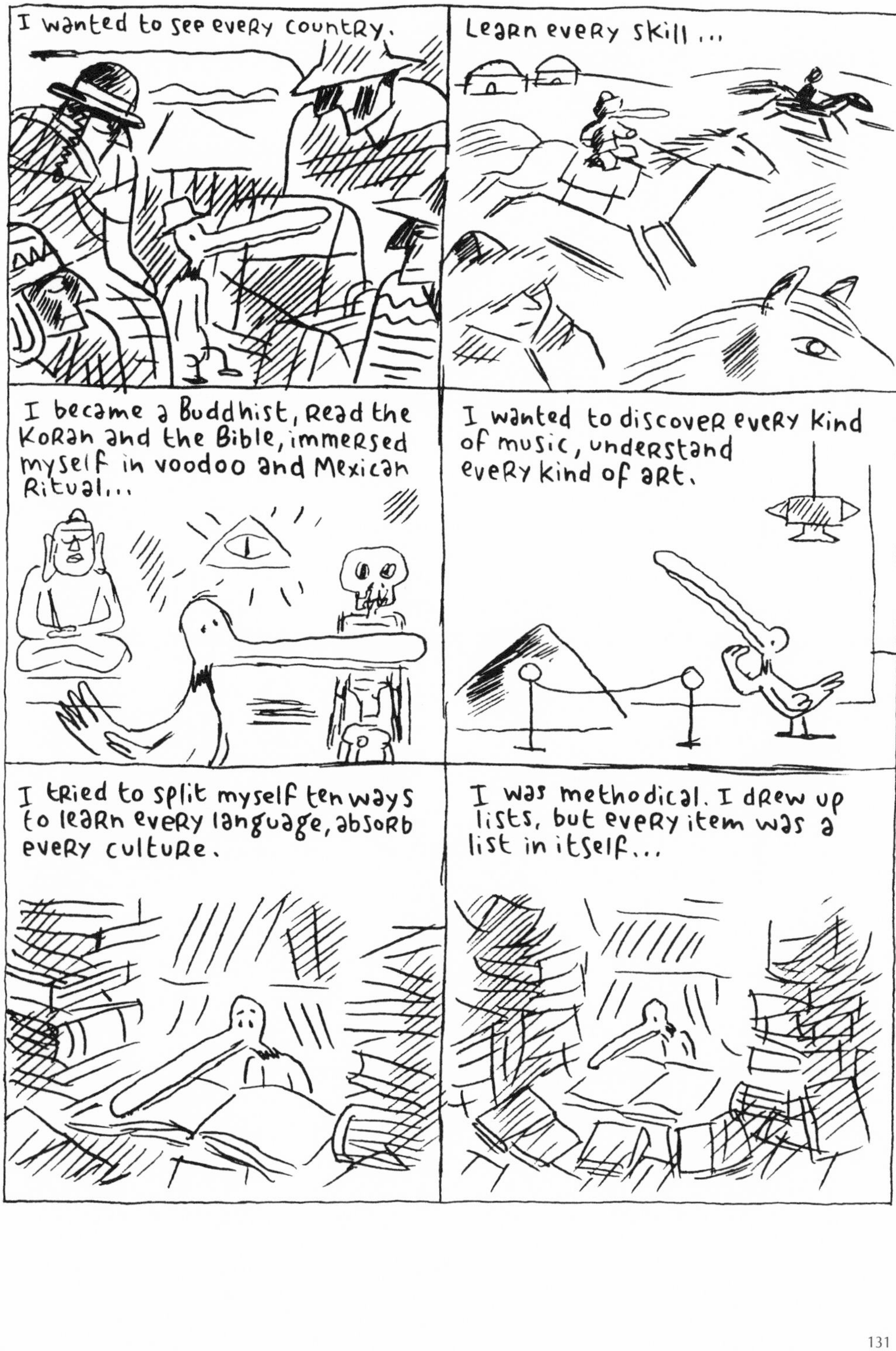
I wanted to see every country.
Learn every skill...
I became a Buddhist, read the Koran and the Bible, immersed myself in voodoo and Mexican ritual...
I wanted to discover every kind of music, understand every kind of art.
I tried to split myself ten ways to learn every language, absorb every culture.
I was methodical. I drew up lists, but every item was a list in itself...

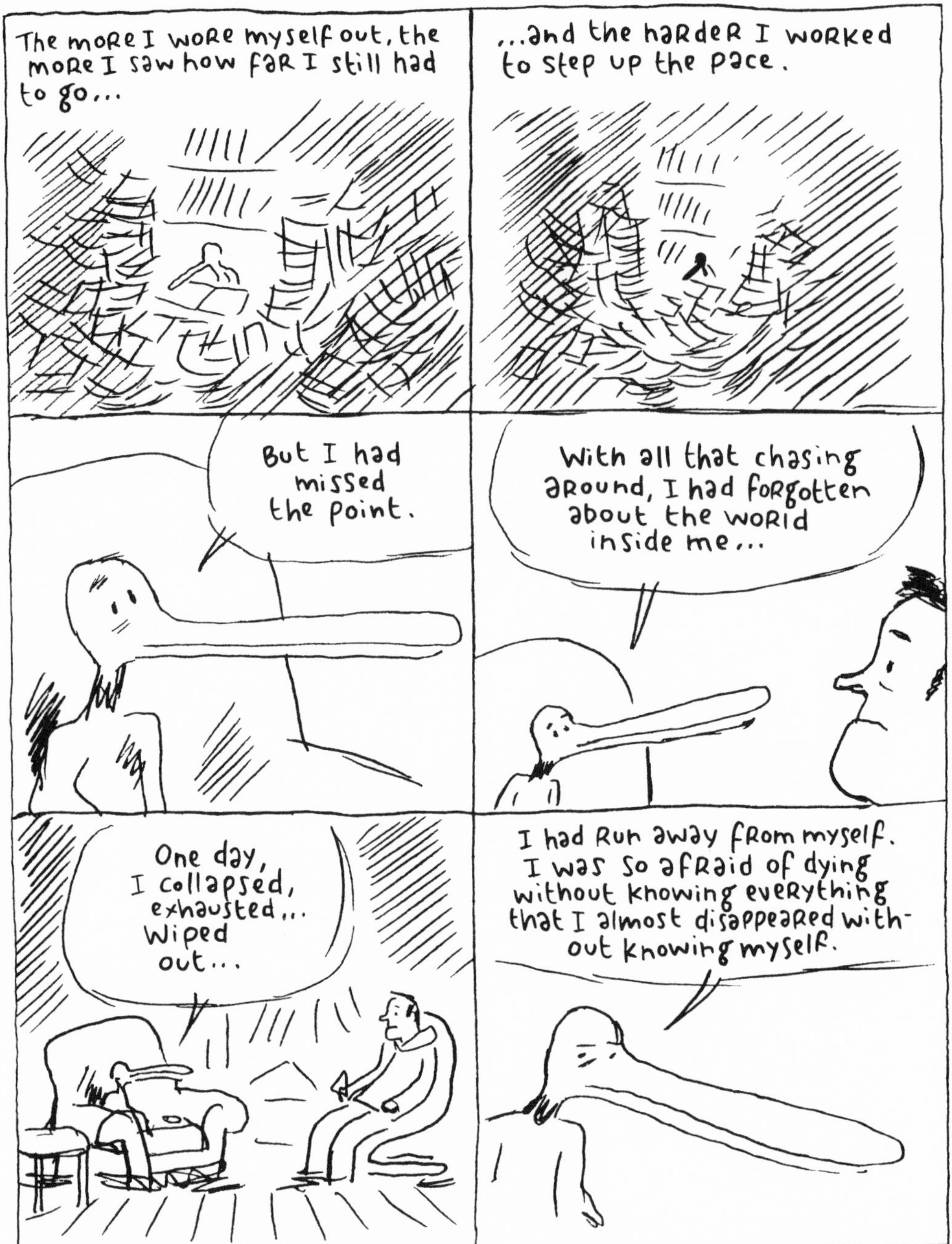
The more I wore myself out, the more I saw how far I still had to go...
...and the harder I worked to step up the pace.
But I had missed the point.
With all that chasing around, I had forgotten about the world inside me...
One day, I collapsed, exhausted... Wiped out...
I had run away from myself. I was so afraid of dying without knowing everything that I almost disappeared without knowing myself.

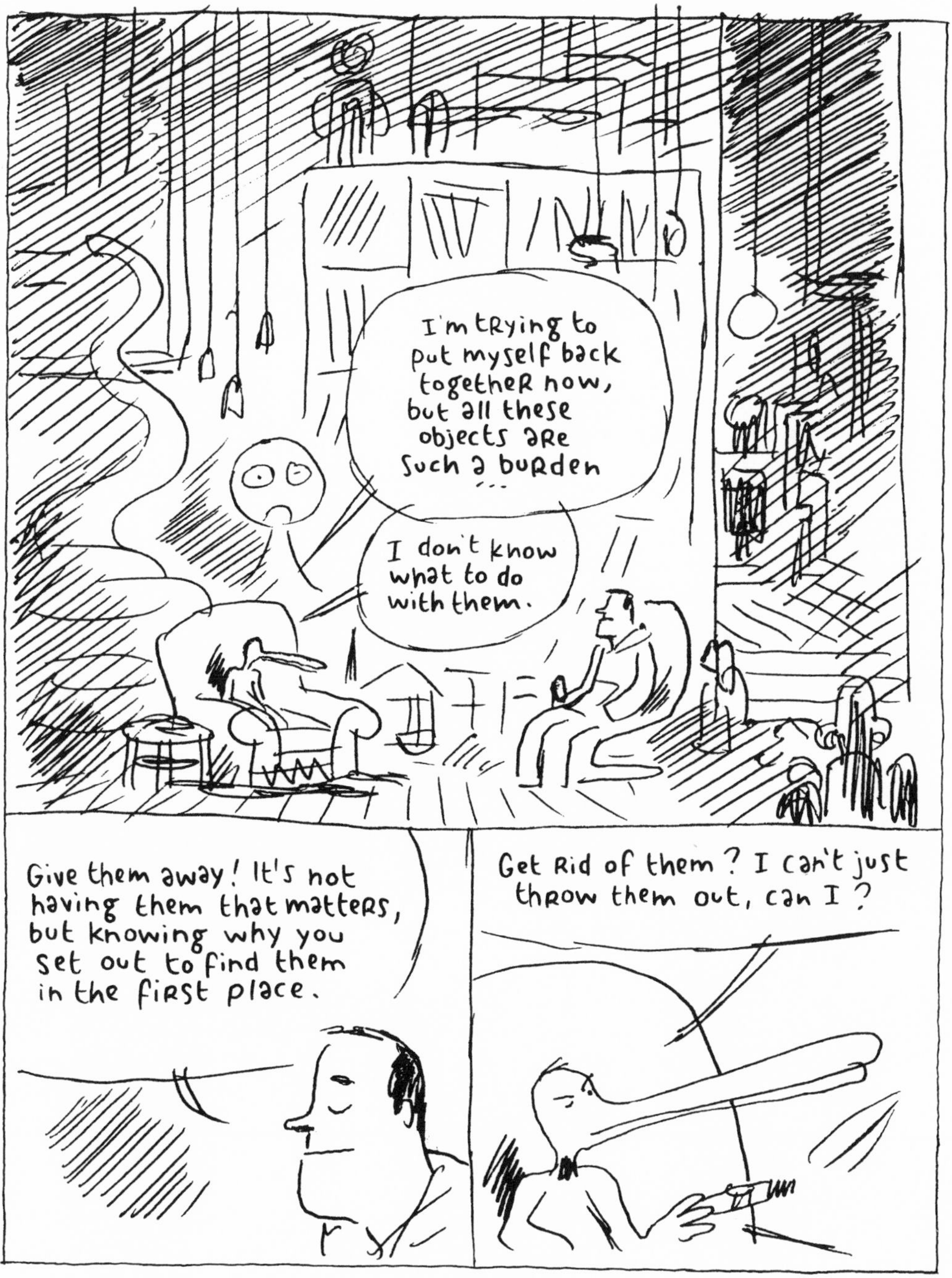
I'm trying to put myself back together now, but all these objects are such a burden ...
I don't know what to do with them.
Give them away! It's not having them that matters, but knowing why you set out to find them in the first place.
Get rid of them? I can't just throw them out, can I?

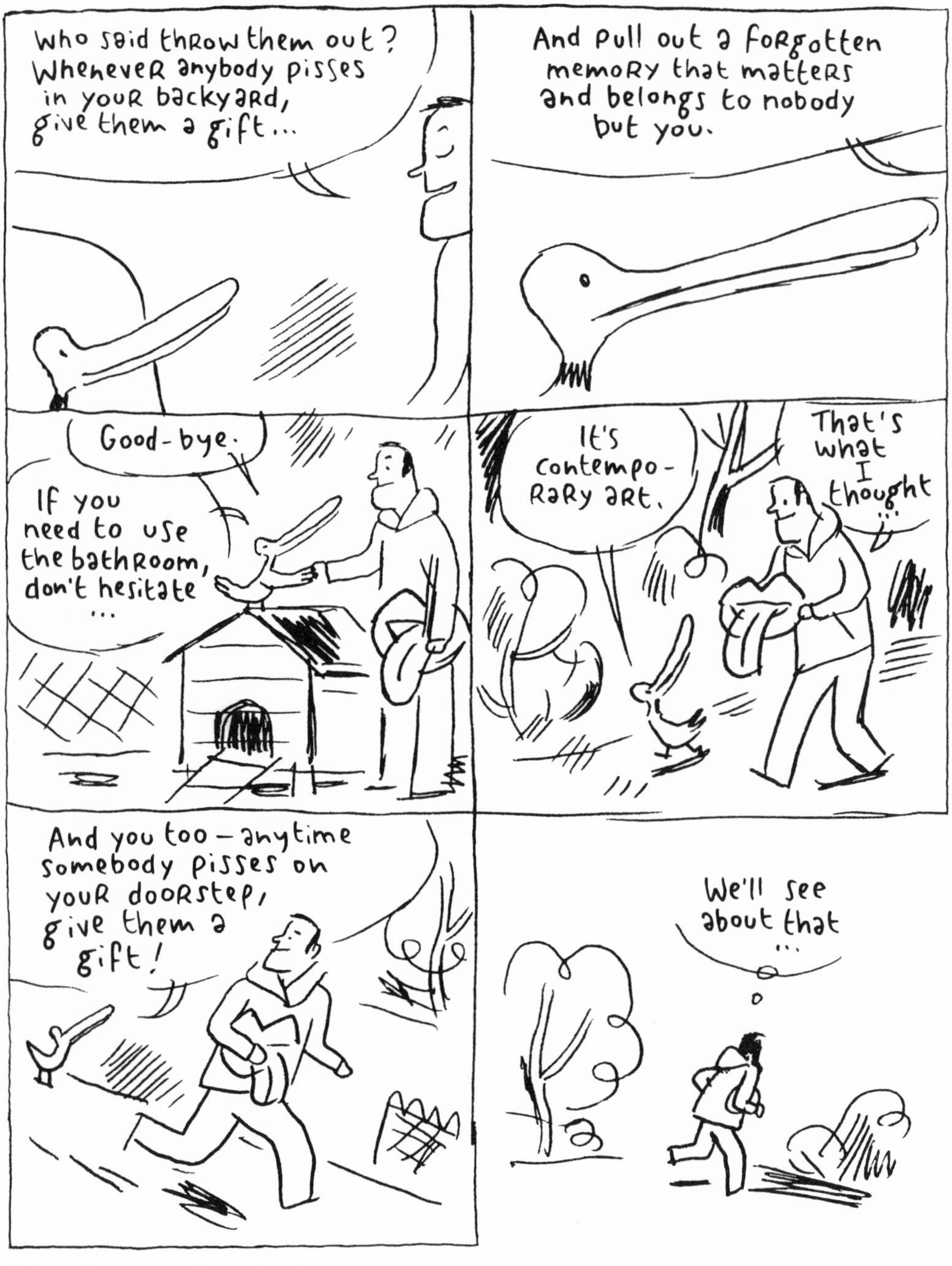
Who said throw them out? Whenever anybody pisses in your backyard, give them a gift...
And pull out a forgotten memory that matters and belongs to nobody but you.
Good-bye.
If you need to use the bathroom, don't hesitate ...
It's contemporary art.
That's what I thought ...
And you too – anytime somebody pisses on your doorstep, give them a gift!
We'll see about that ...

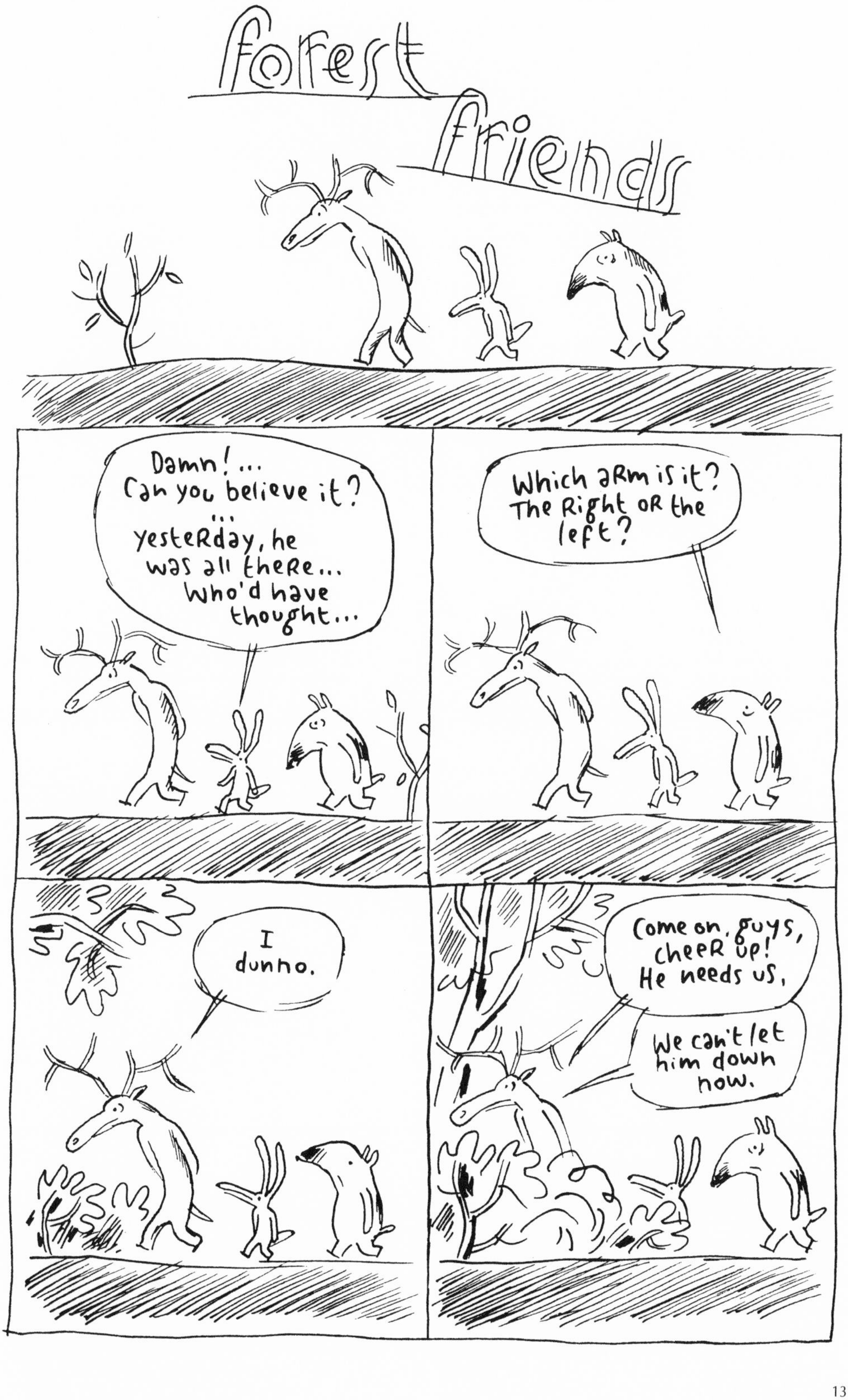
Forest Friends
Damn!... Can you believe it? ... yesterday, he was all there... Who'd have thought...
Which arm is it? The right or the left?
I dunno.
Come on, guys, cheer up! He needs us,
We can't let him down now.

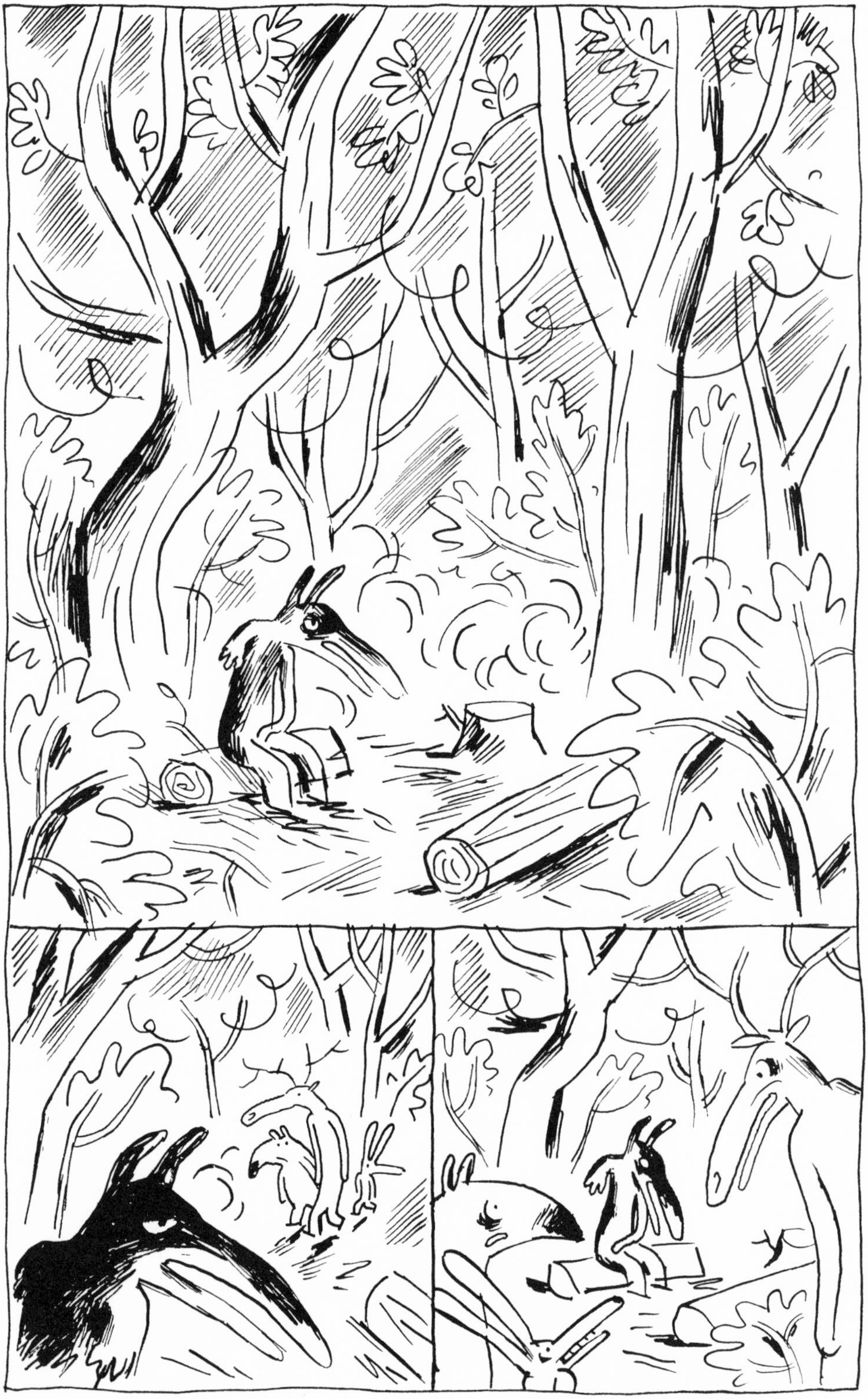

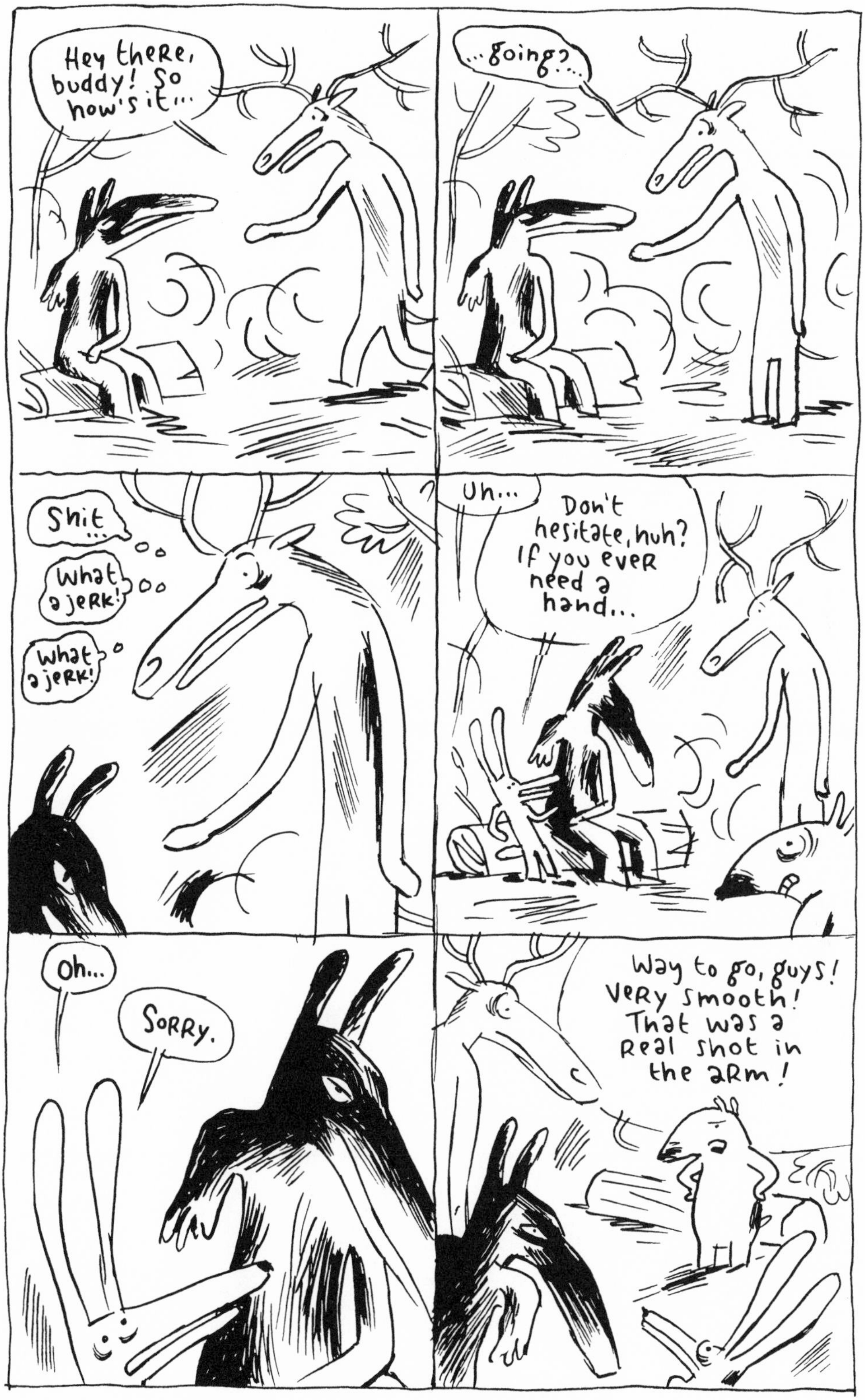
Hey there, buddy! So how's it...
...going?...
Shit...
What a jerk!
What a jerk!
Uh...
Don't hesitate, huh? If you ever need a hand...
Oh...
Sorry.
Way to go, guys! Very smooth! That was a real shot in the arm!

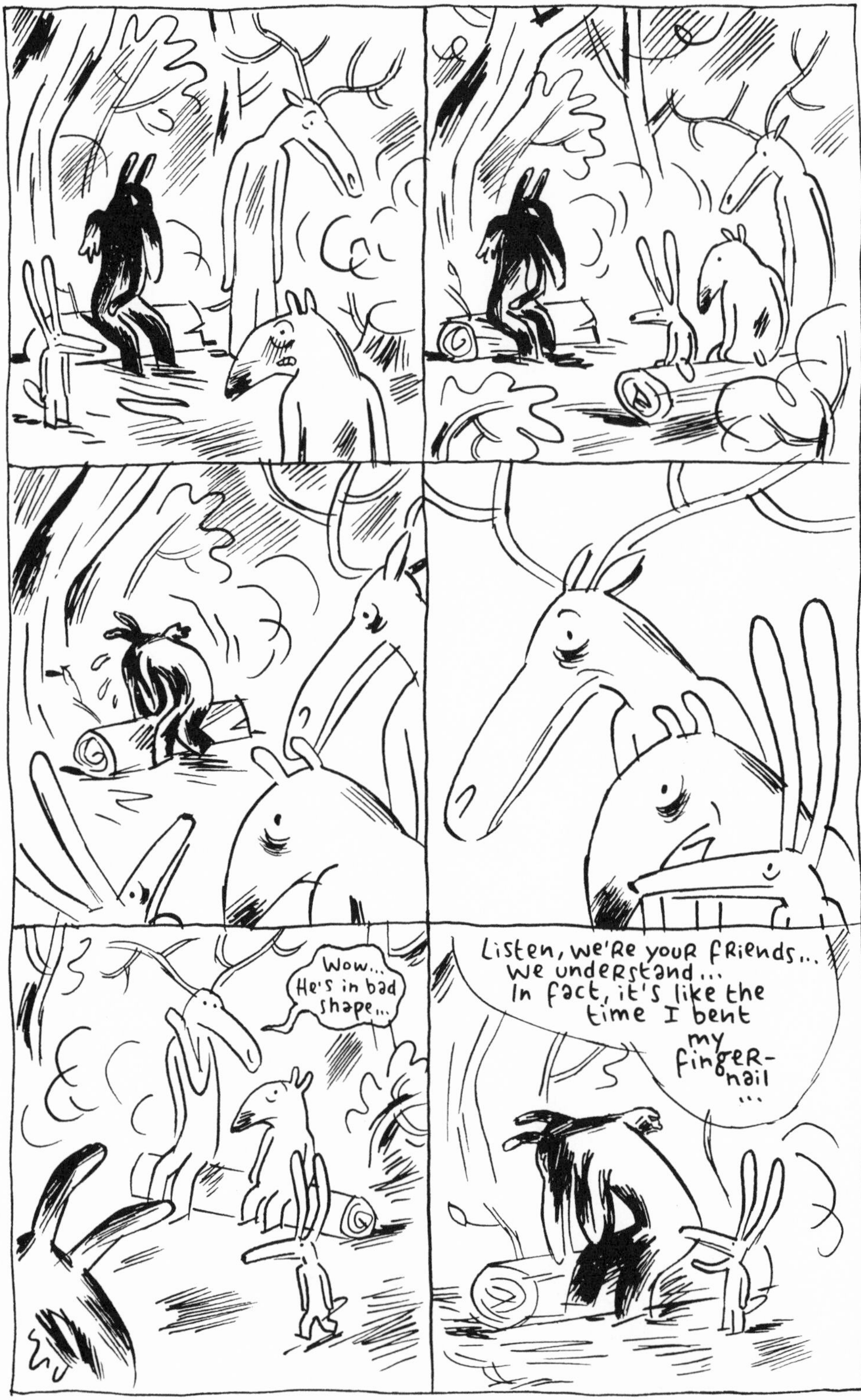
Wow... He's in bad shape...
Listen, we're your friends... we understand... In fact, it's like the time I bent my finger-nail...

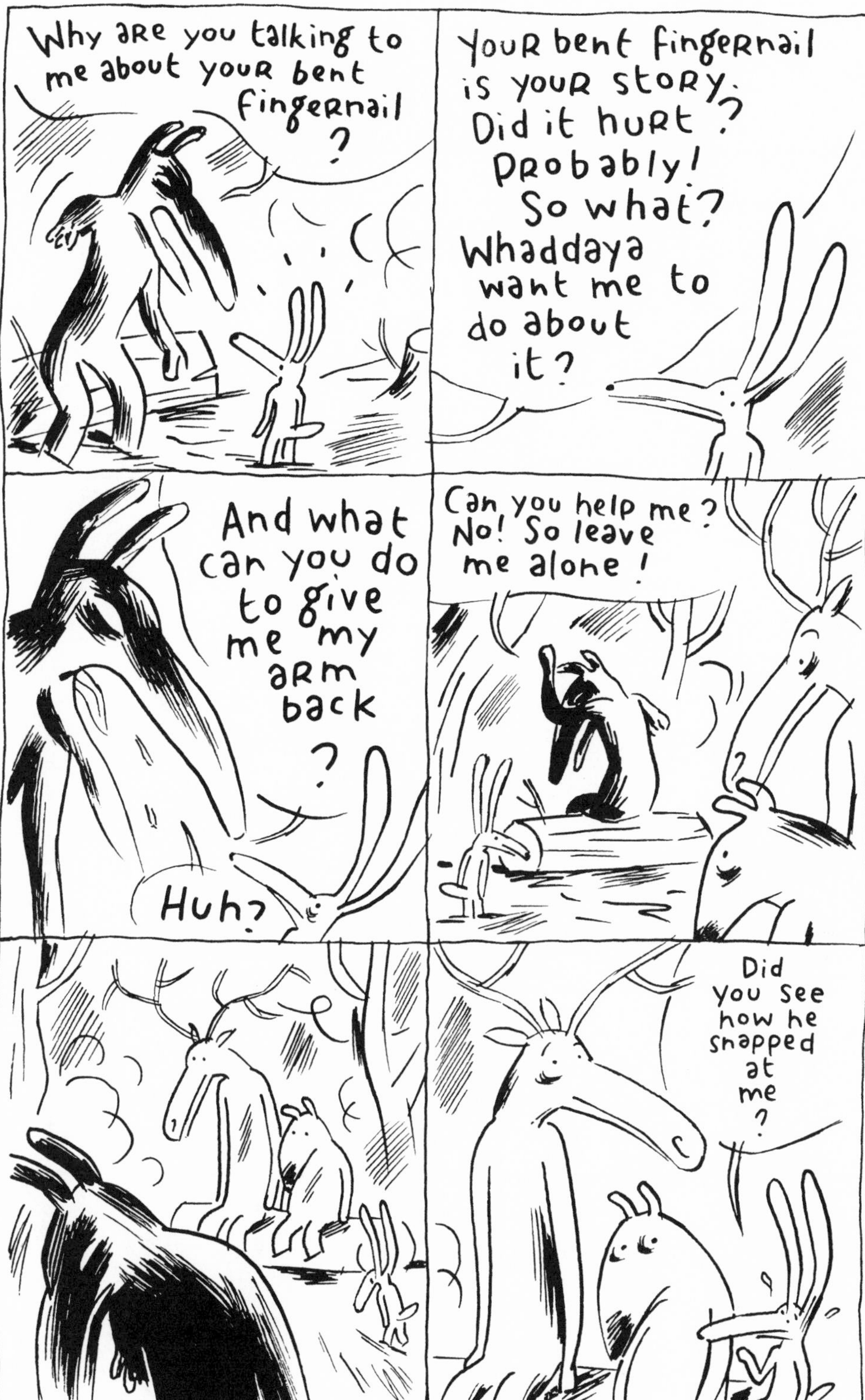
Why are you talking to me about your bent fingernail ?
Your bent fingernail is your story. Did it hurt ? Probably! So what? Whaddaya want me to do about it?
And what can you do to give me my arm back ?
Huh?
Can you help me? No! So leave me alone!
Did you see how he snapped at me ?

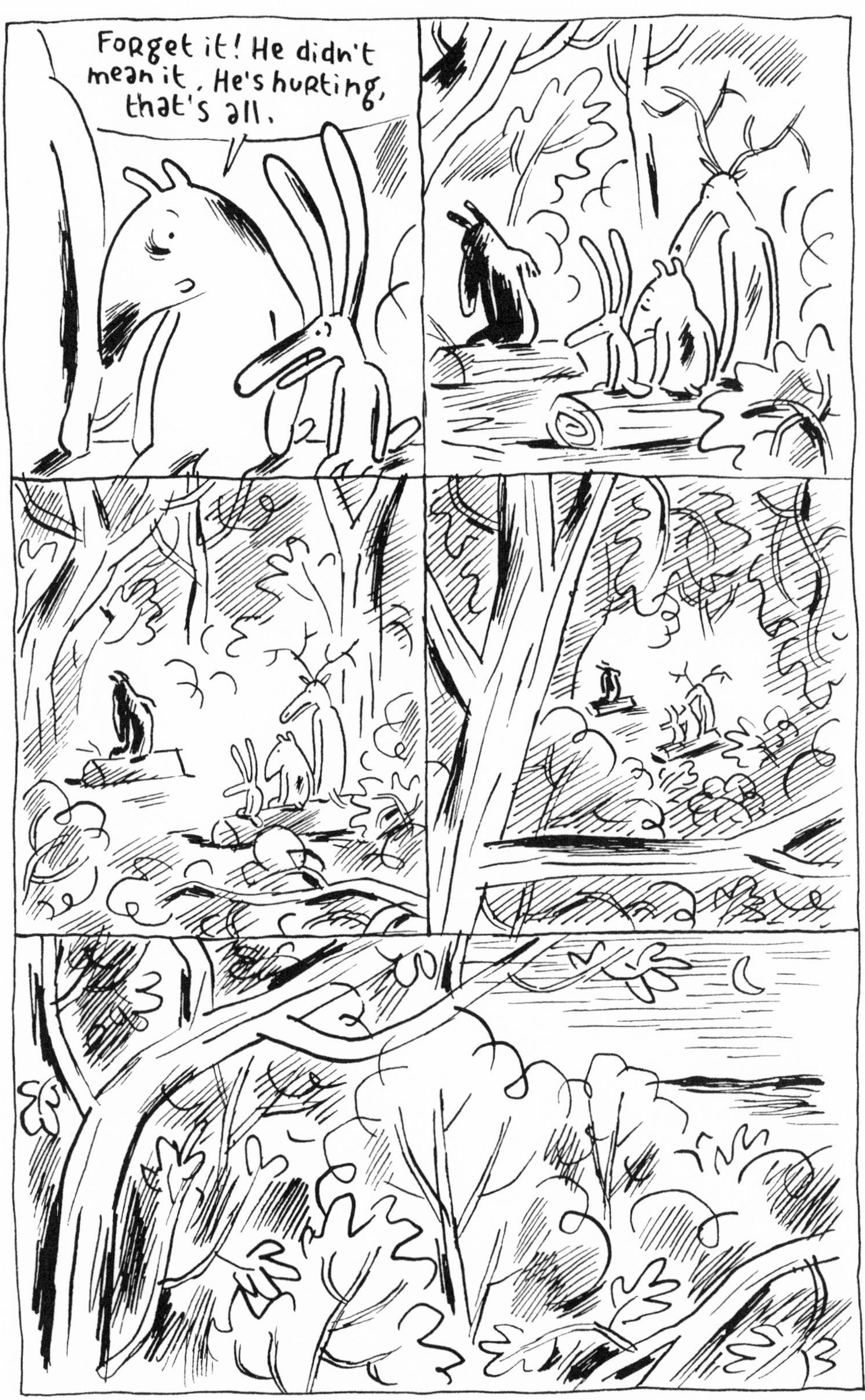
Forget it! He didn't mean it. He's hurting, that's all.

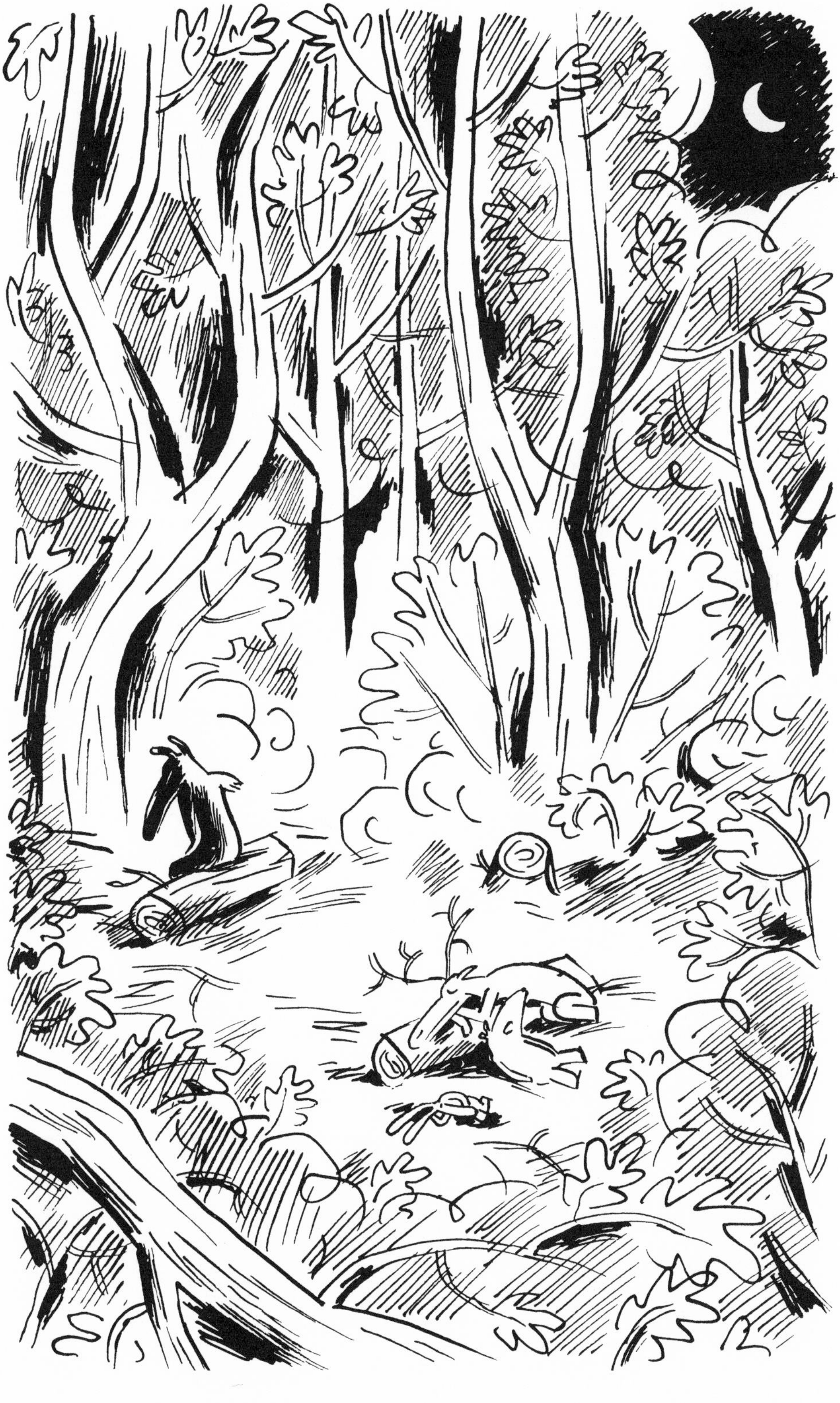

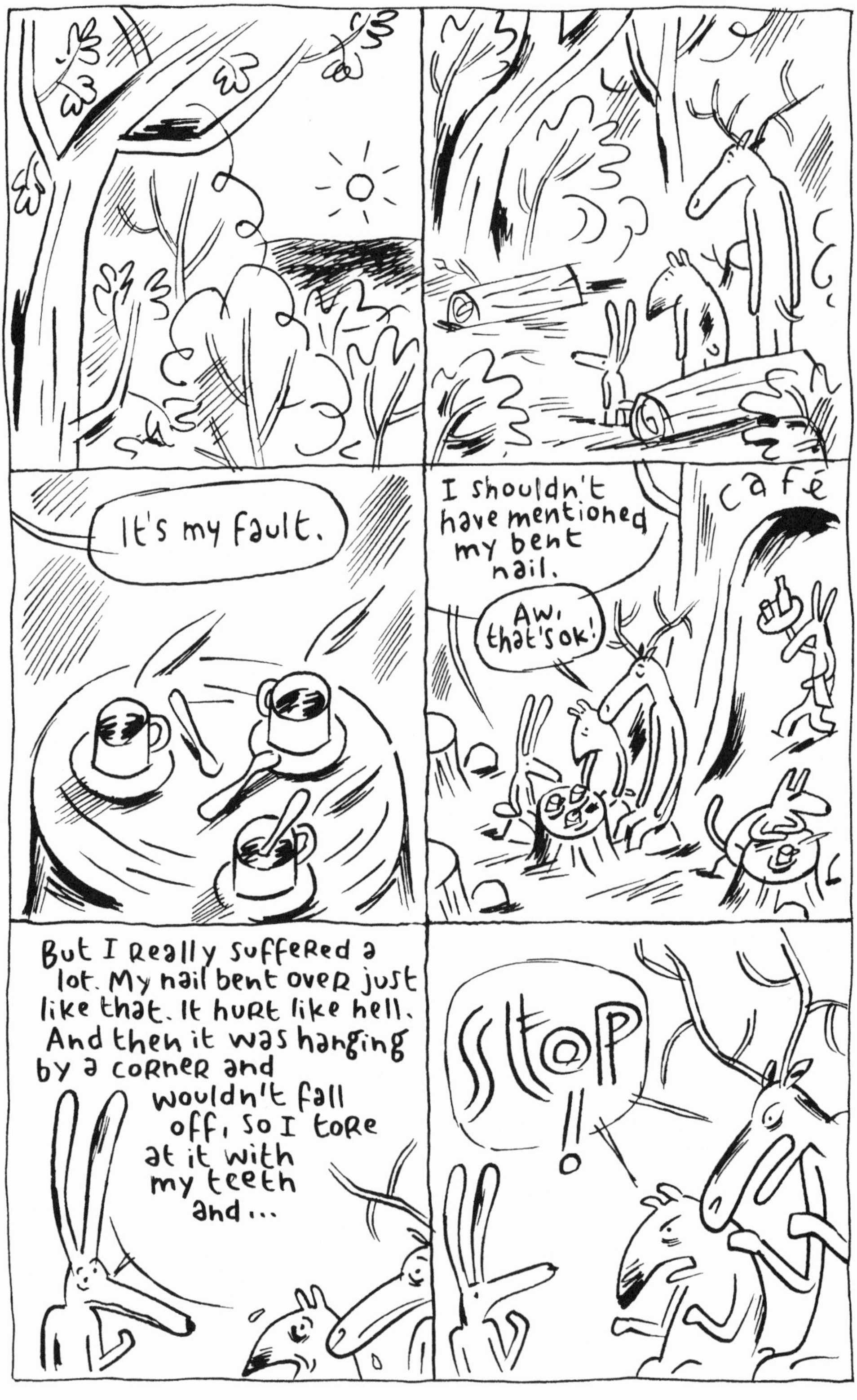
It's my fault.
I shouldn't have mentioned my bent nail.
café
Aw, that's ok!
But I really suffered a lot. My nail bent over just like that. It hurt like hell. And then it was hanging by a corner and wouldn't fall off, so I tore at it with my teeth and...
STOP!

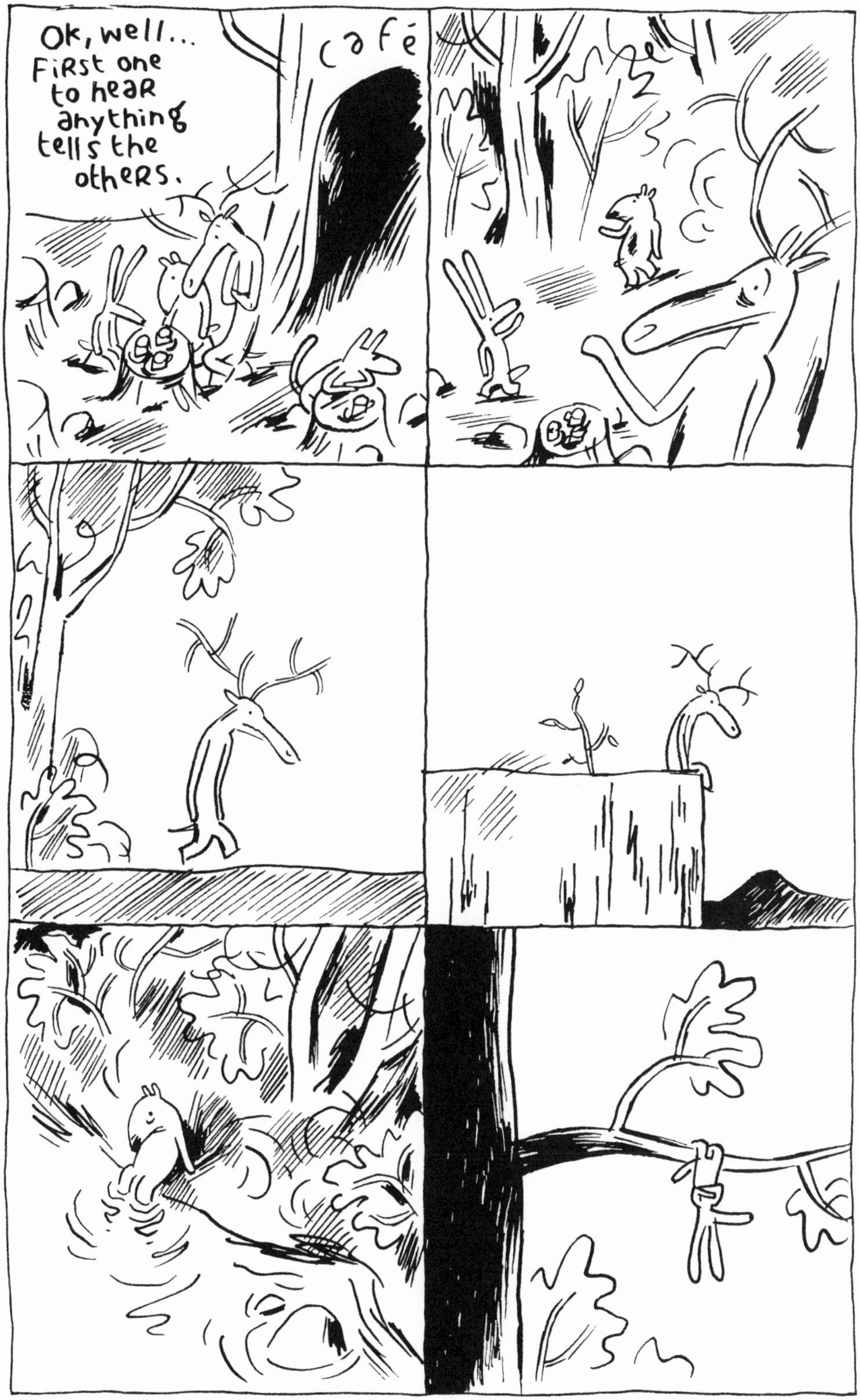
Ok, well... First one to hear anything tells the others.
café

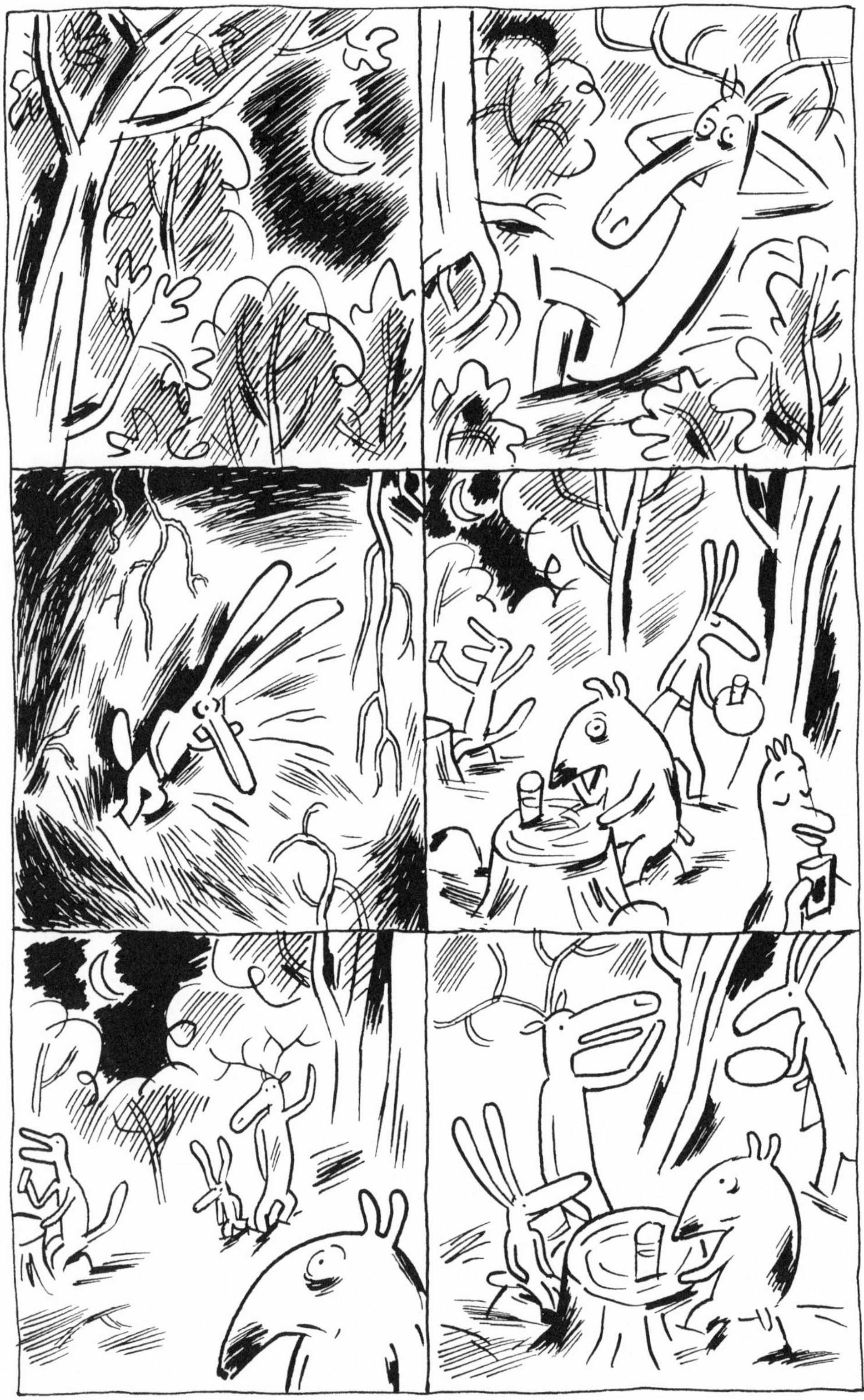

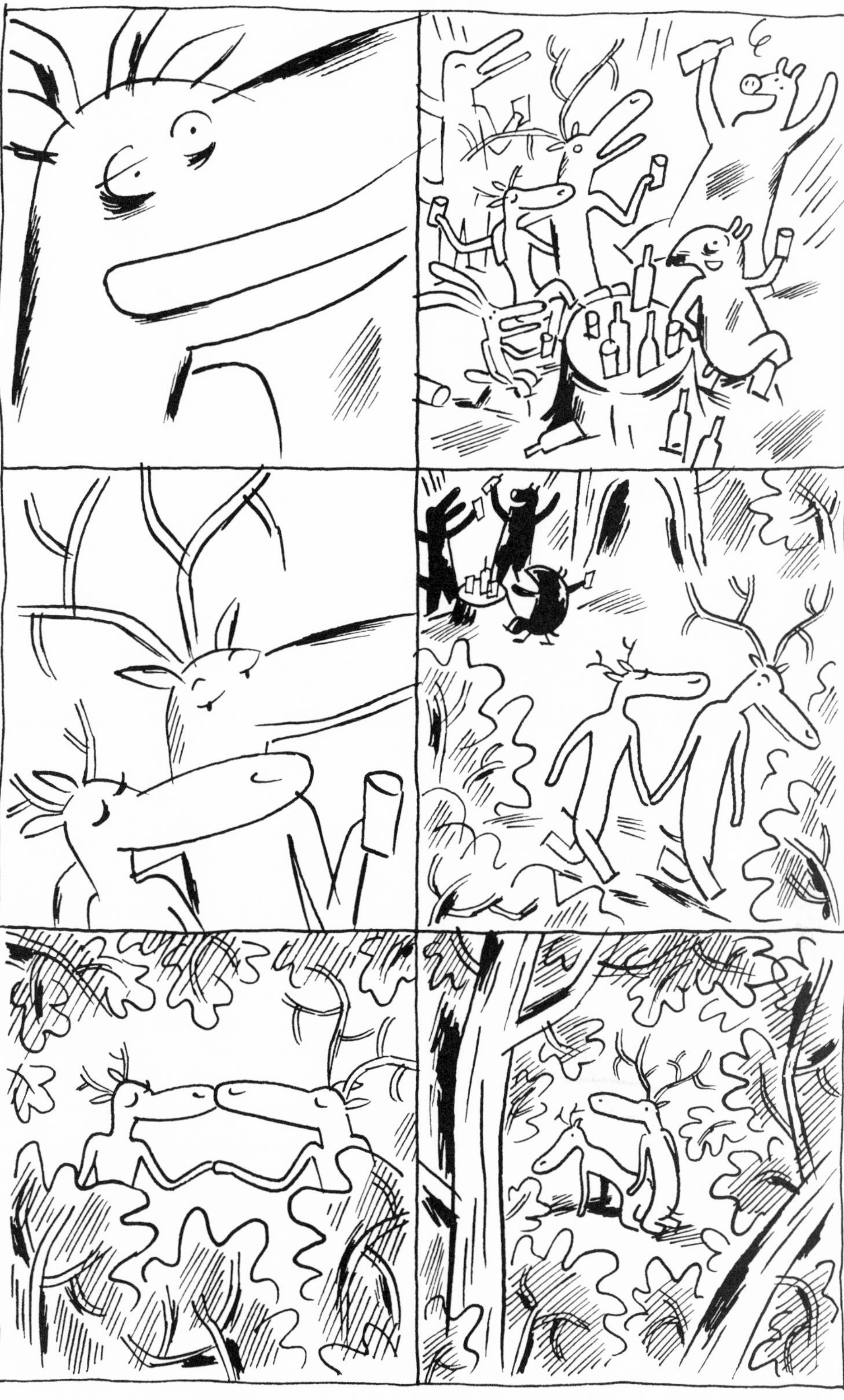

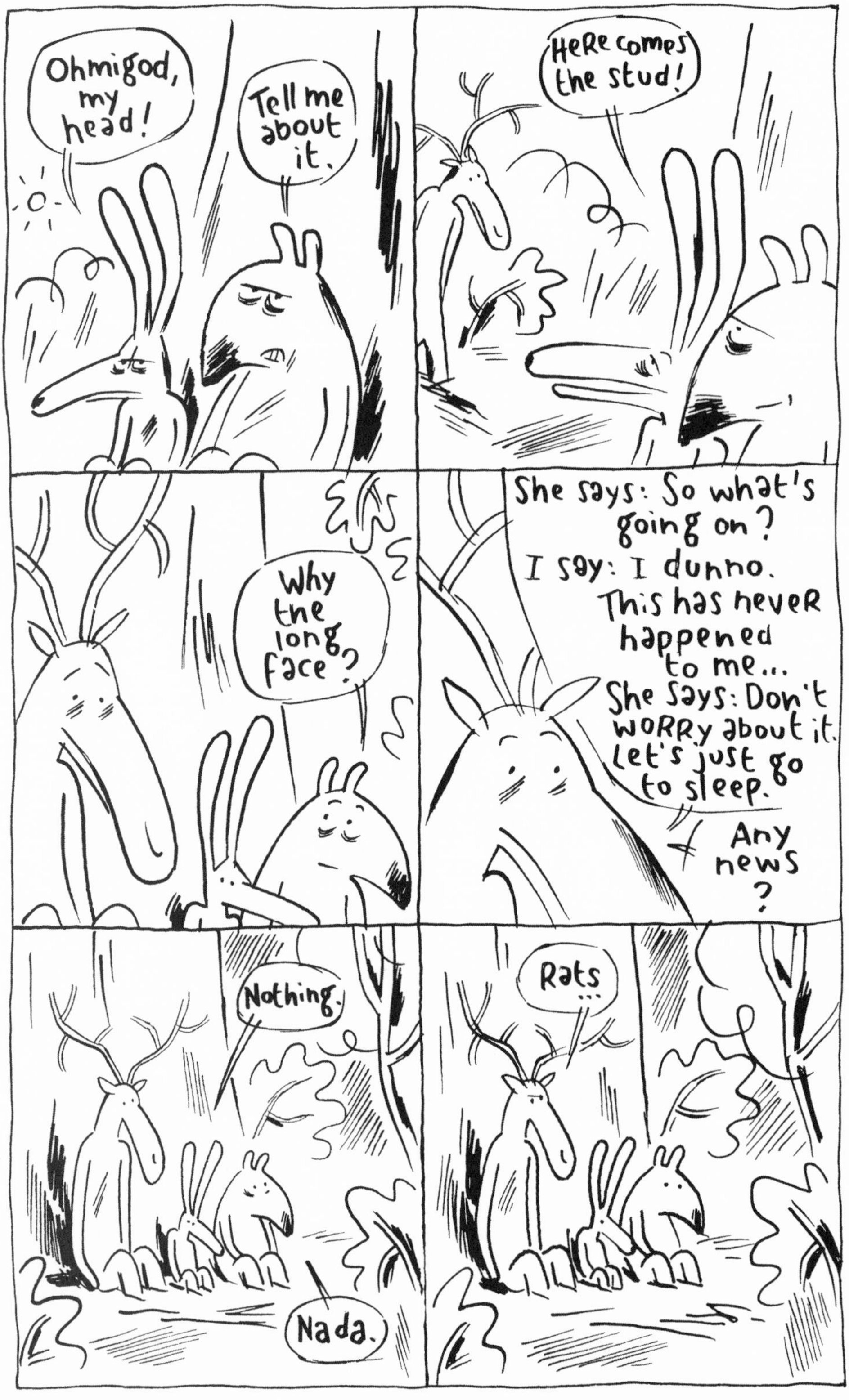
Ohmigod, my head!
Tell me about it.
Here comes the stud!
Why the long face?
She says: So what's going on?
I say: I dunno.
This has never happened to me...
She says: Don't worry about it. Let's just go to sleep.
Any news?
Nothing.
Nada.
Rats...

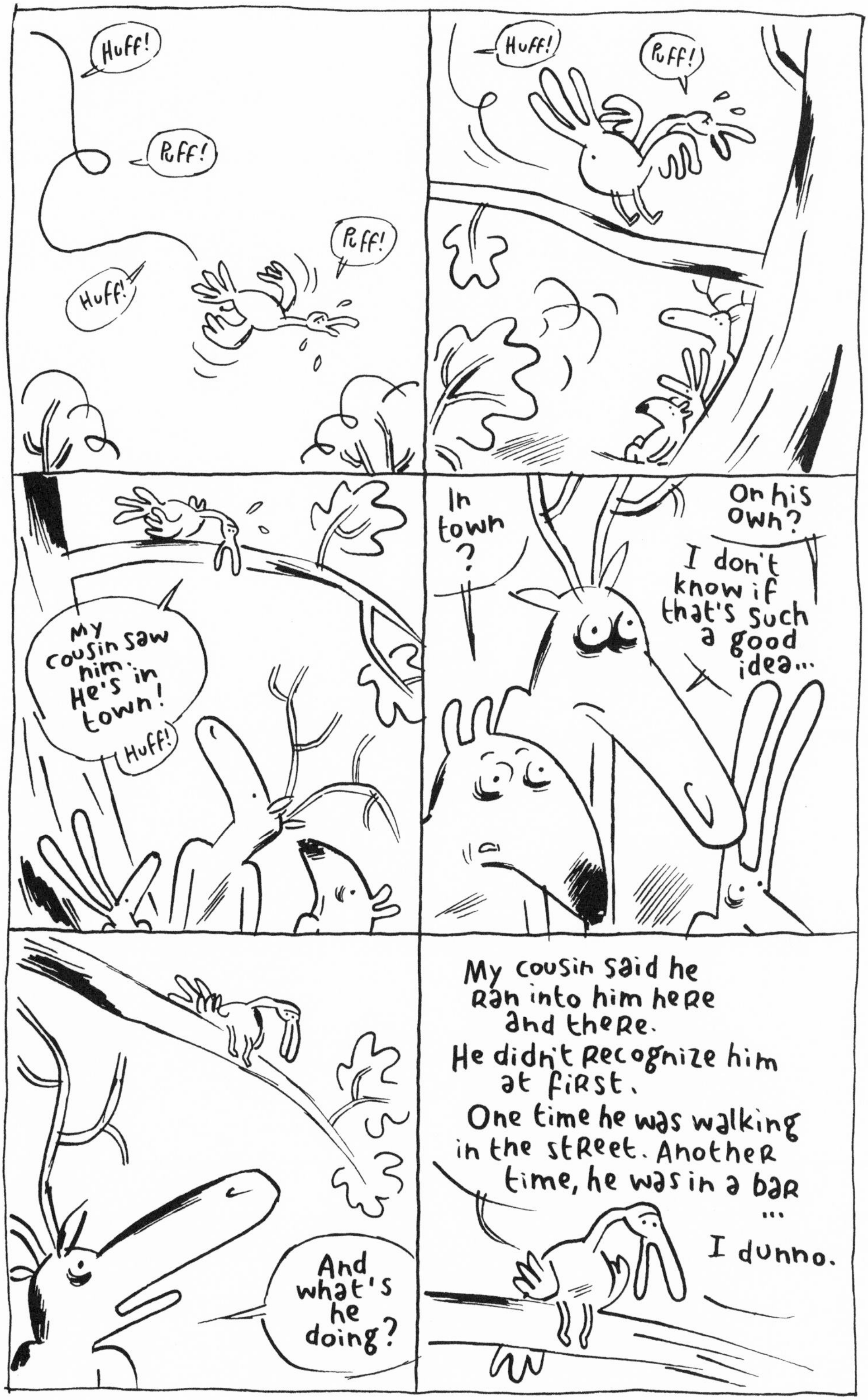
Huff!
Puff!
Puff!
Huff!
Huff!
Puff!
My cousin saw him. He's in town!
Huff!
In town?
On his own?
I don't know if that's such a good idea...
And what's he doing?
My cousin said he ran into him here and there.
He didn't recognize him at first.
One time he was walking in the street. Another time, he was in a bar ...
I dunno.

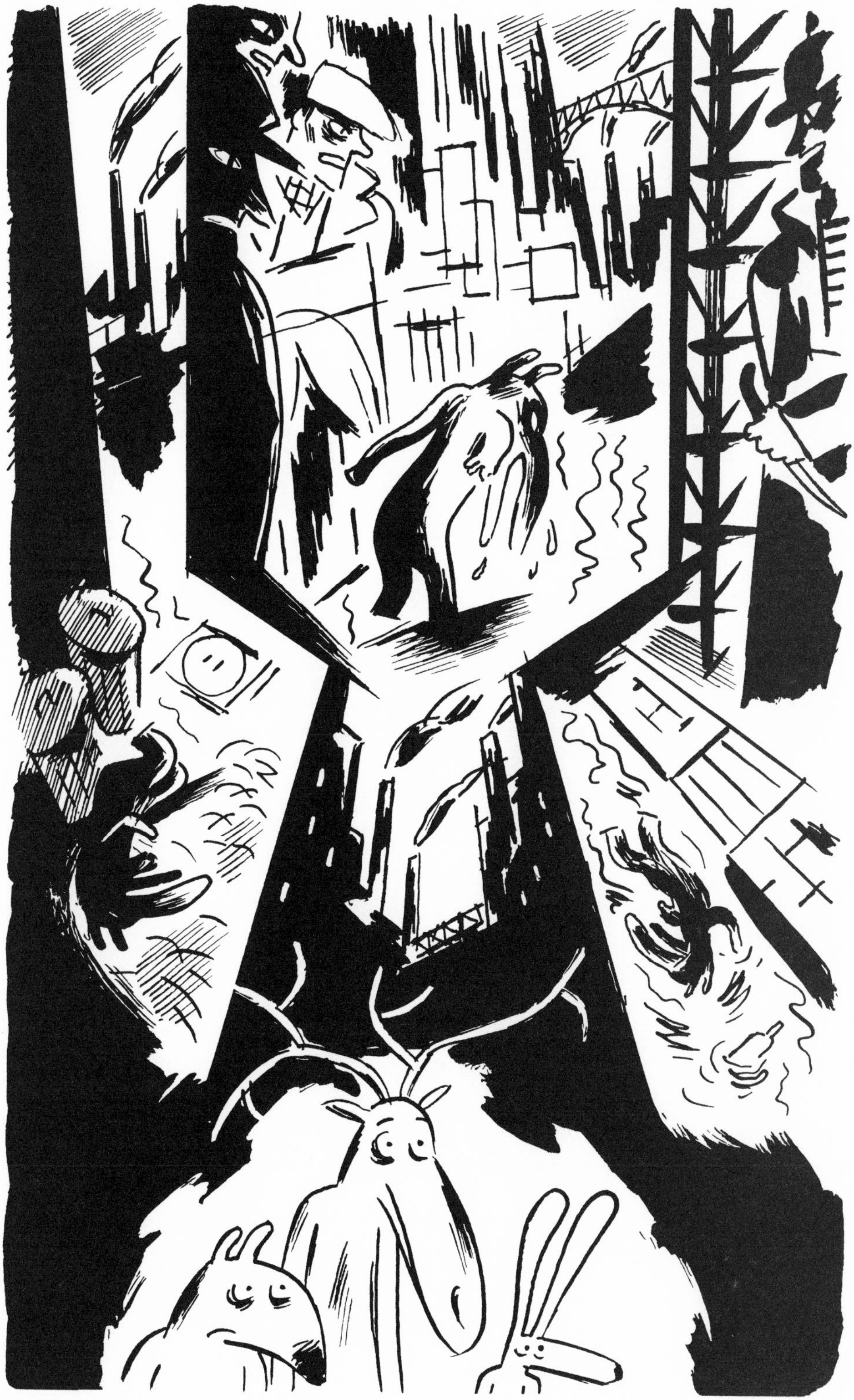

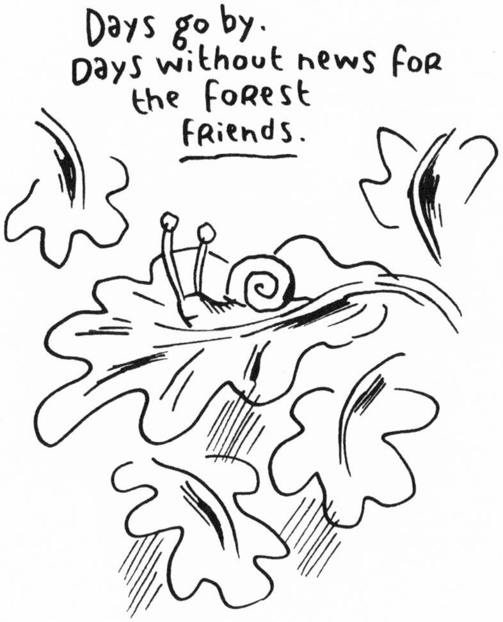
Days go by.
Days without news for the forest friends.

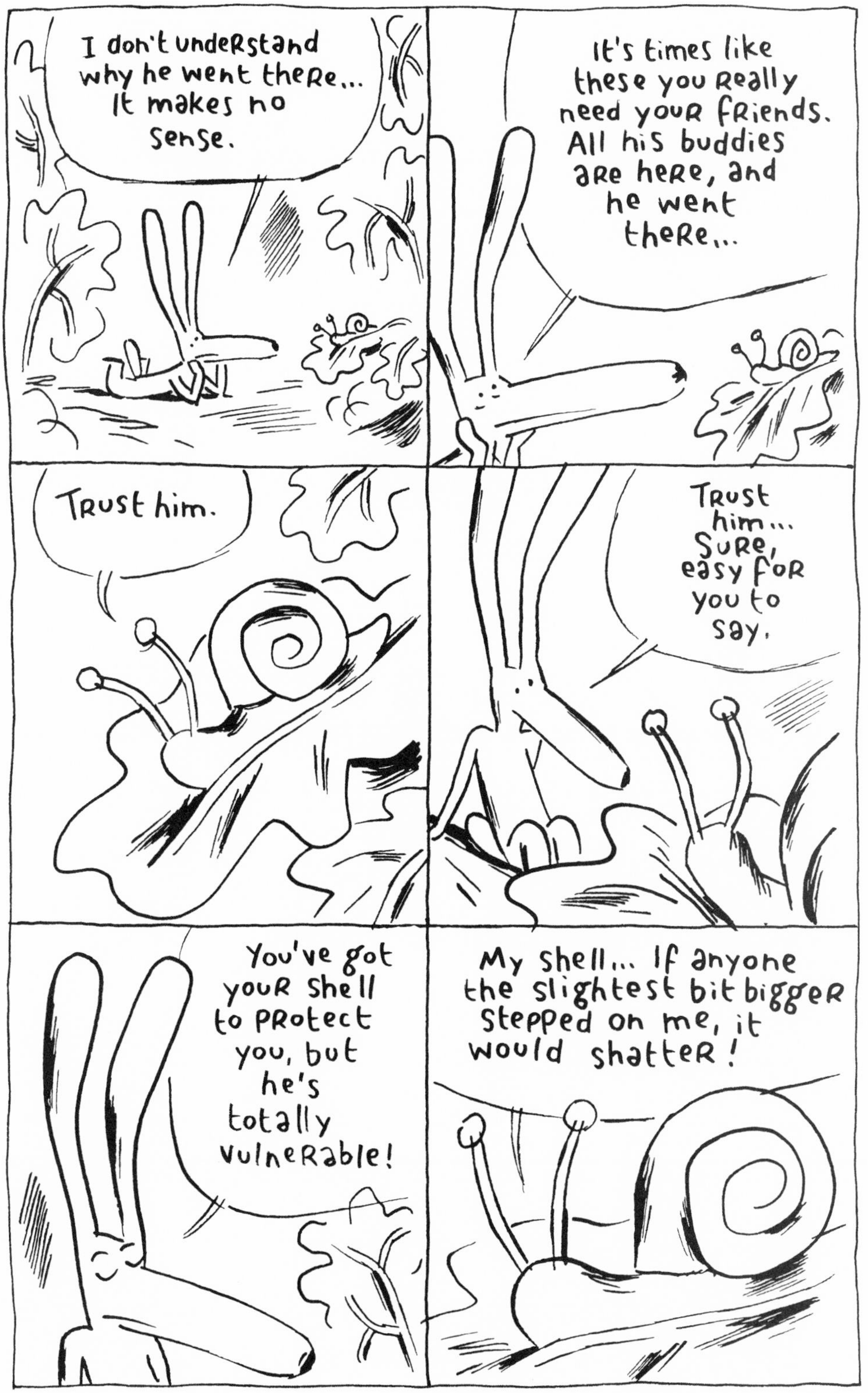
I don't understand why he went there... It makes no sense.
It's times like these you really need your friends. All his buddies are here, and he went there...
Trust him.
Trust him... Sure, easy for you to say.
You've got your shell to protect you, but he's totally vulnerable!
My shell... If anyone the slightest bit bigger stepped on me, it would shatter!

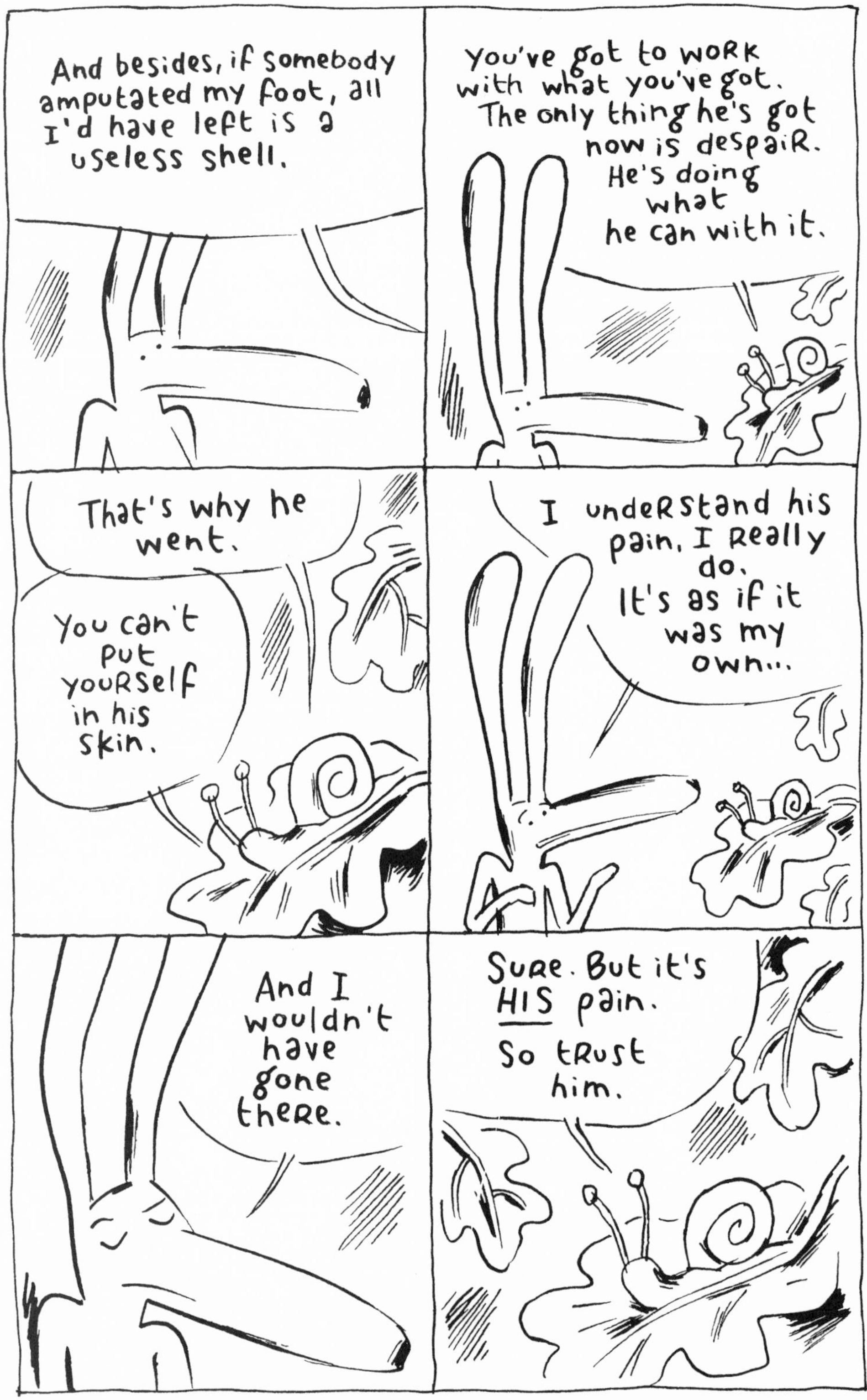
And besides, if somebody amputated my foot, all I'd have left is a useless shell.
You've got to work with what you've got. The only thing he's got now is despair. He's doing what he can with it.
That's why he went.
You can't put yourself in his skin.
I understand his pain, I really do. It's as if it was my own...
And I wouldn't have gone there.
Sure. But it's HIS pain.
So trust him.

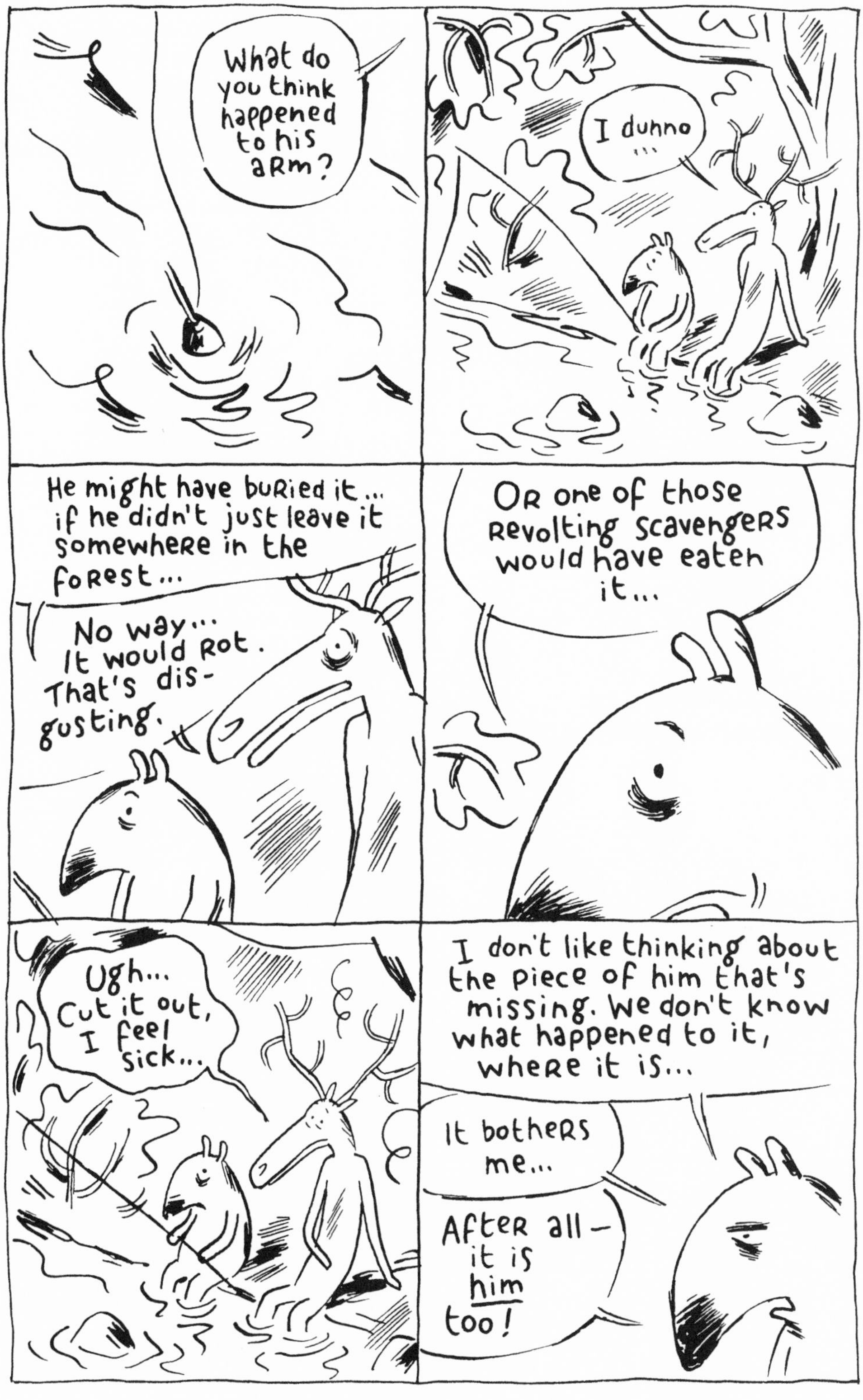
What do you think happened to his arm?
I dunno ...
He might have buried it... if he didn't just leave it somewhere in the forest...
No way... It would rot. That's disgusting.
Or one of those revolting scavengers would have eaten it...
Ugh... Cut it out, I feel sick...
I don't like thinking about the piece of him that's missing. We don't know what happened to it, where it is...
It bothers me...
After all — it is him too!

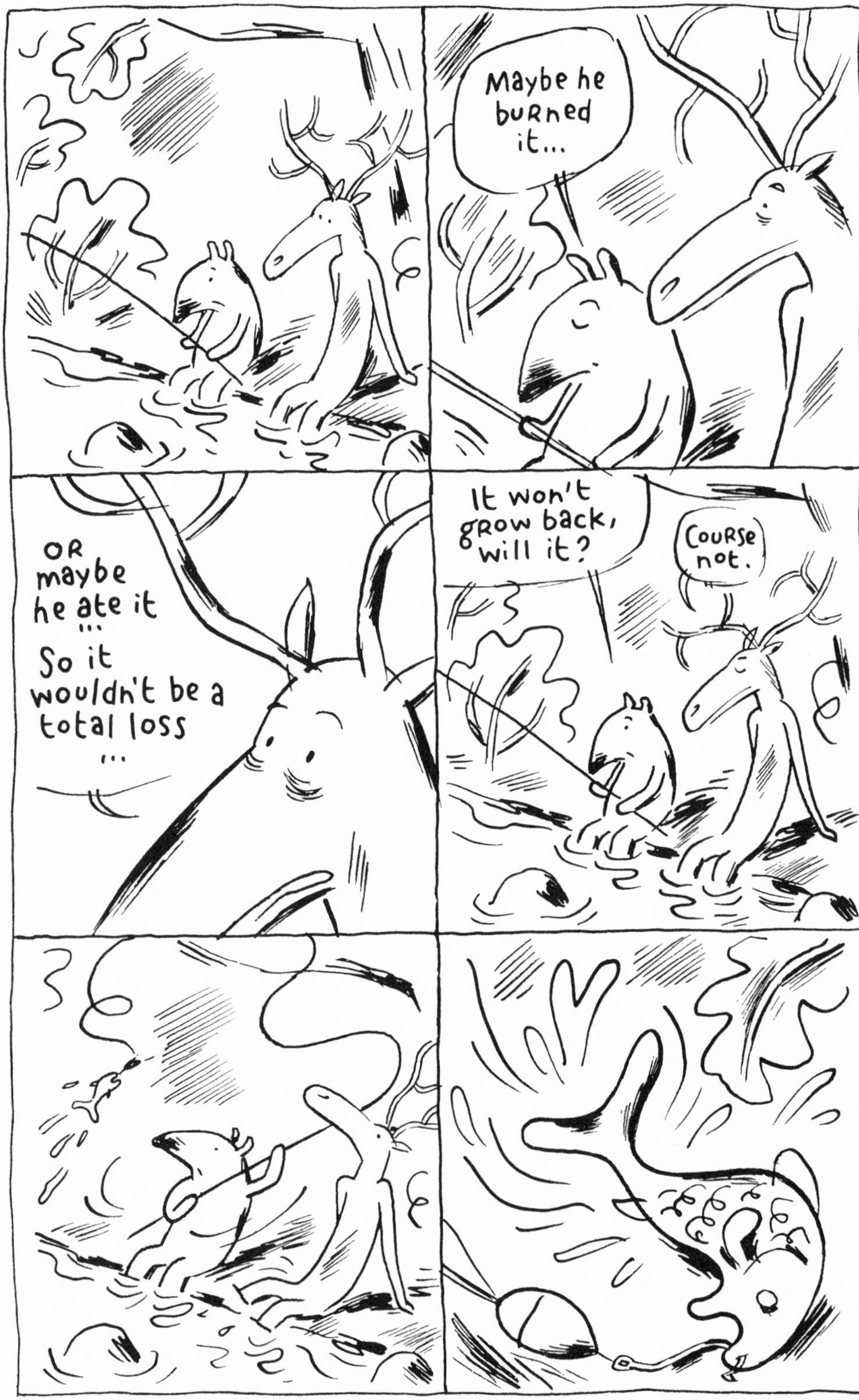
Maybe he burned it...
OR maybe he ate it ... So it wouldn't be a total loss ...
It won't grow back, will it?
Course not.

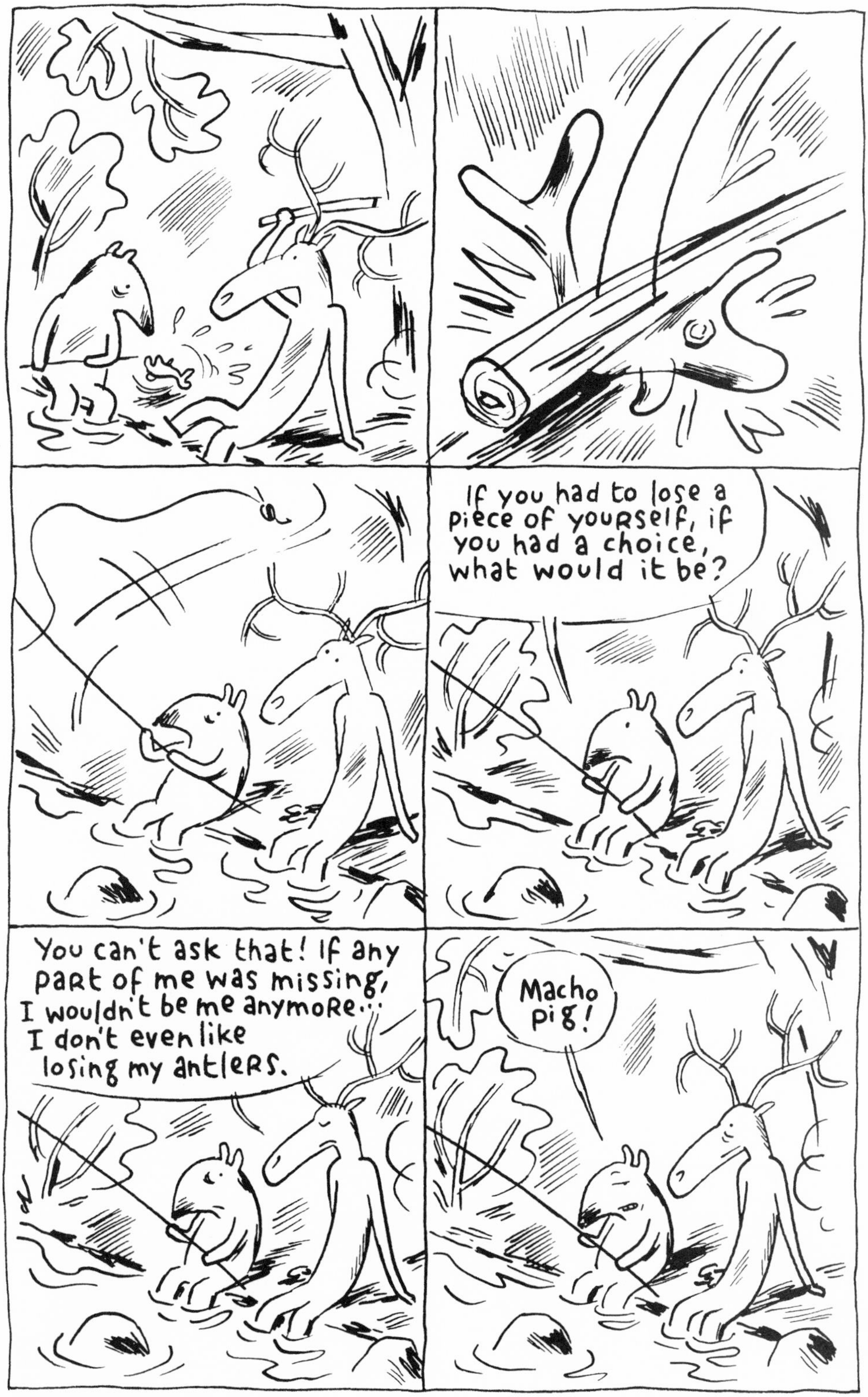

If you had to lose a piece of yourself, if you had a choice, what would it be?
You can't ask that! If any part of me was missing, I wouldn't be me anymore... I don't even like losing my antlers.
Macho pig!

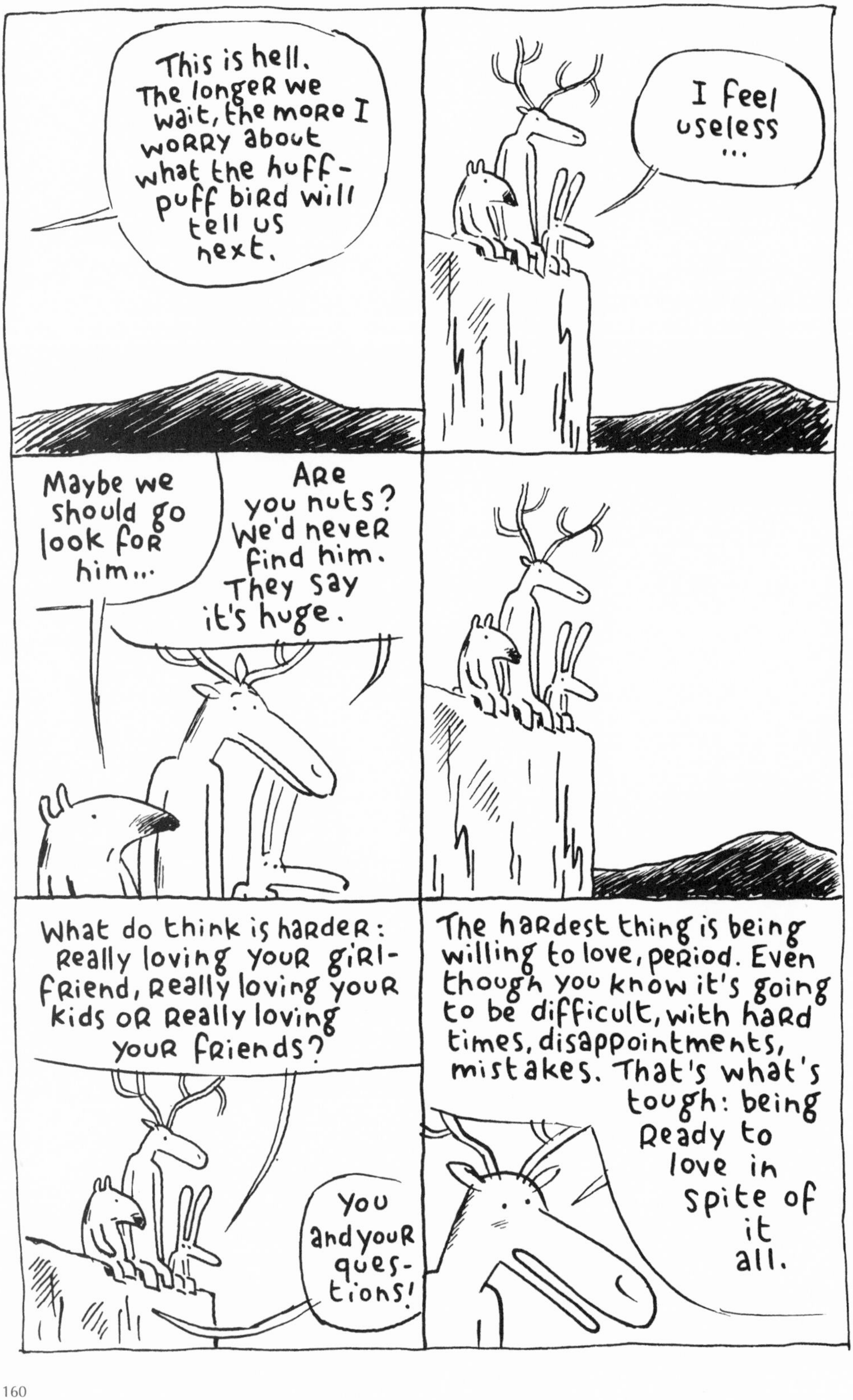
This is hell. The longer we wait, the more I worry about what the huff-puff bird will tell us next.
I feel useless ...
Maybe we should go look for him...
Are you nuts? We'd never find him. They say it's huge.
What do think is harder: Really loving your girlfriend, really loving your kids or really loving your friends?
You and your questions!
The hardest thing is being willing to love, period. Even though you know it's going to be difficult, with hard times, disappointments, mistakes. That's what's tough: being ready to love in spite of it all.

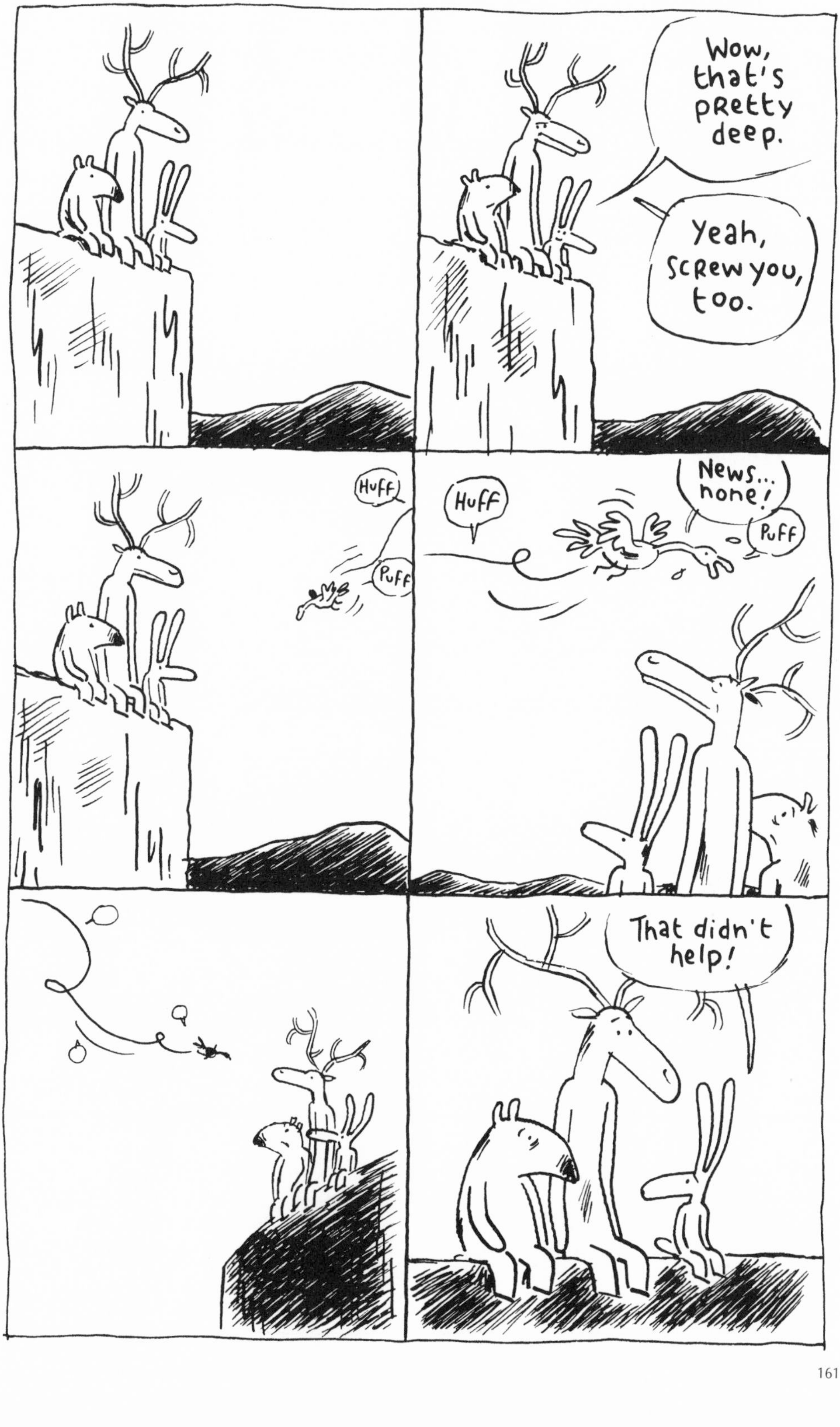
Wow, that's pretty deep.
Yeah, screw you, too.
Huff
Puff
Huff
News... none!
Puff
That didn't help!

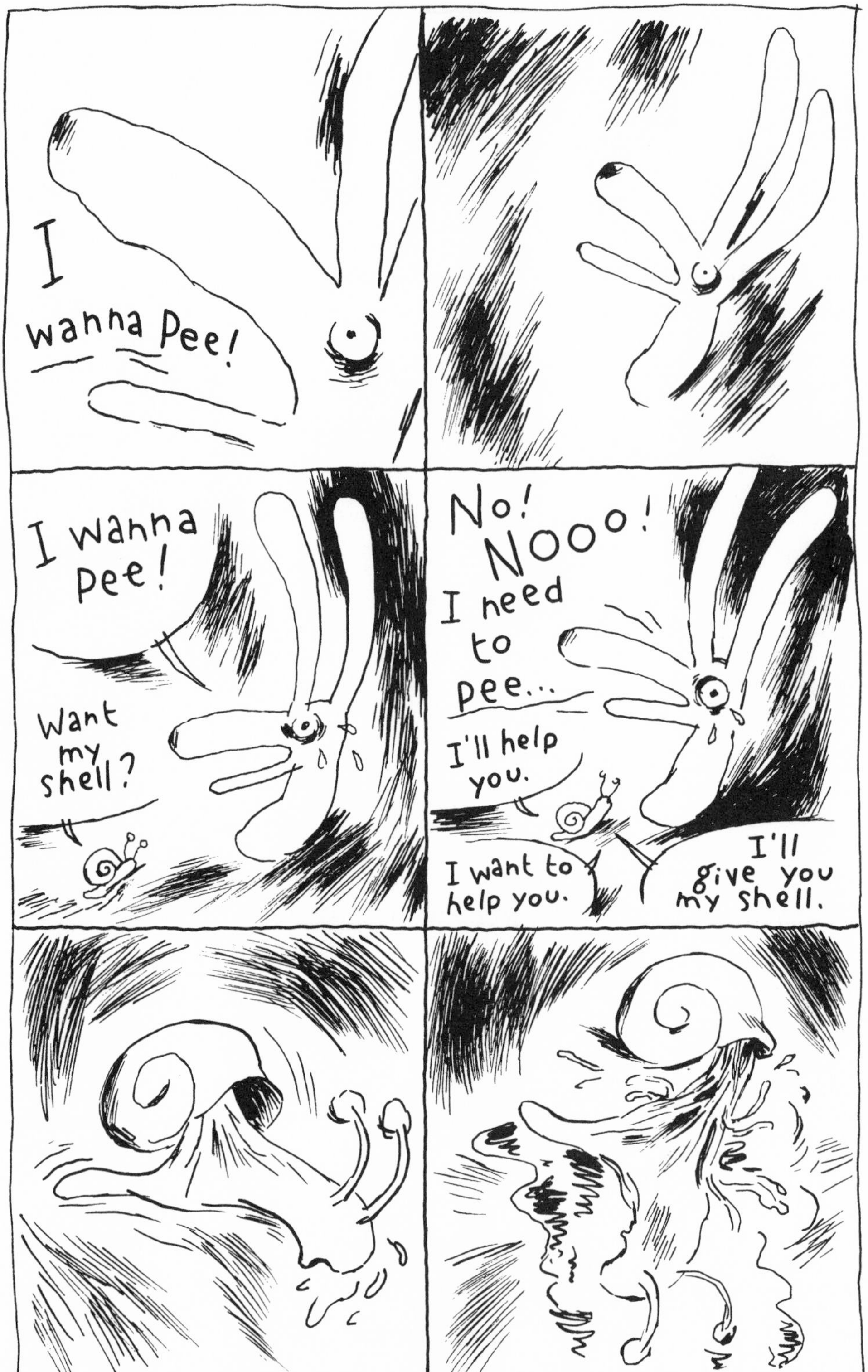
I wanna pee!
I wanna pee!
Want my shell?
No! NOOO! I need to pee...
I'll help you.
I want to help you.
I'll give you my shell.

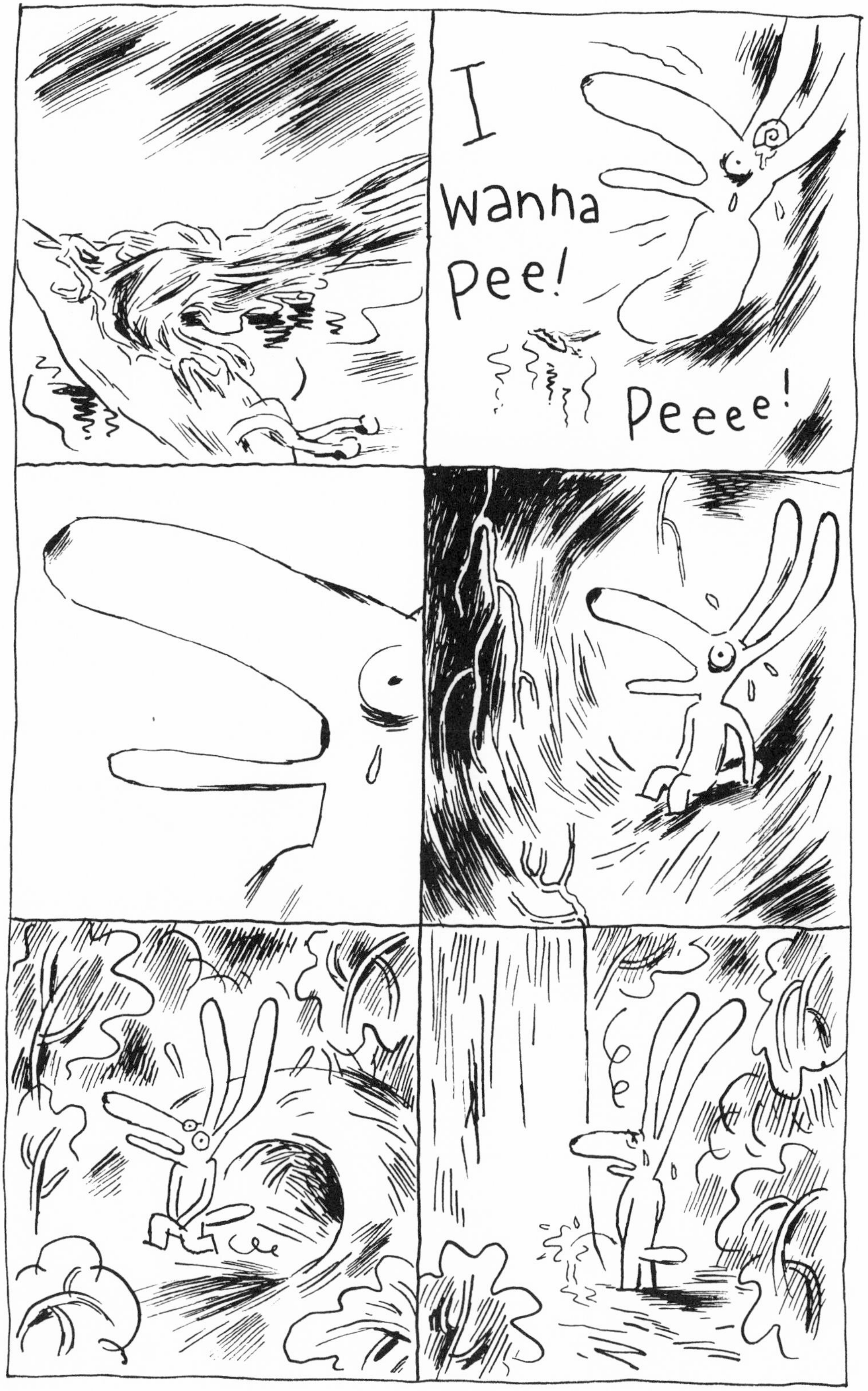
I wanna pee!
Peeee!

Weeks go by
Weeks without news for our forest friends...
Nothing!
Huff
Weeks with good days.
With a little help from my friends
Weeks with bad days.
Weeks with totally normal days.

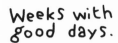

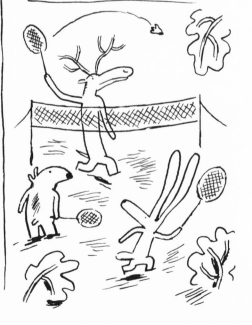

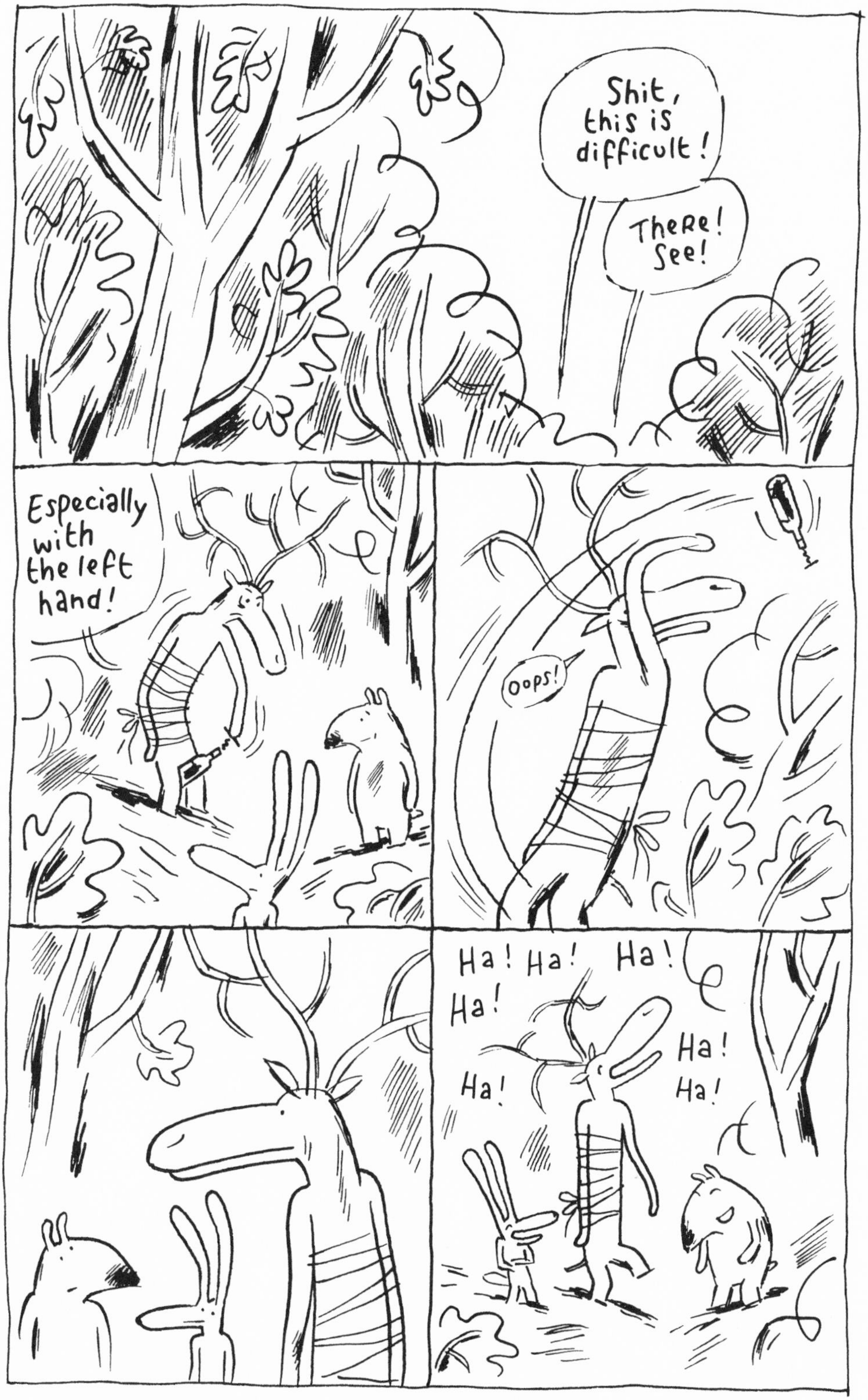
Shit, this is difficult!
There! See!
Especially with the left hand!
Oops!
Ha! Ha! Ha! Ha!
Ha!
Ha! Ha!

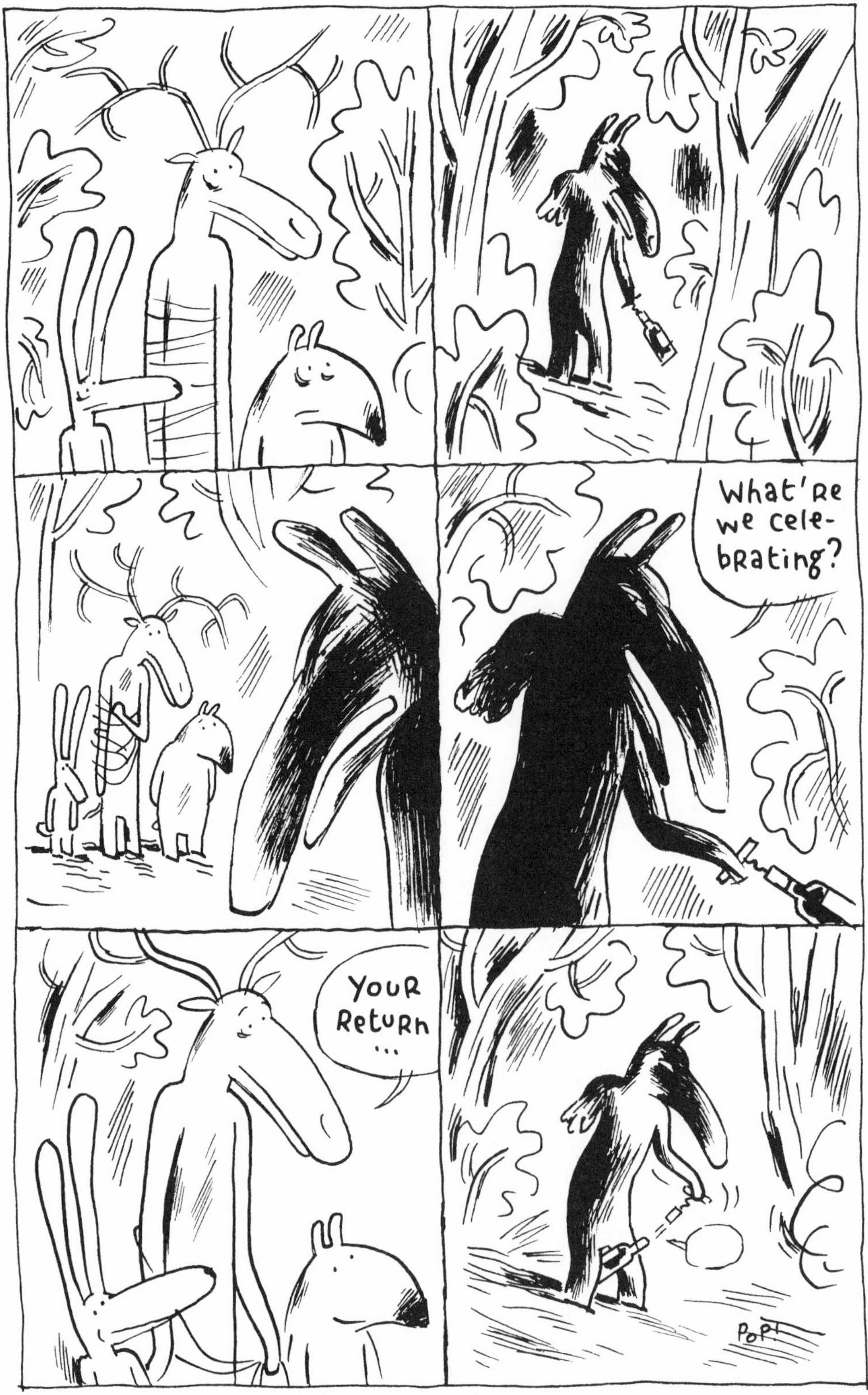
What're we celebrating?
Your Return ...
POP!

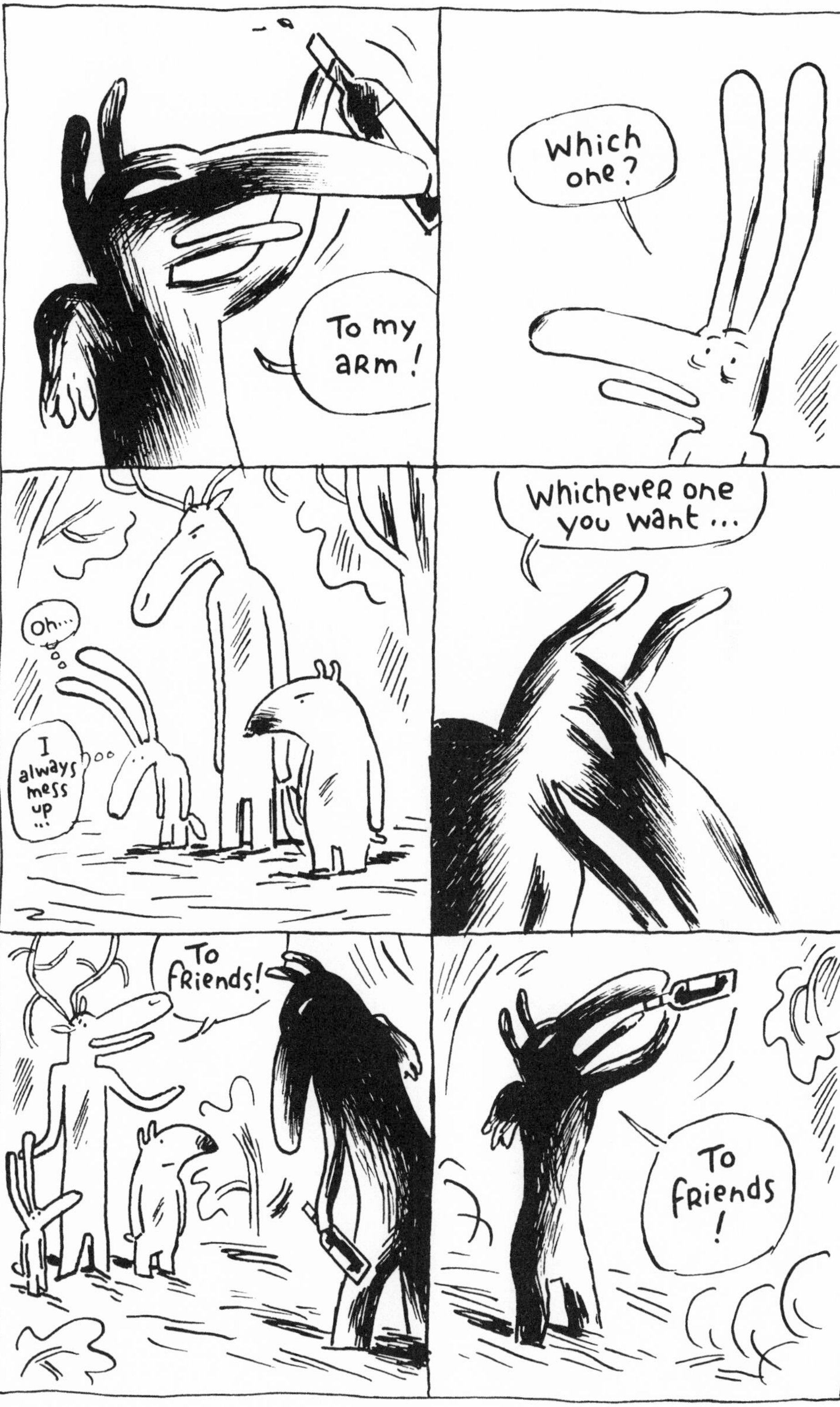
To my arm!
Which one?
Oh...
I always mess up...
Noo
Whichever one you want...
To friends!
To friends!

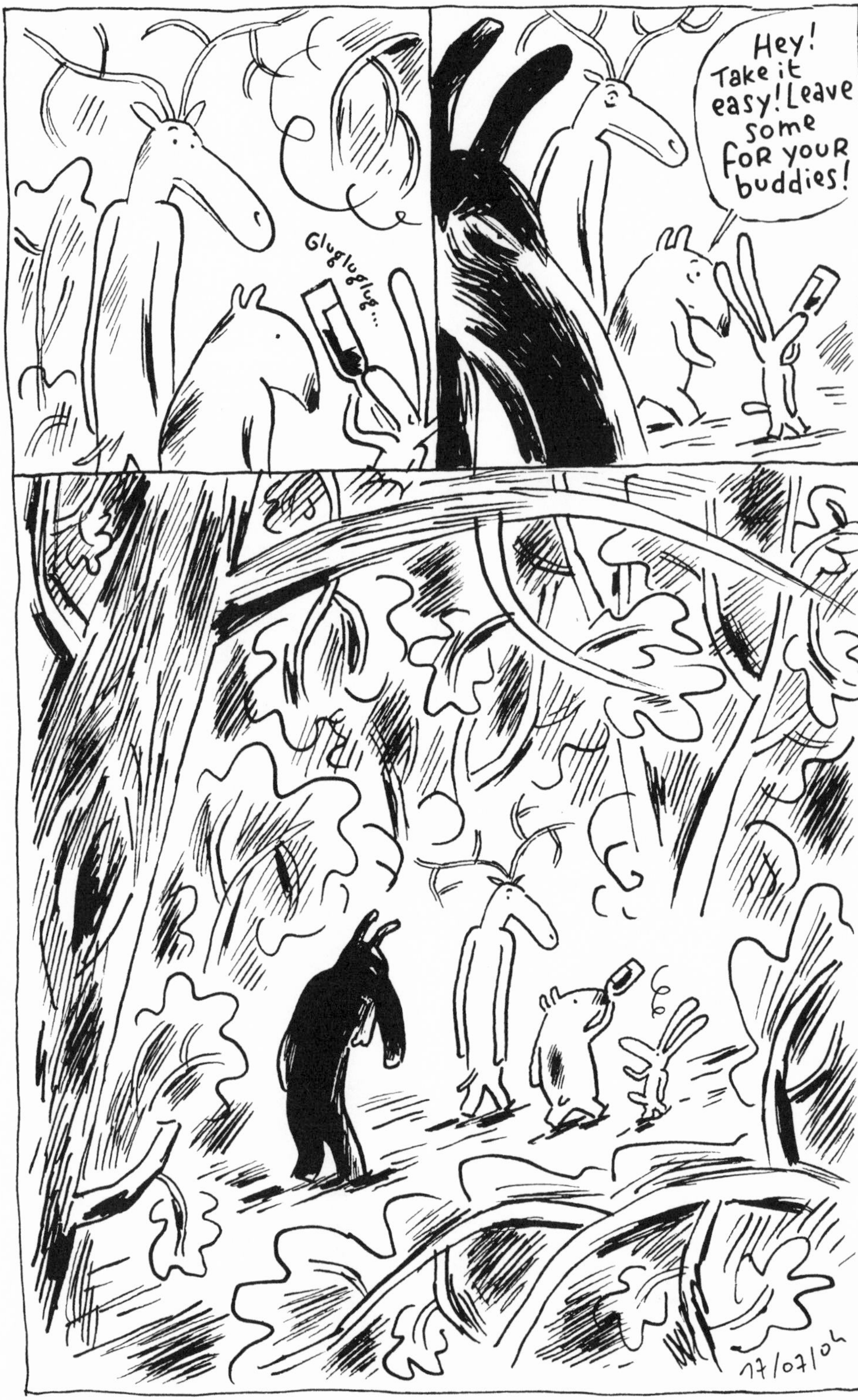
Gluglugluglug...
Hey! Take it easy! Leave some for your buddies!
17/07/04

Lucha Libre

Love Catch

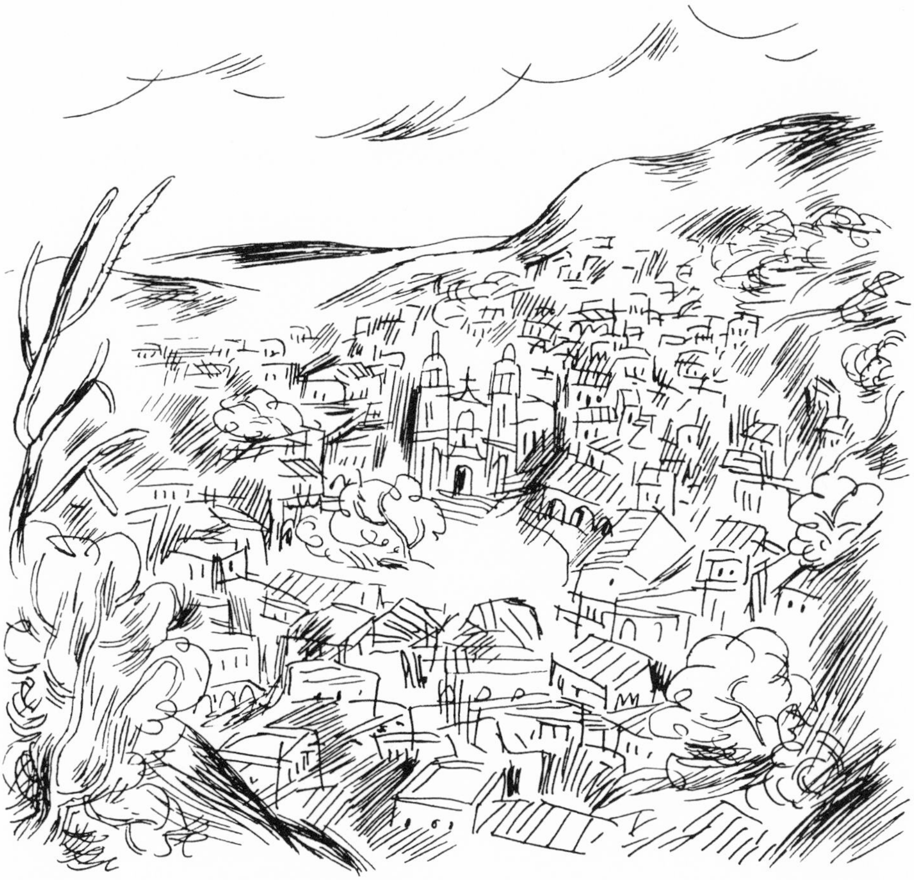

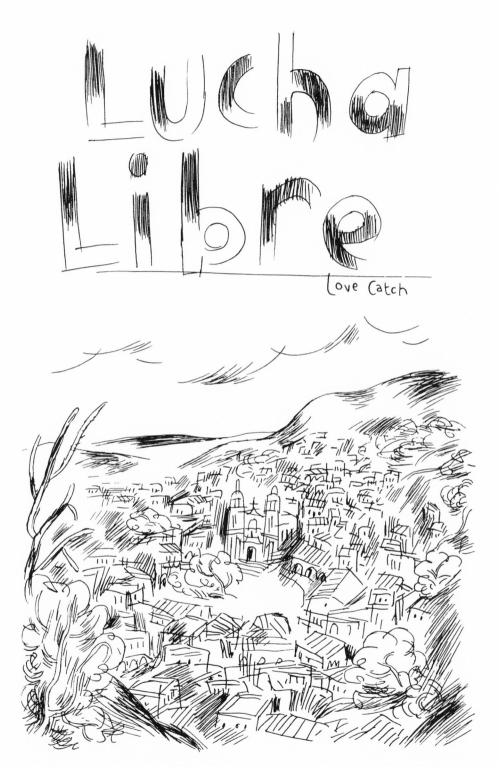

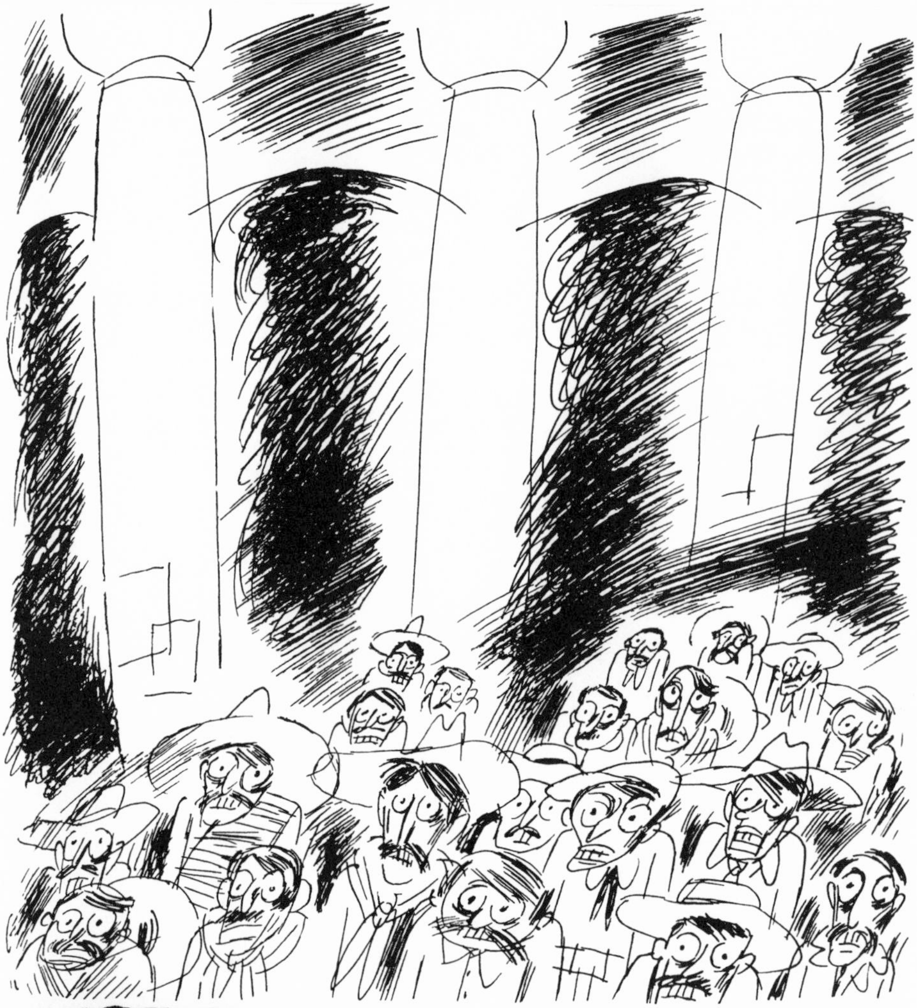

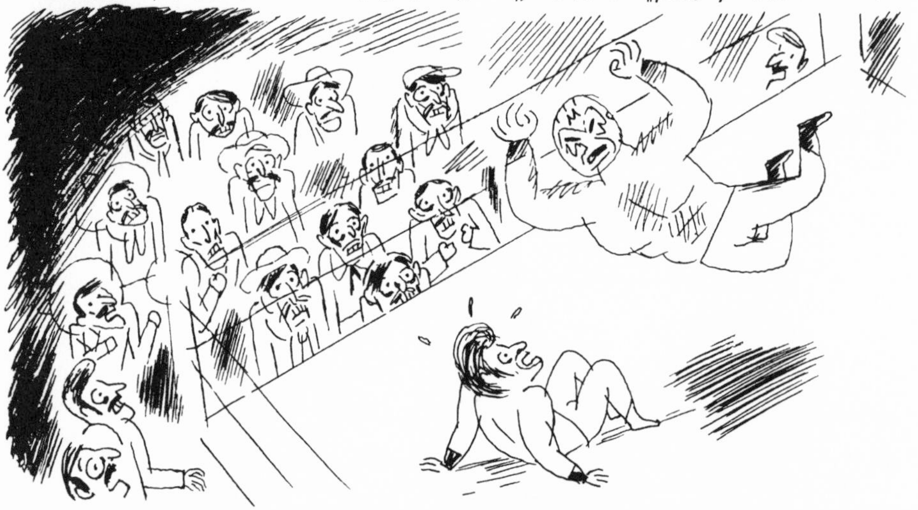

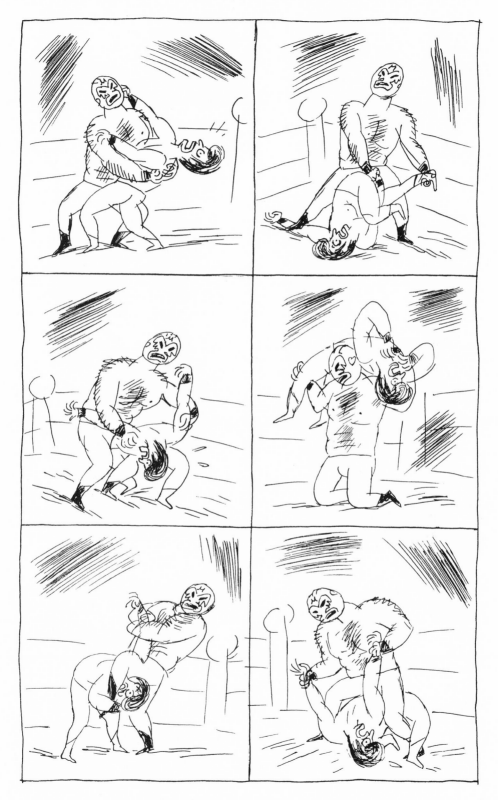

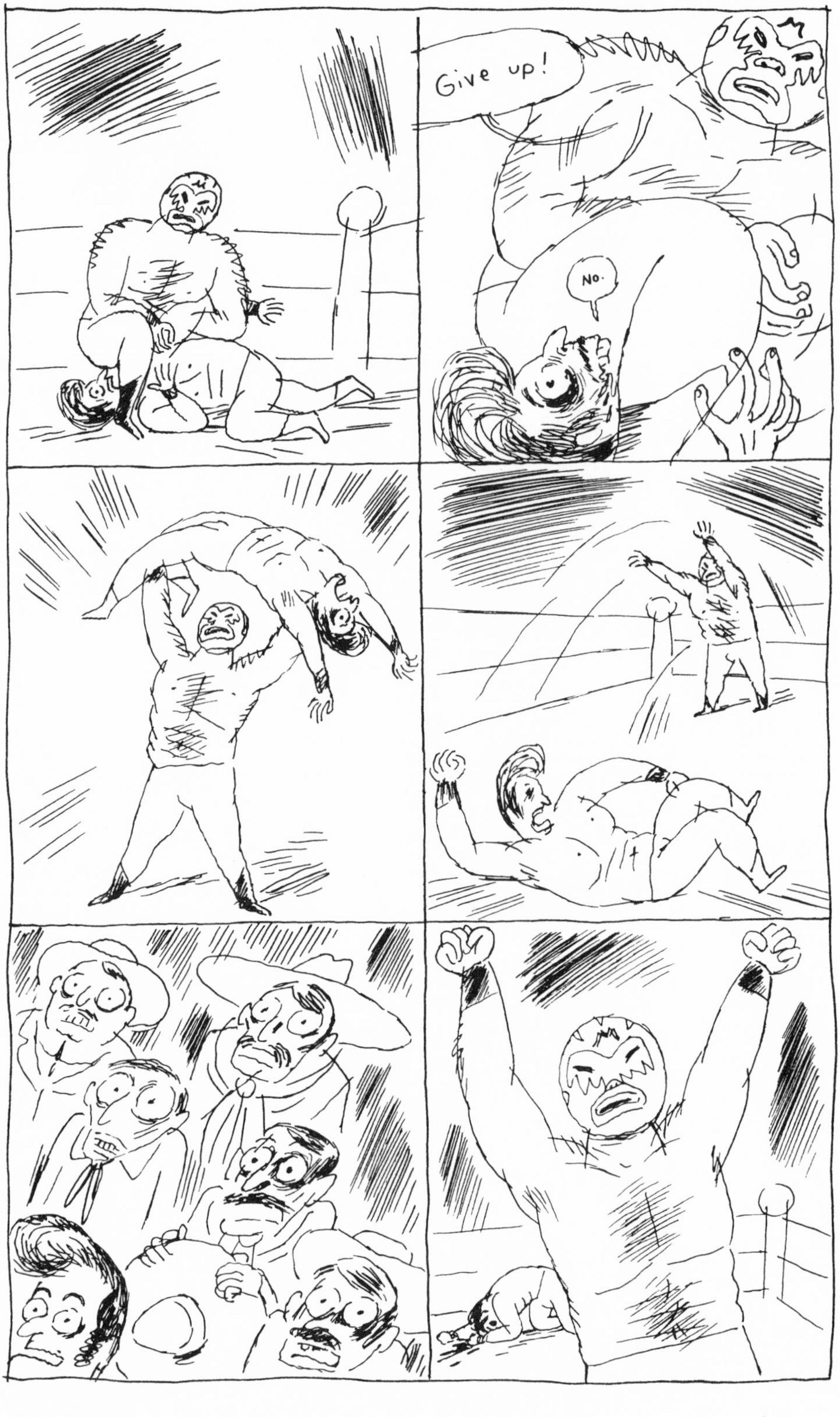
Give up!
No.

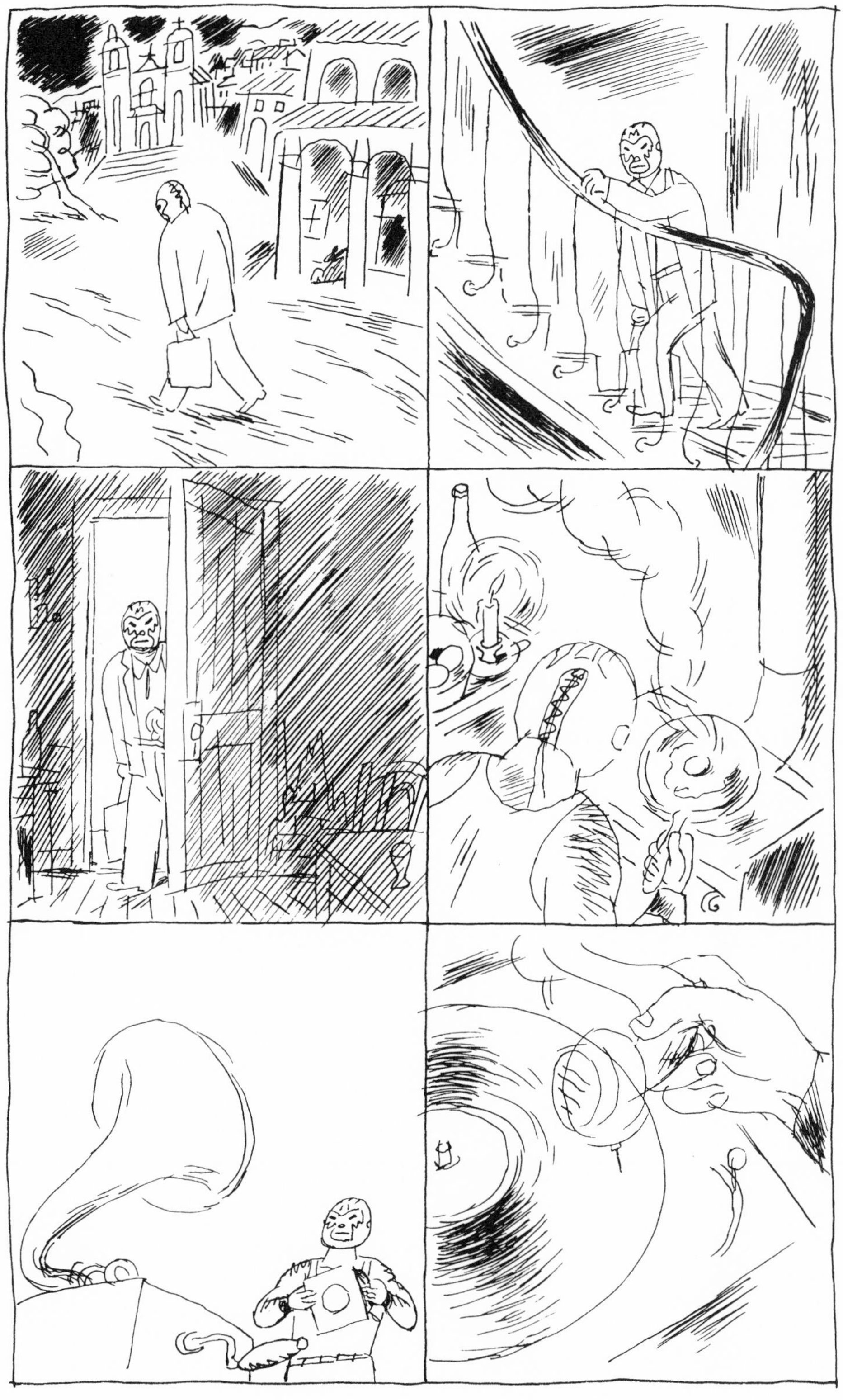

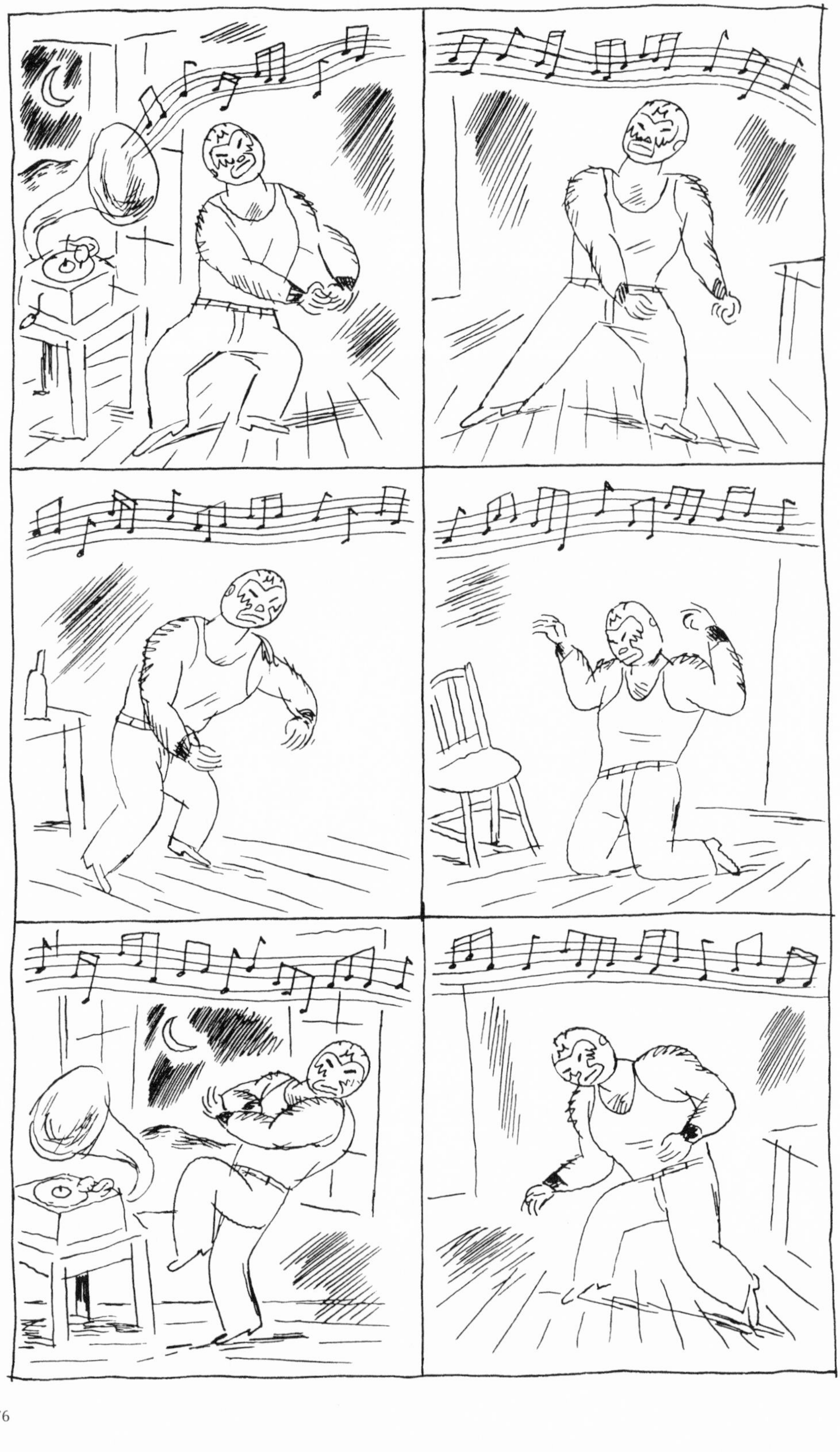

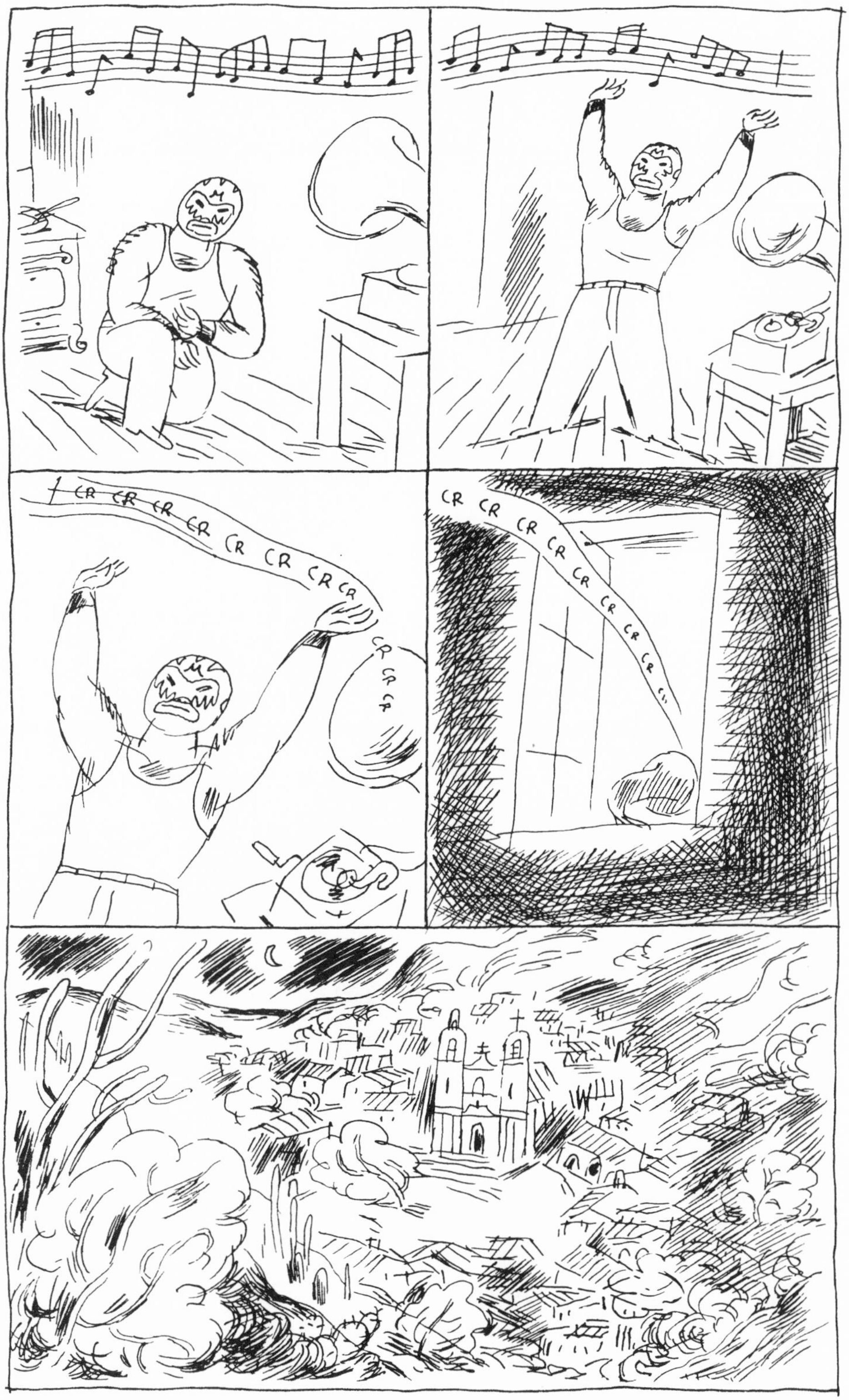
CR CR CR CR CR CR CR CR CR CR CR
CR CR CR CR CR CR CR CR

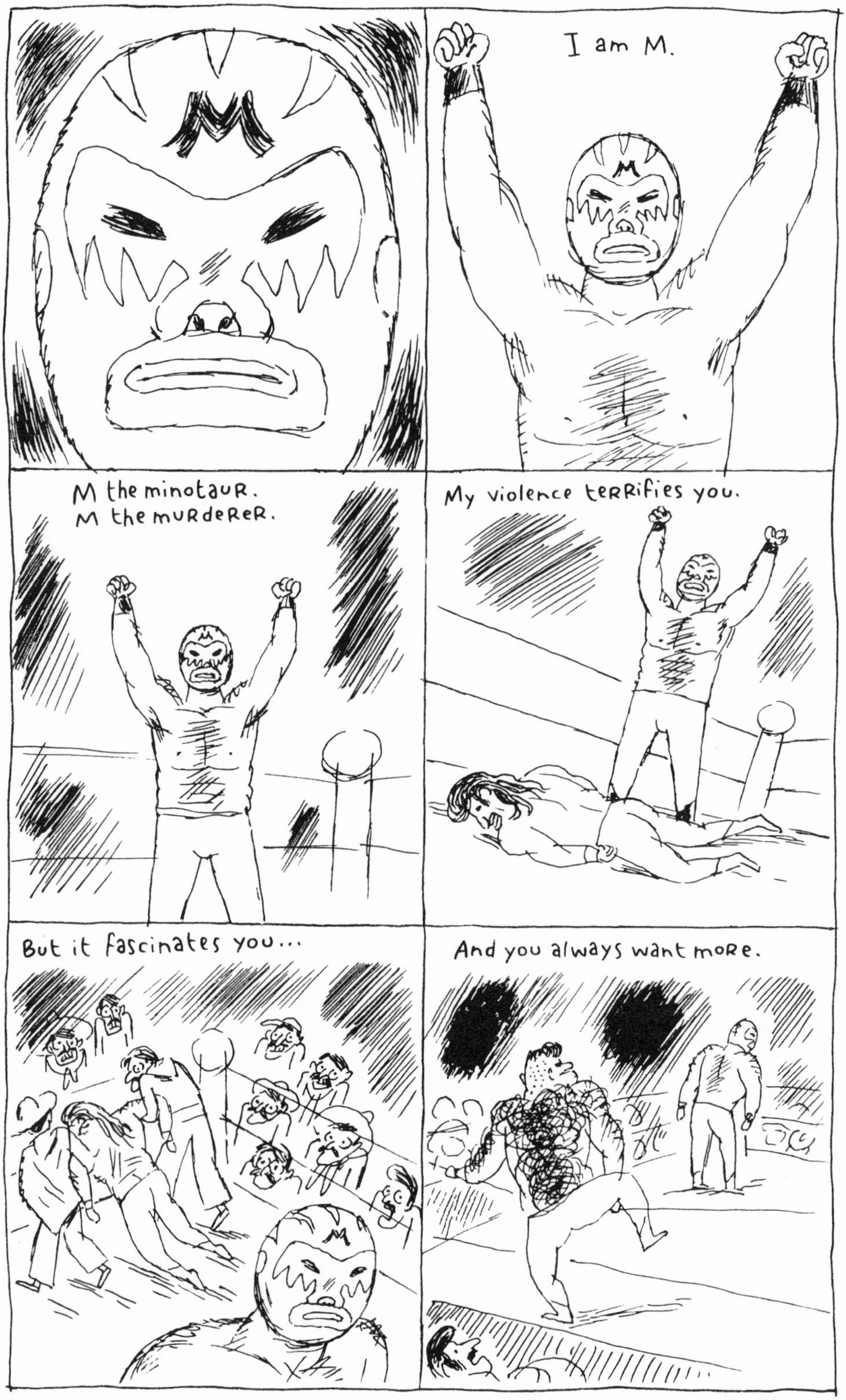
I am M.
M the minotaur.
M the murderer.
My violence terrifies you.
But it fascinates you...
And you always want more.

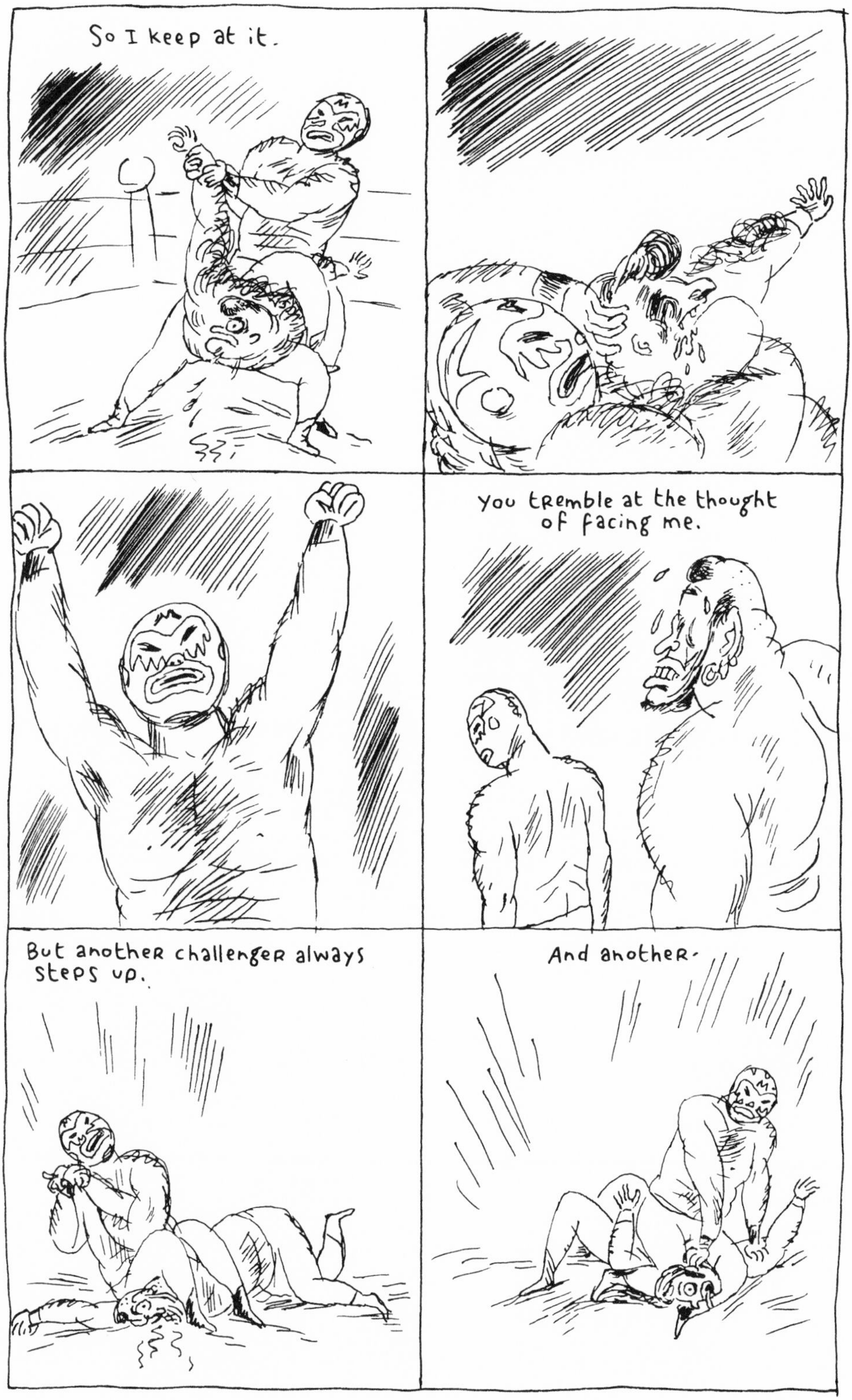
So I keep at it.
You tremble at the thought of facing me.
But another challenger always steps up.
And another.

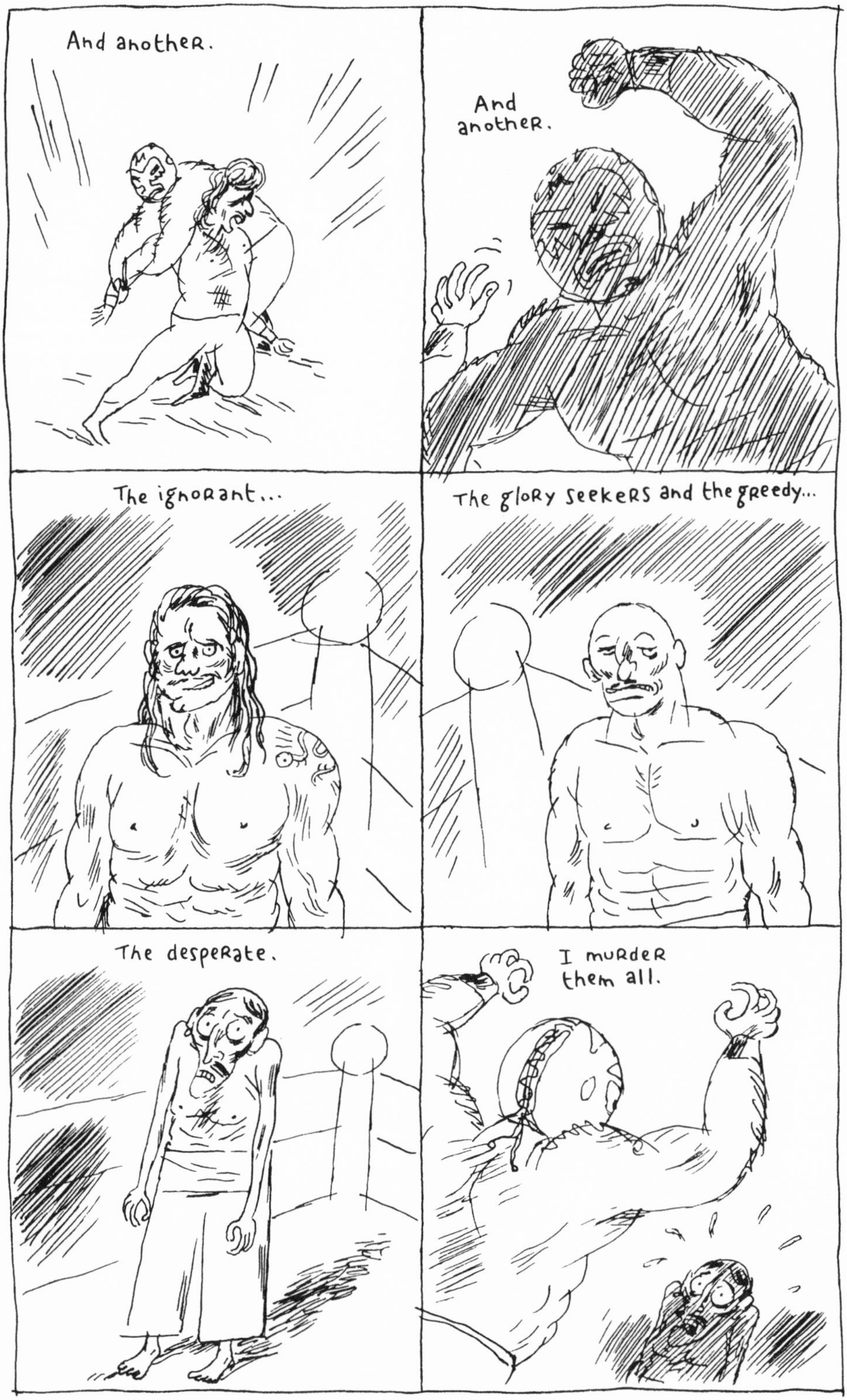
And another.
And another.
The ignorant...
The glory seekers and the greedy...
The desperate.
I murder them all.

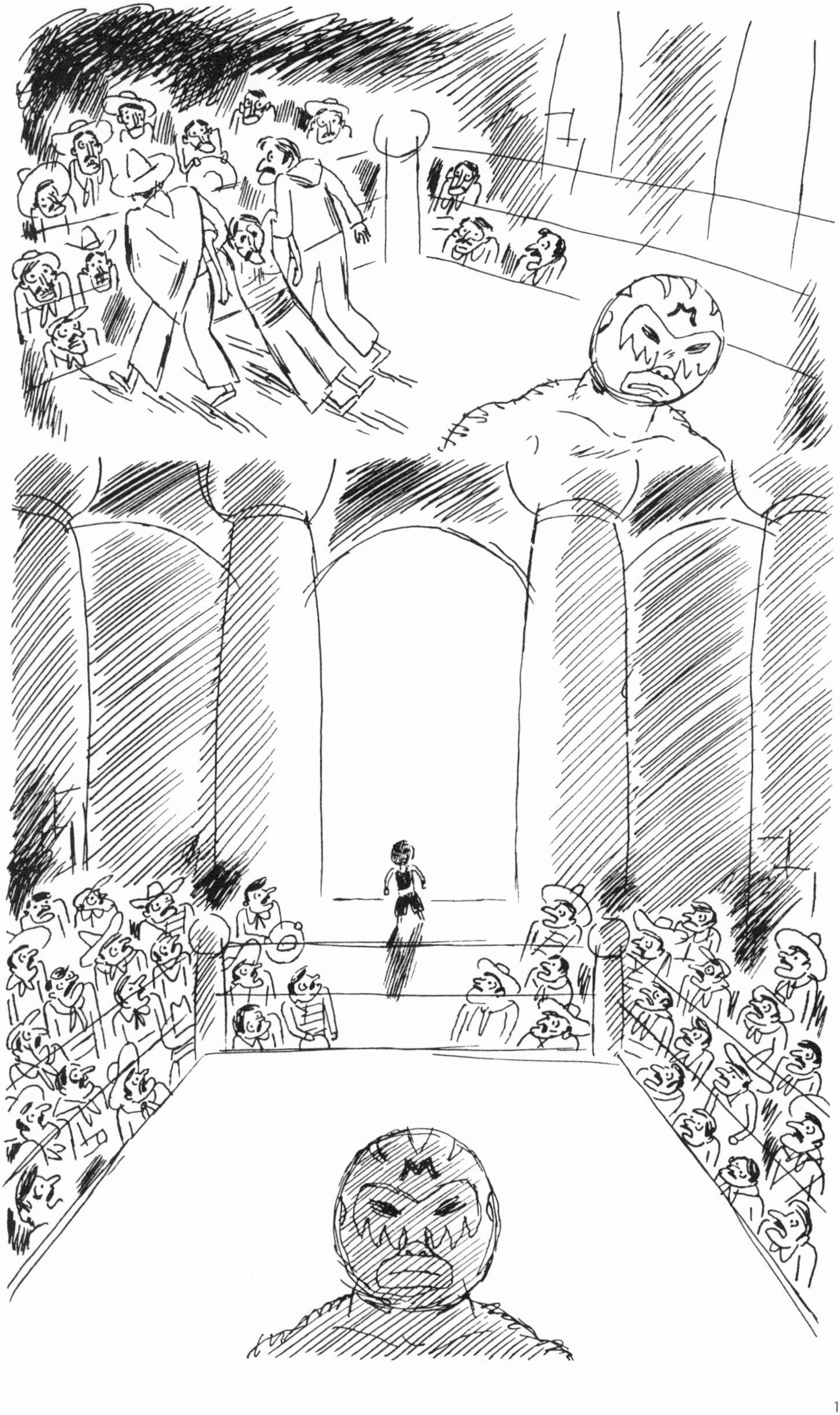

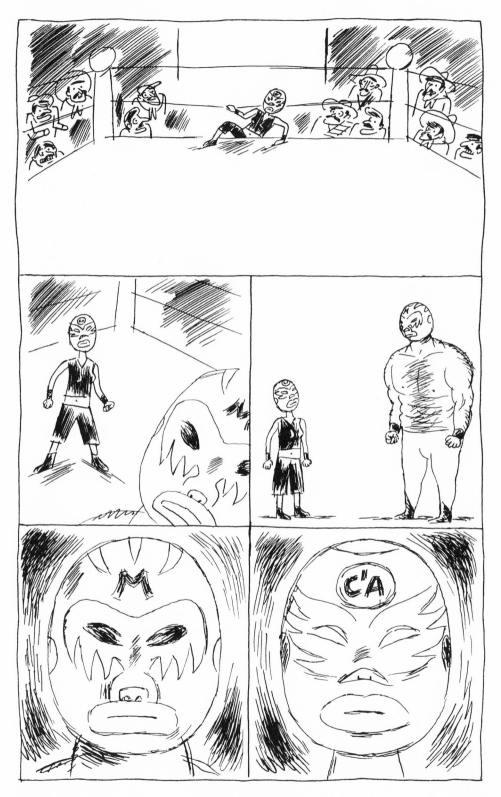

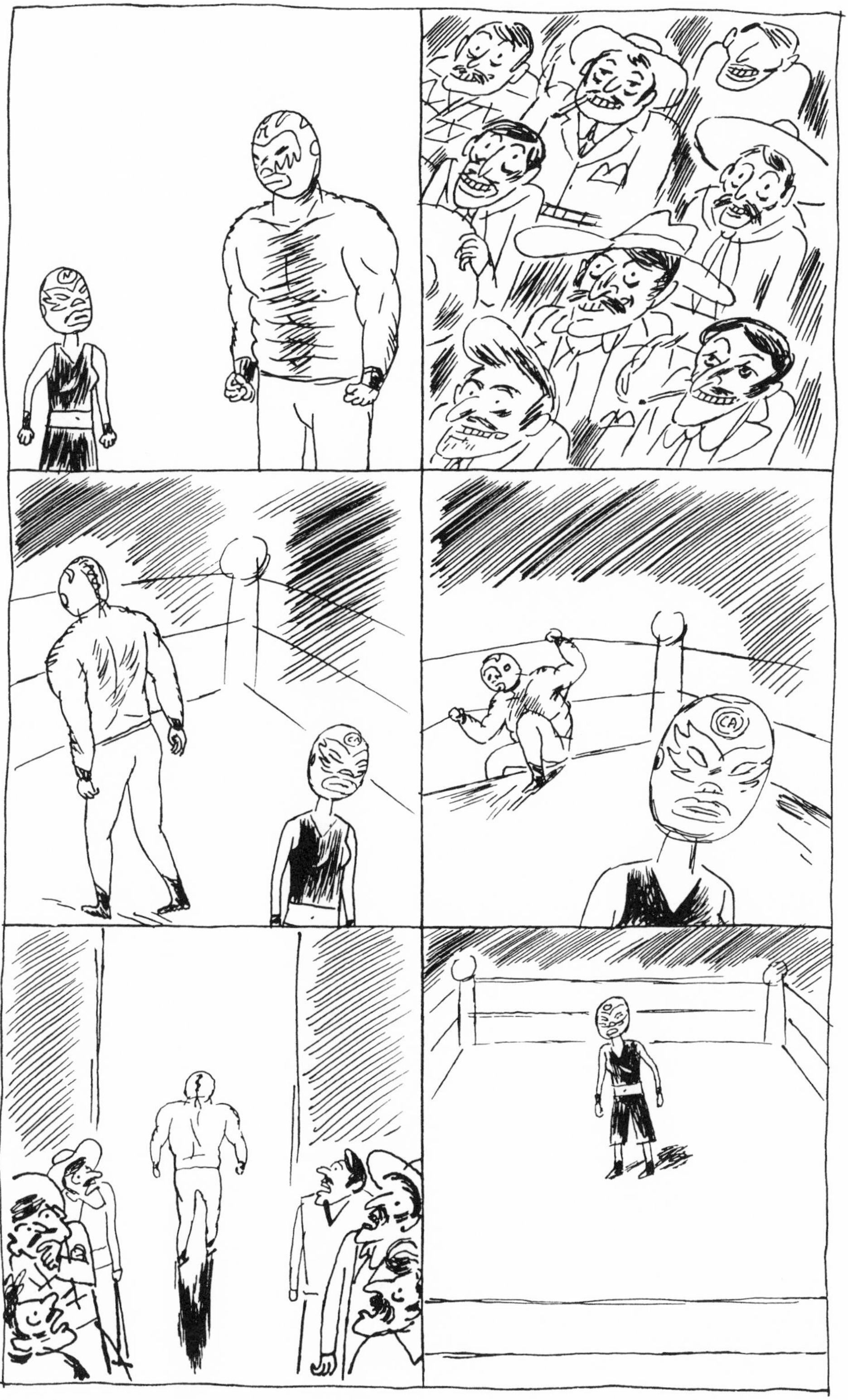

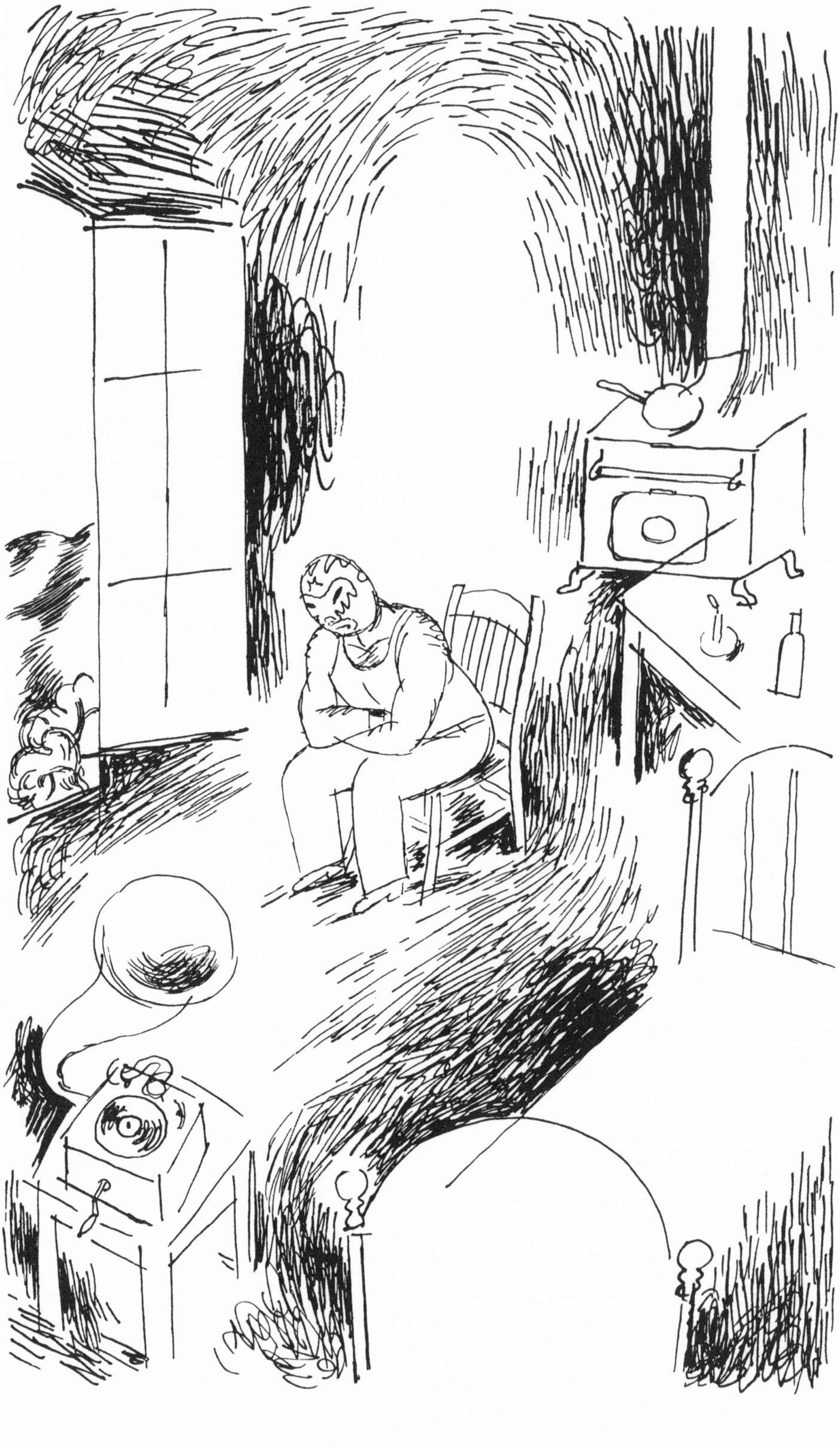

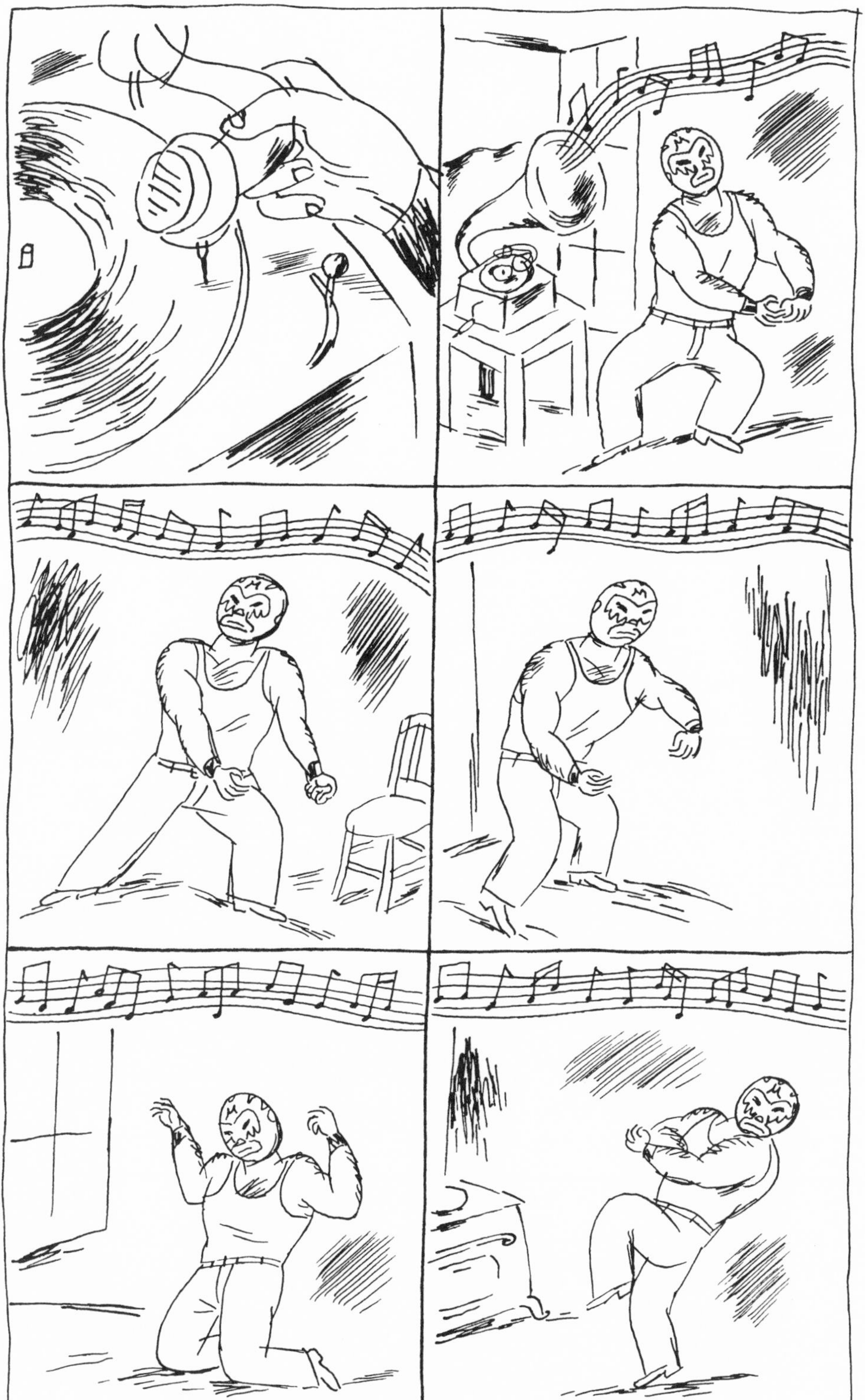

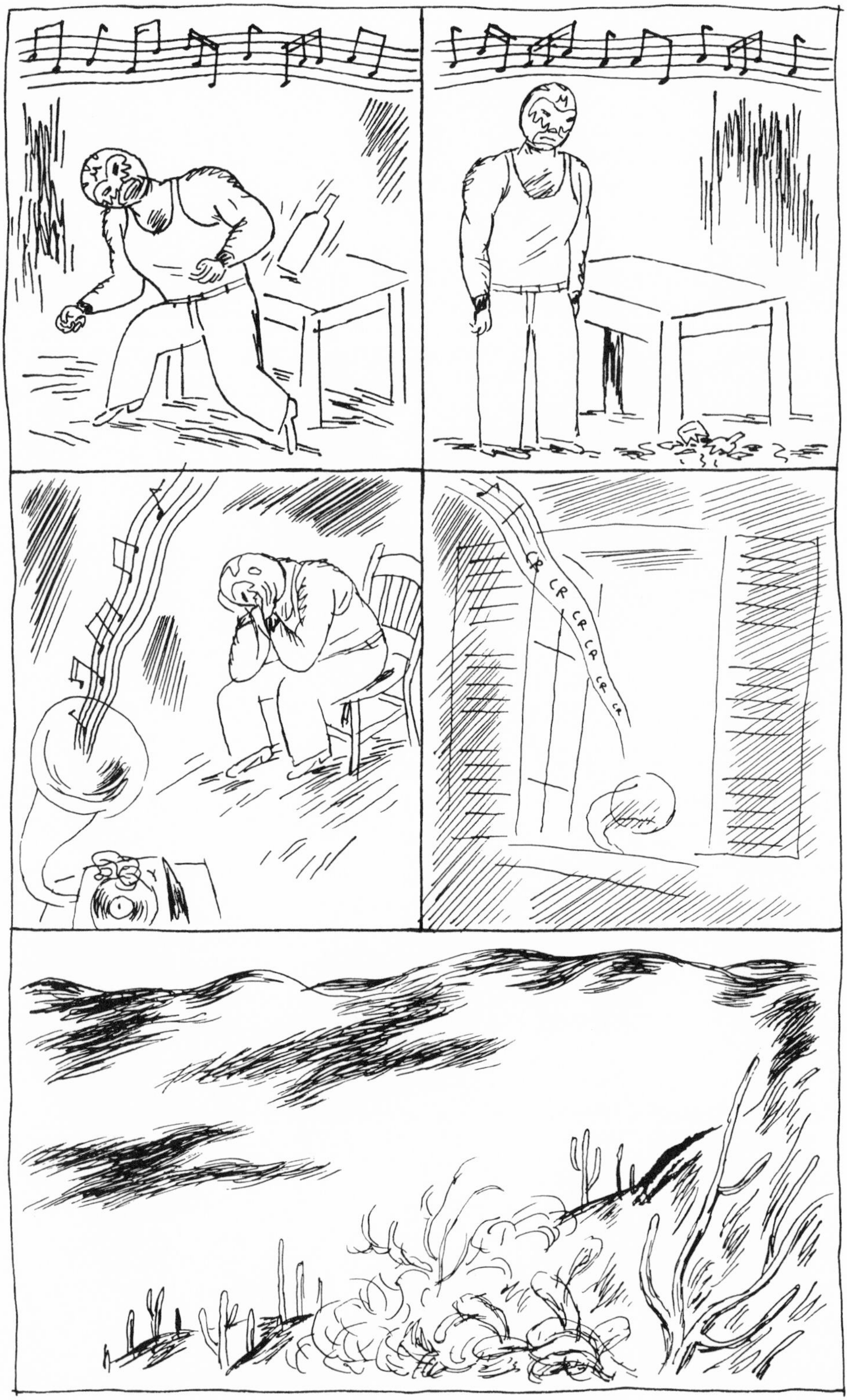
CR CR CR CR CR CR

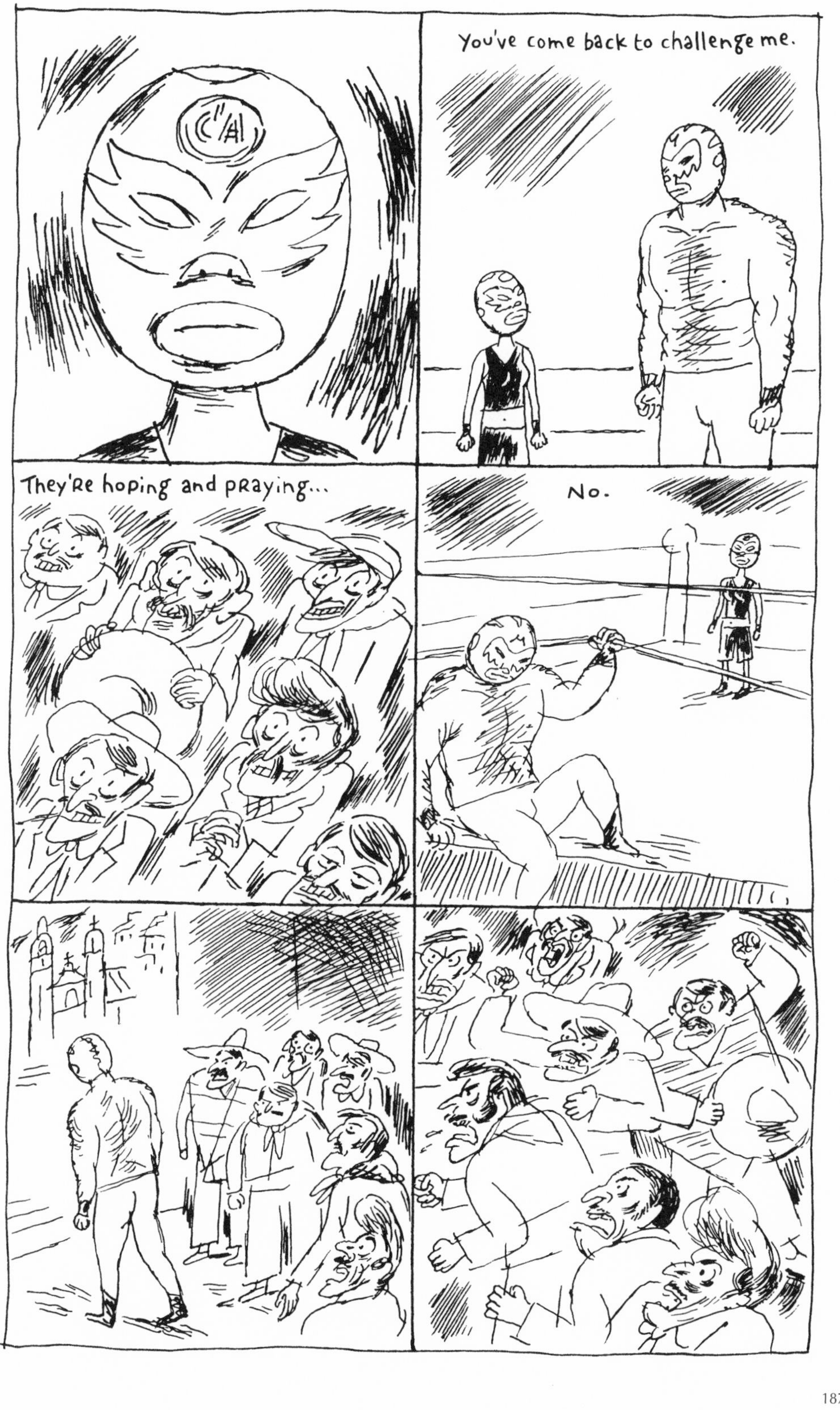
You've come back to challenge me.
They're hoping and praying...
No.

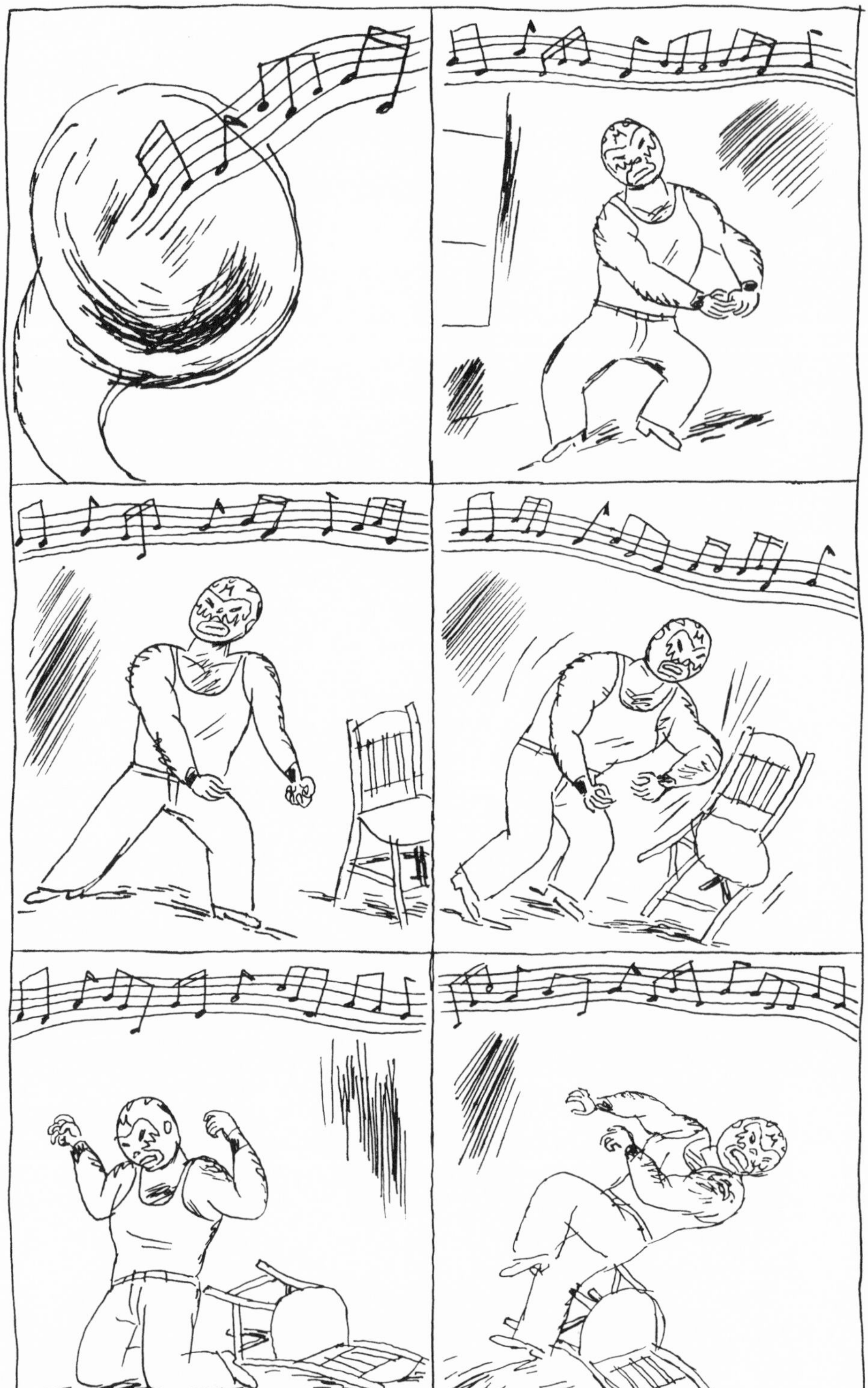

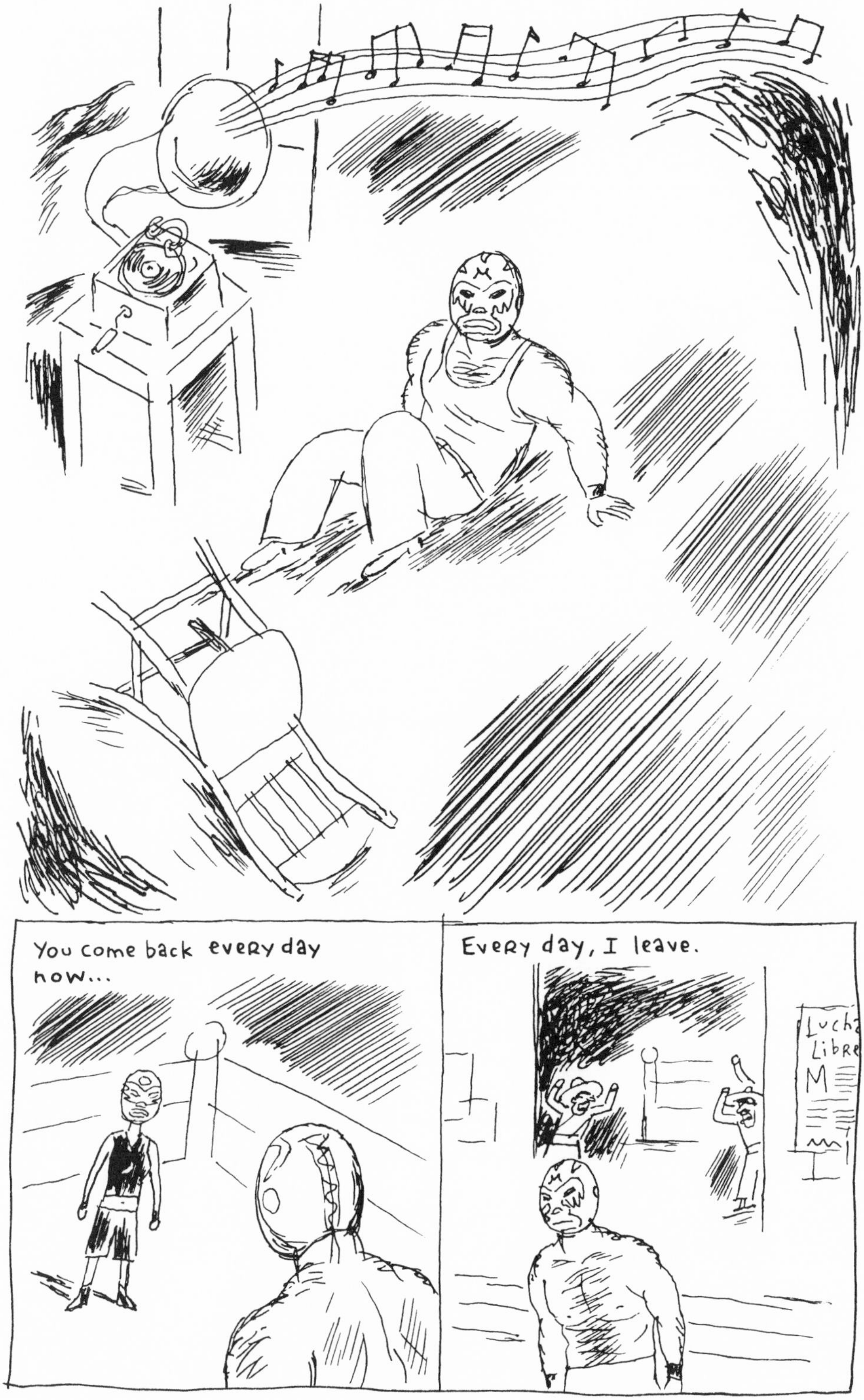
You come back every day now...
Every day, I leave.

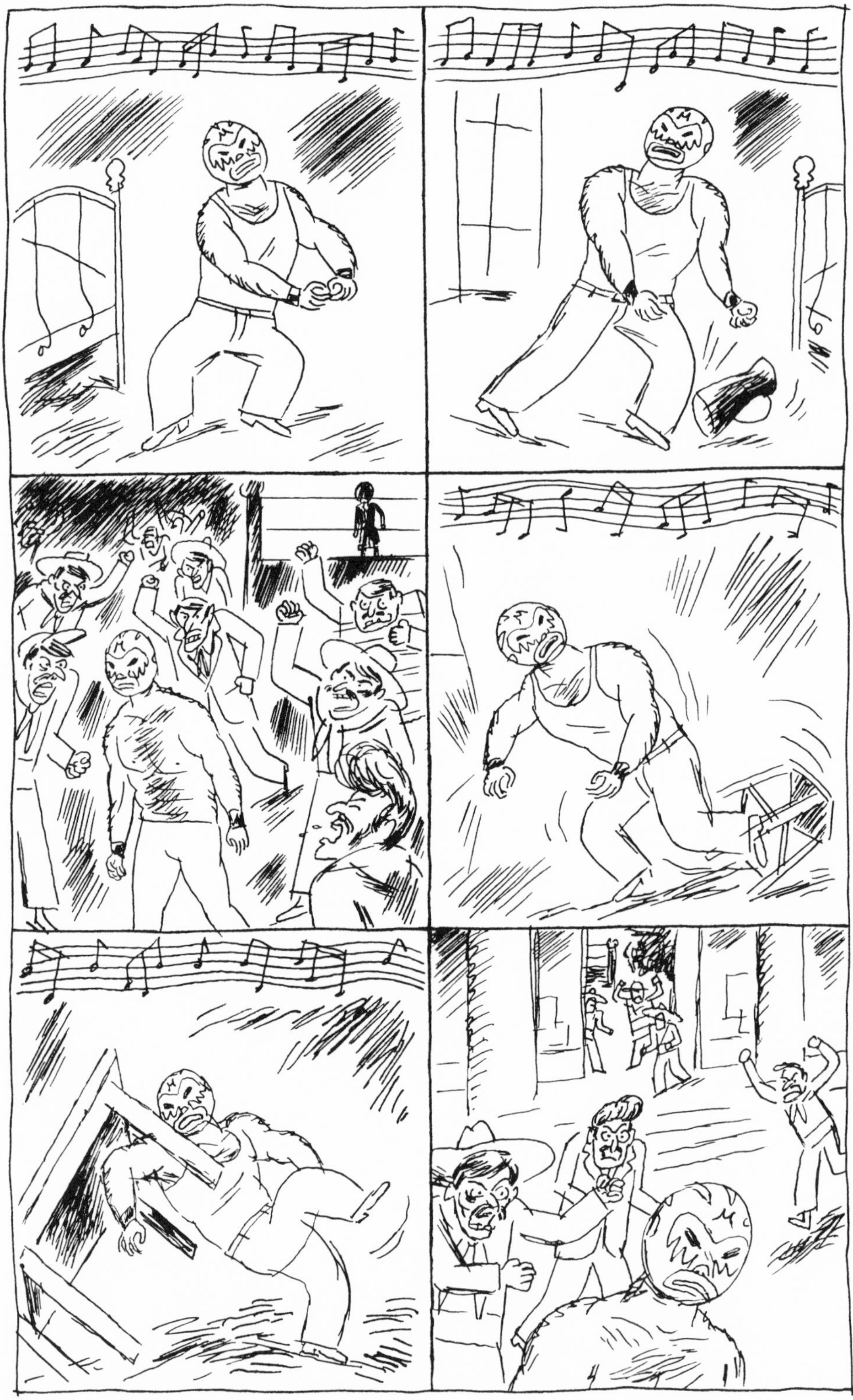

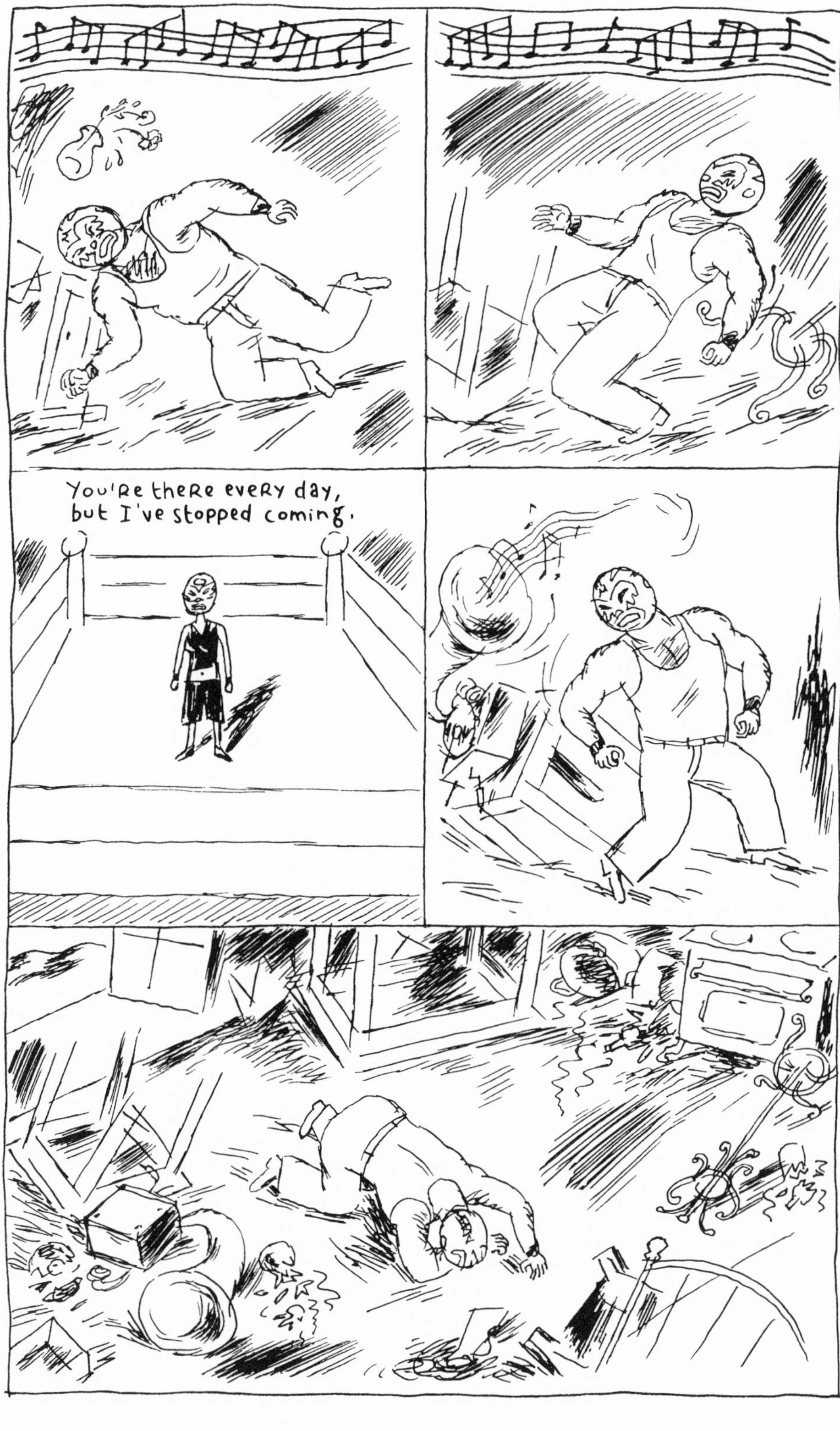
You're there every day,
but I've stopped coming.

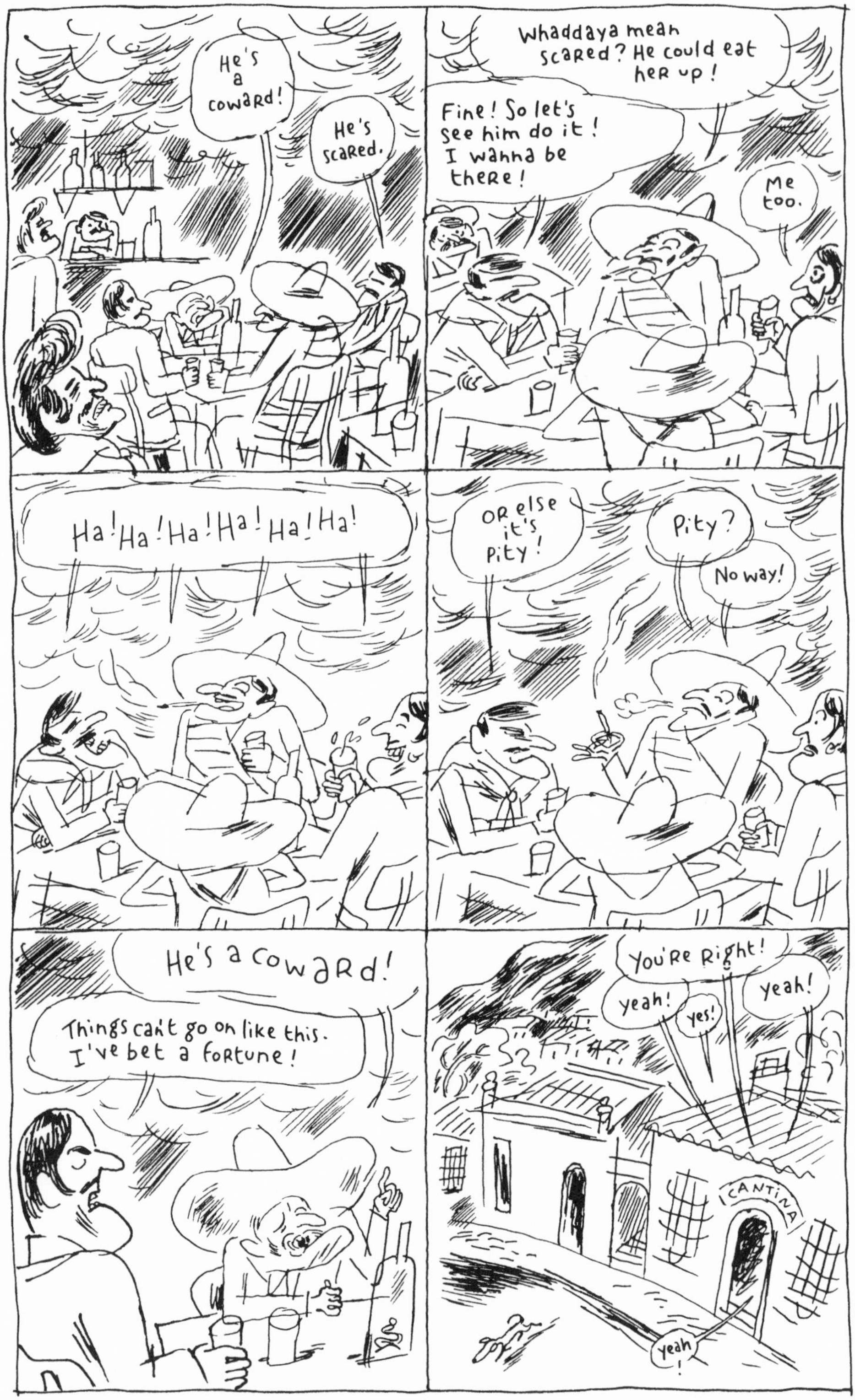
He's a coward!
He's scared.
Whaddaya mean scared? He could eat her up!
Fine! So let's see him do it! I wanna be there!
Me too.
Ha! Ha! Ha! Ha! Ha! Ha!
OR else it's pity!
Pity?
No way!
He's a coward!
Things can't go on like this. I've bet a fortune!
You're Right!
yeah!
Yes!
Yeah!
CANTINA
yeah!

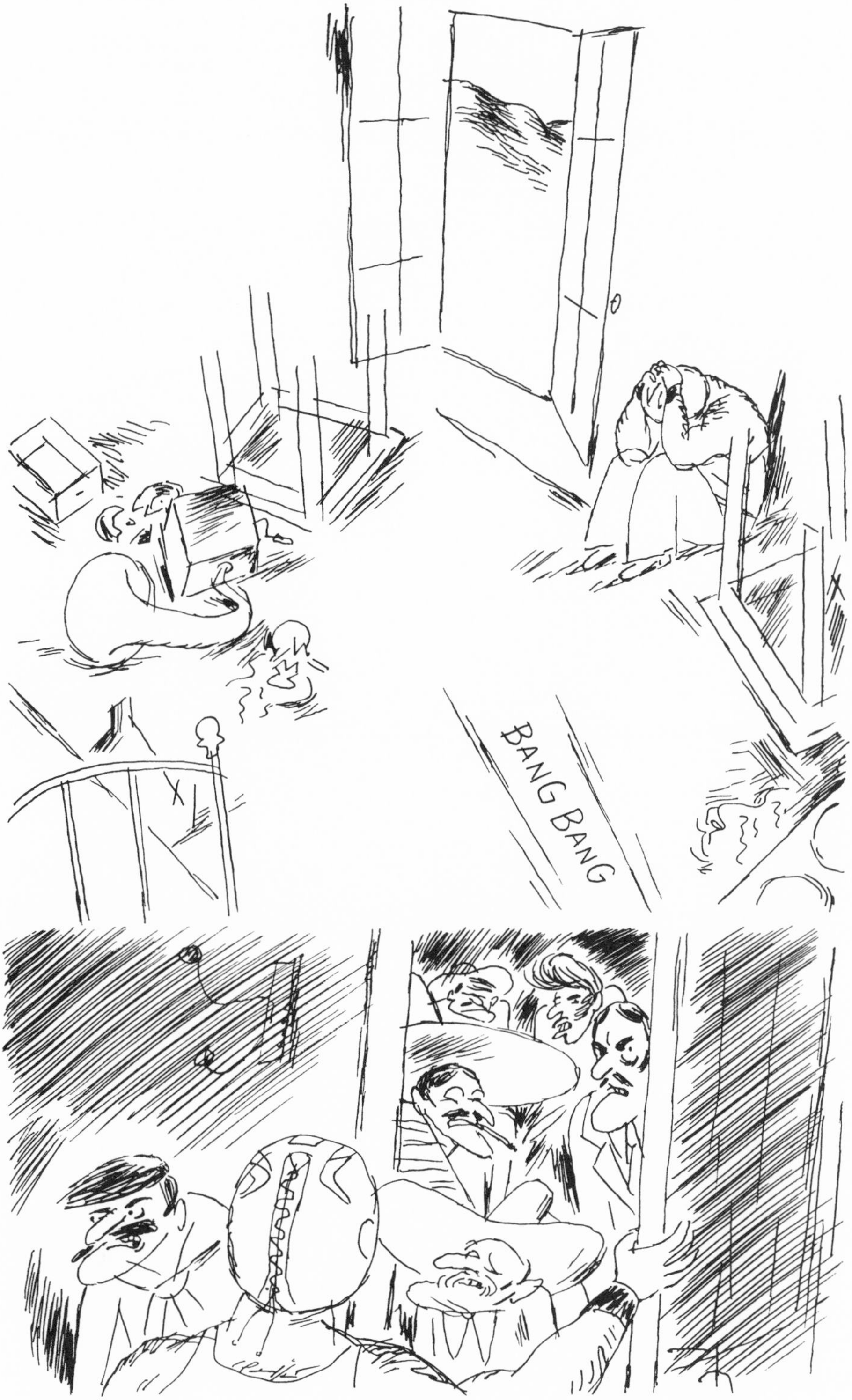
BANG BANG

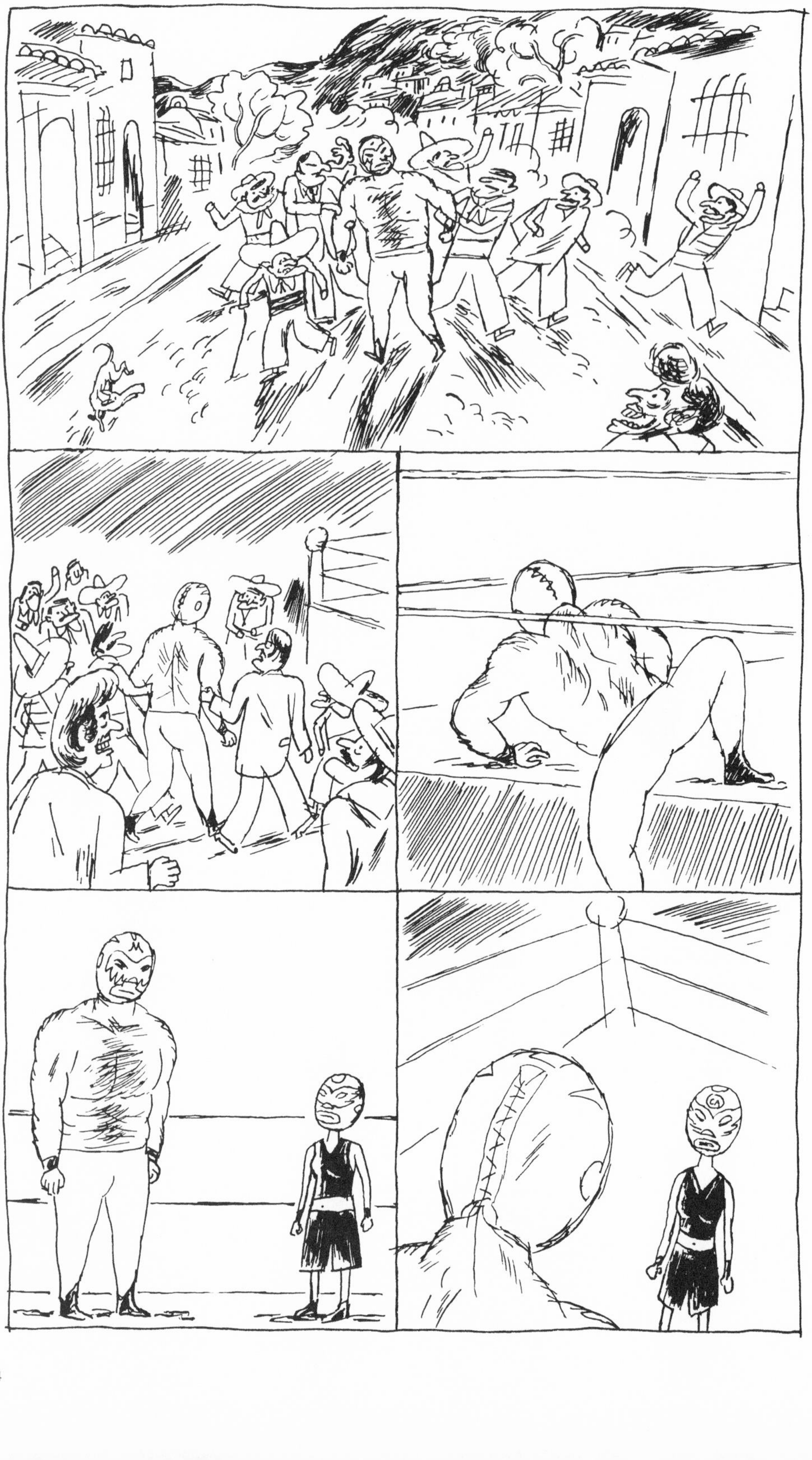

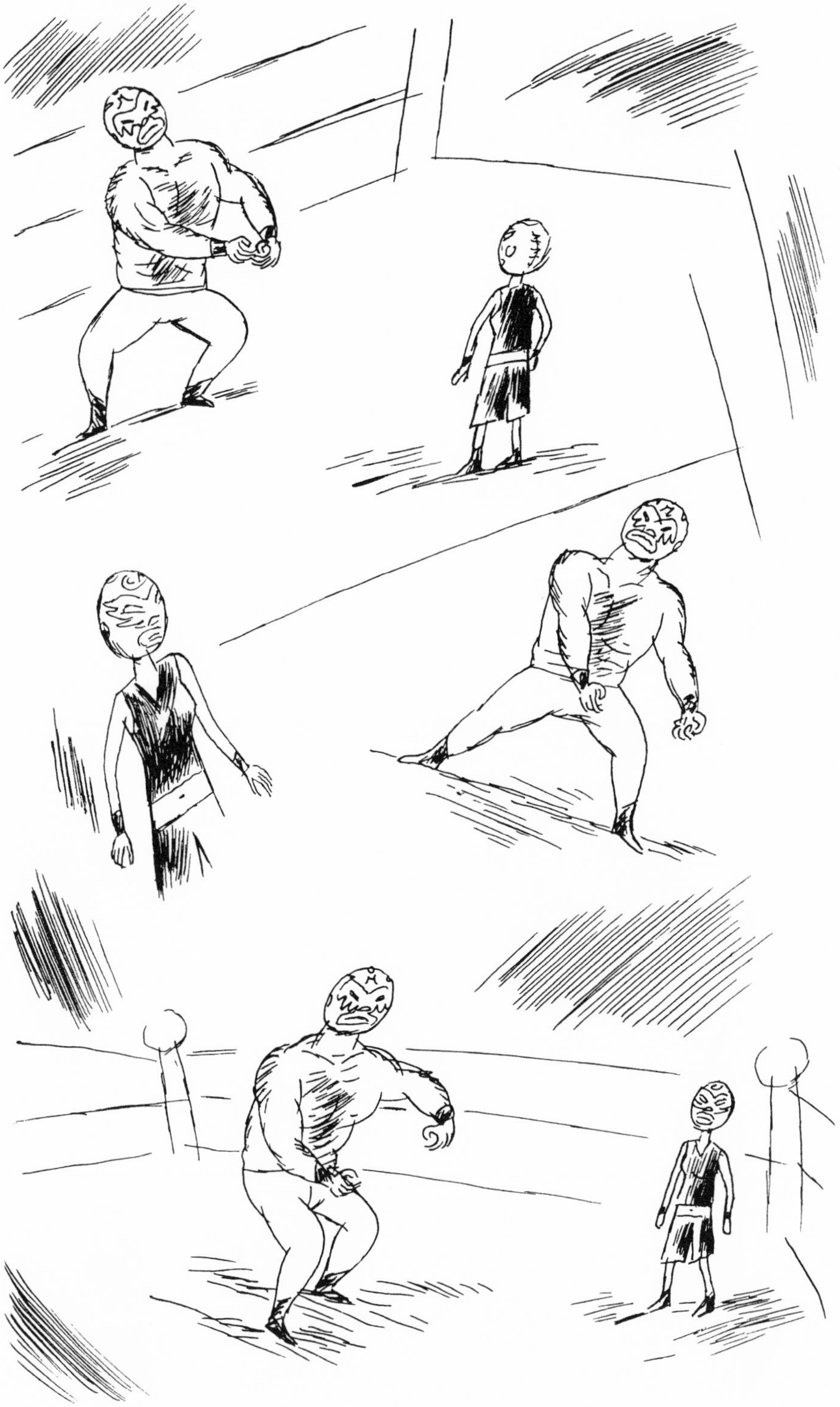

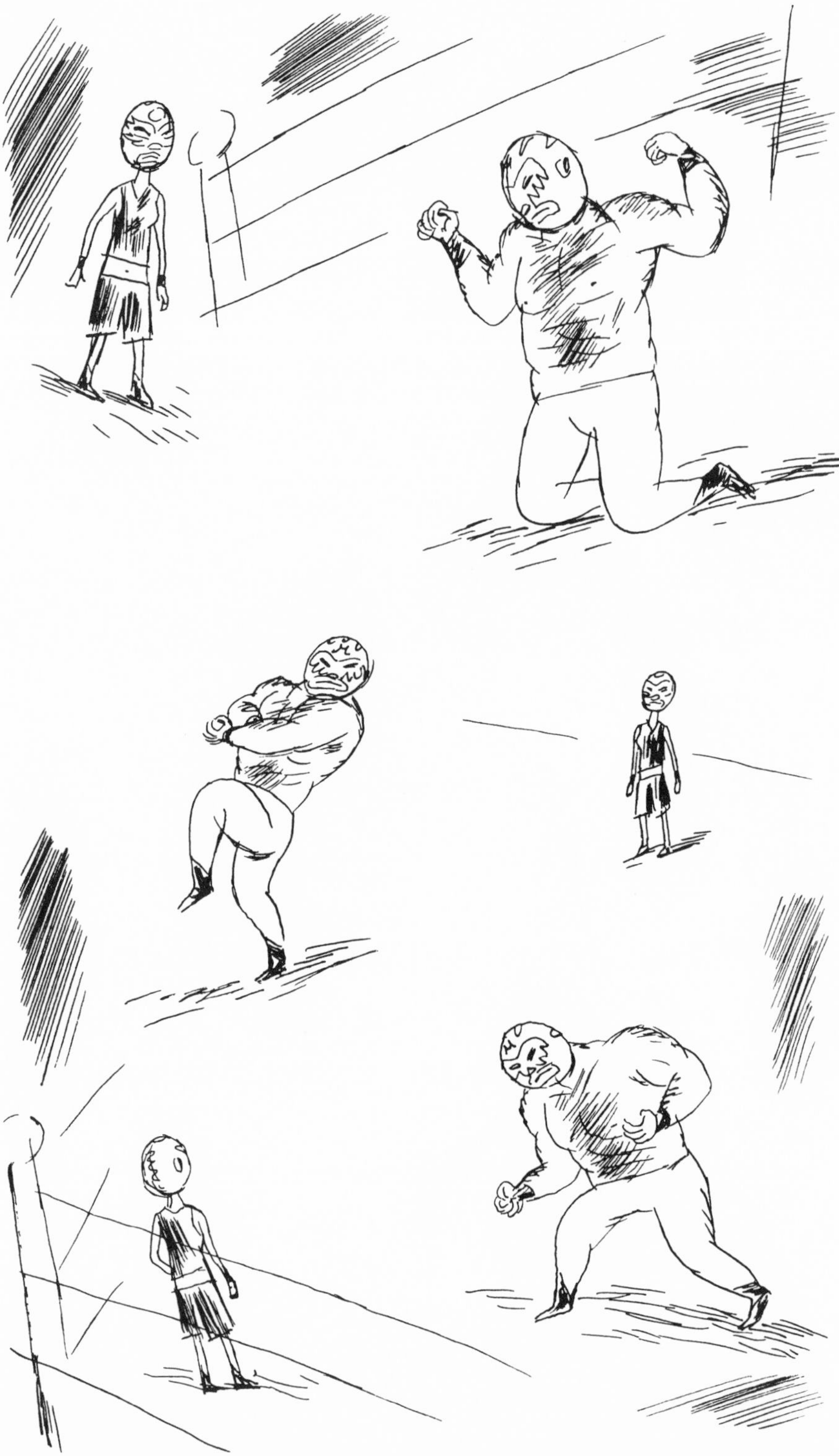

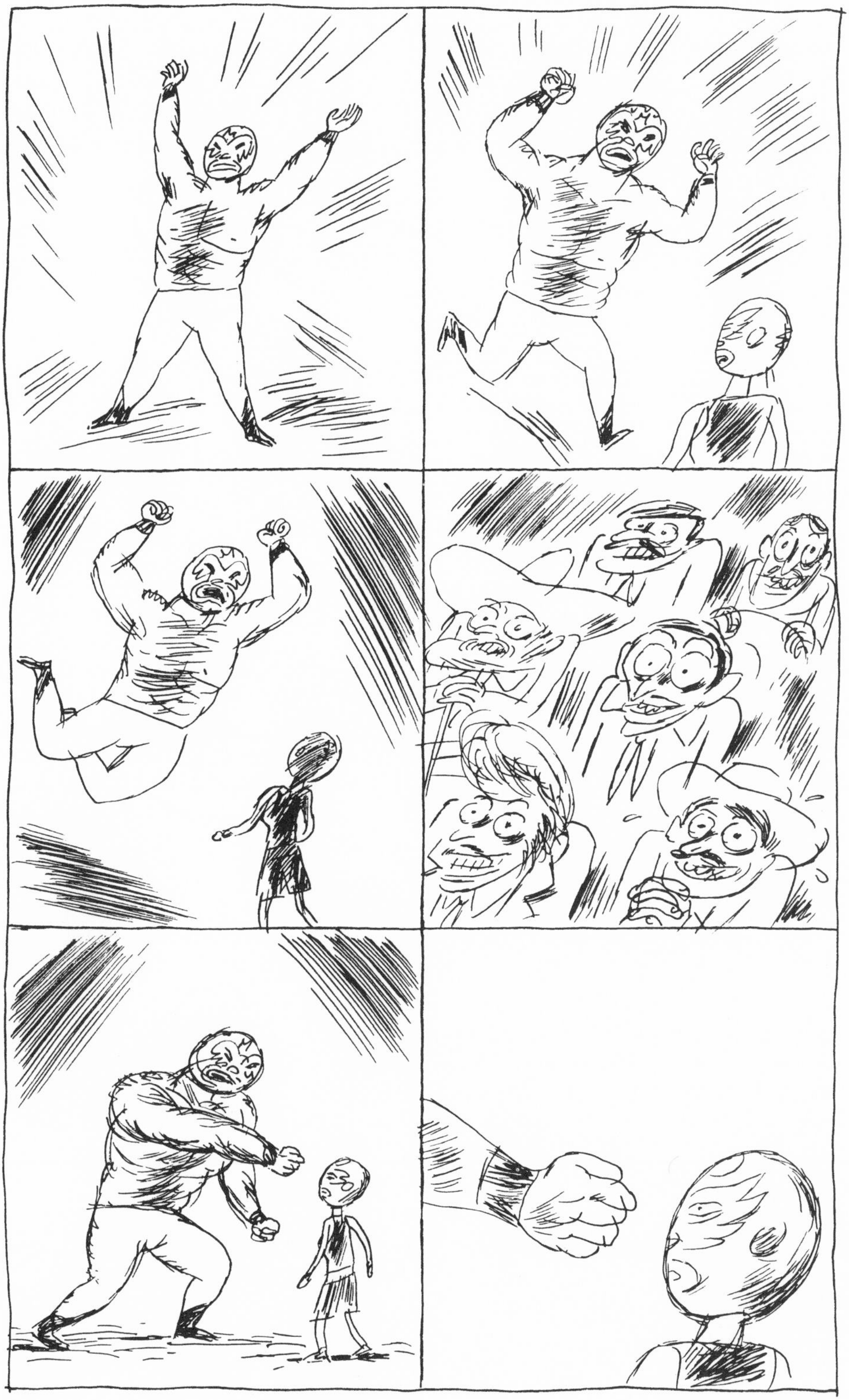

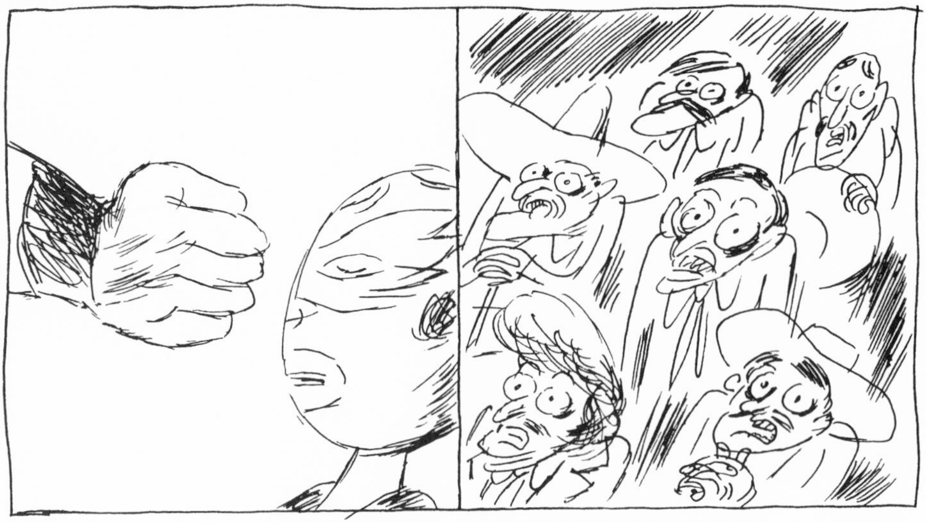

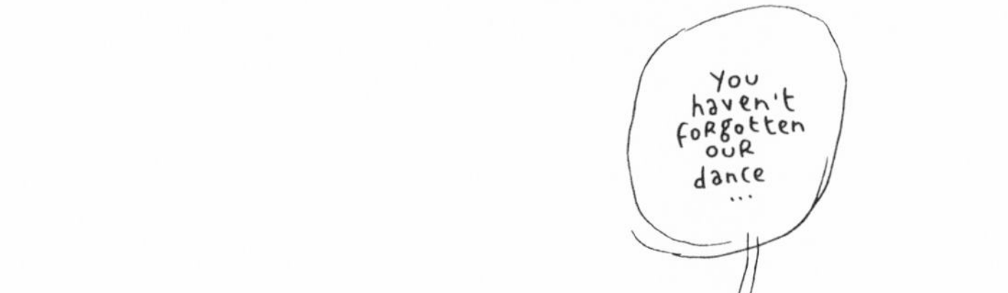
You haven't forgotten our dance ...

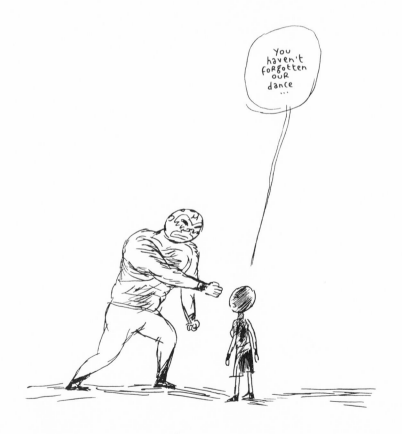

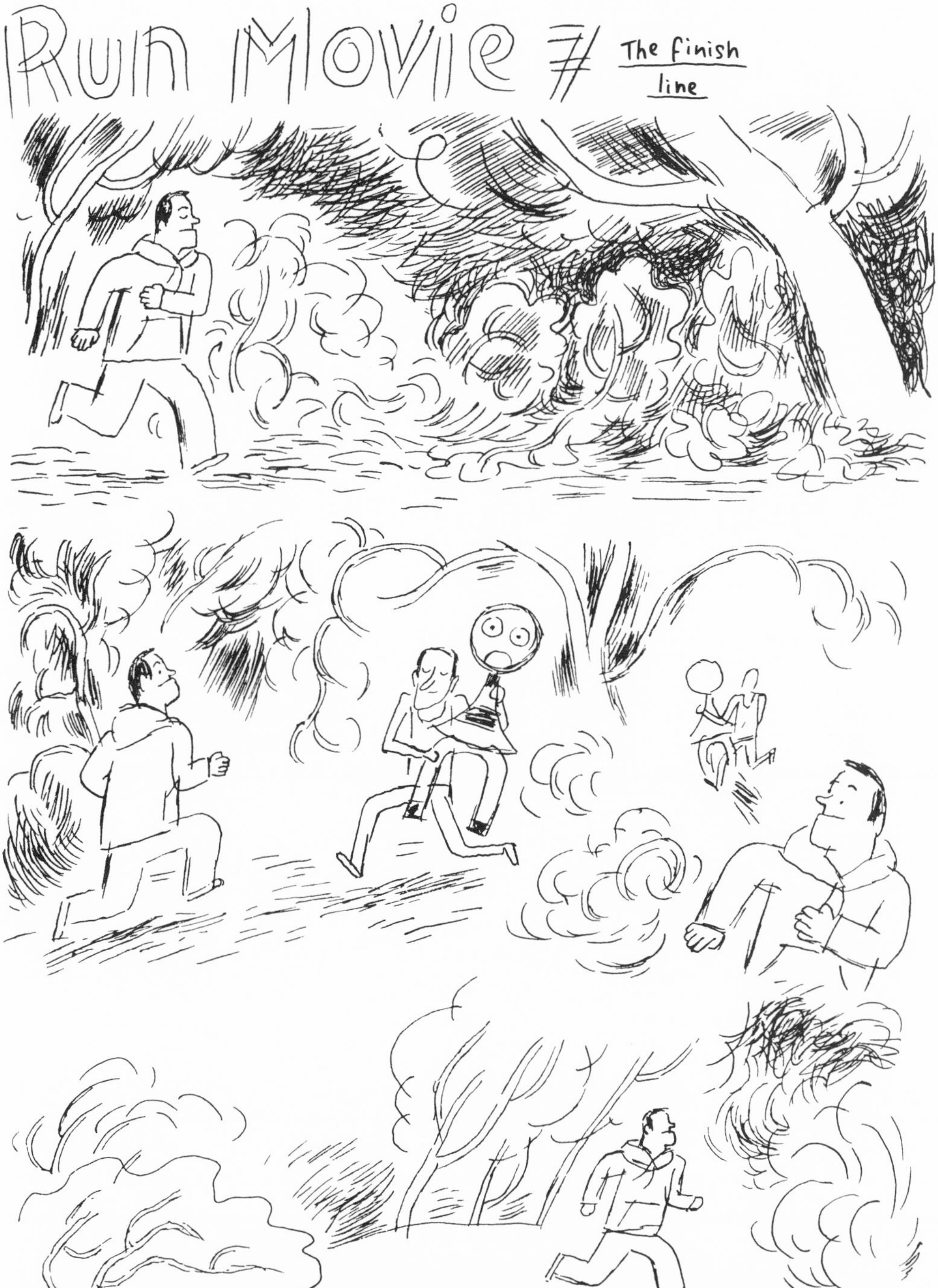
Run Movie 7
The finish line

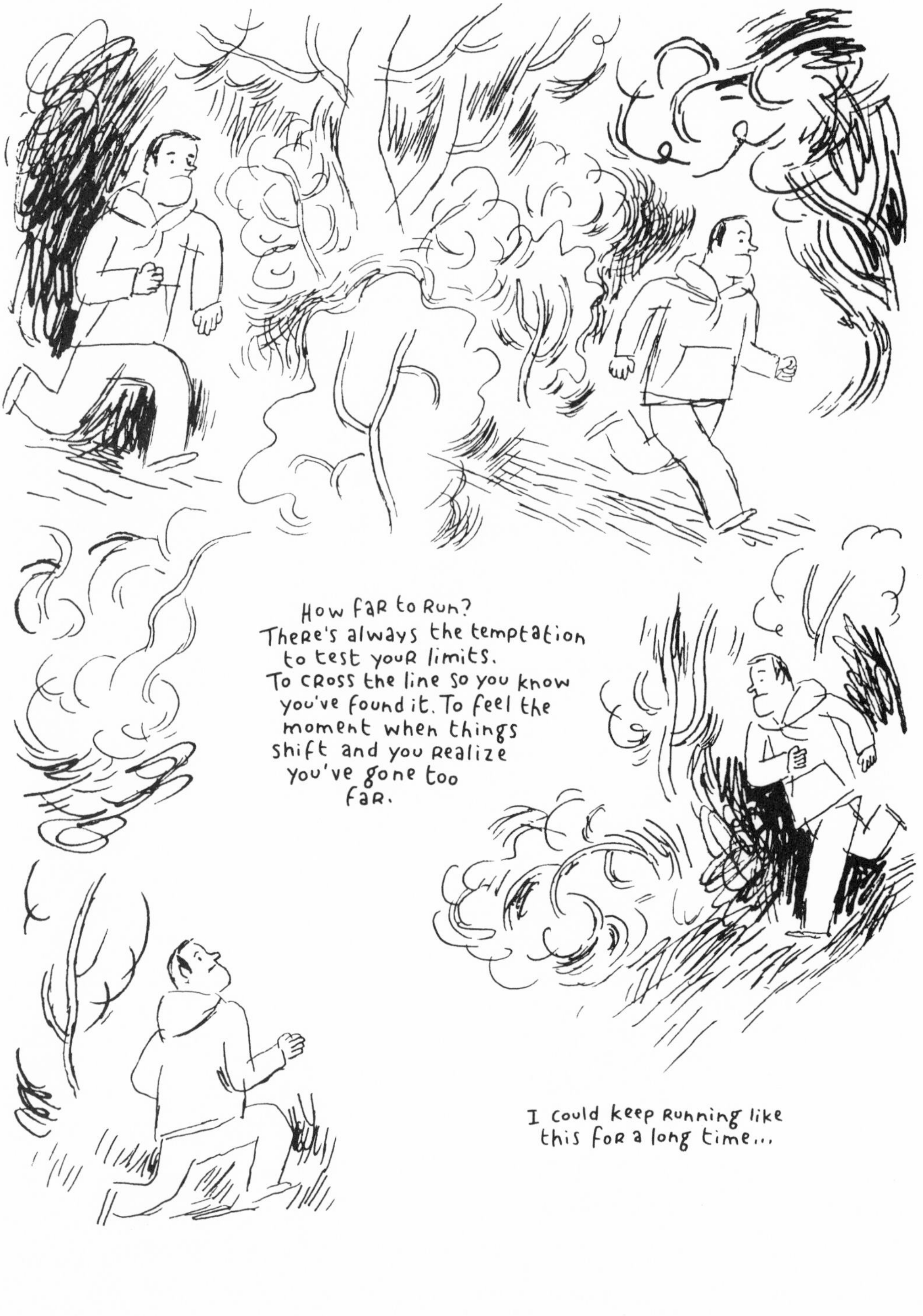
How far to run?
There's always the temptation to test your limits.
To cross the line so you know you've found it. To feel the moment when things shift and you realize you've gone too far.
I could keep running like this for a long time...

Sooner or later, you've got
to know when to stop.

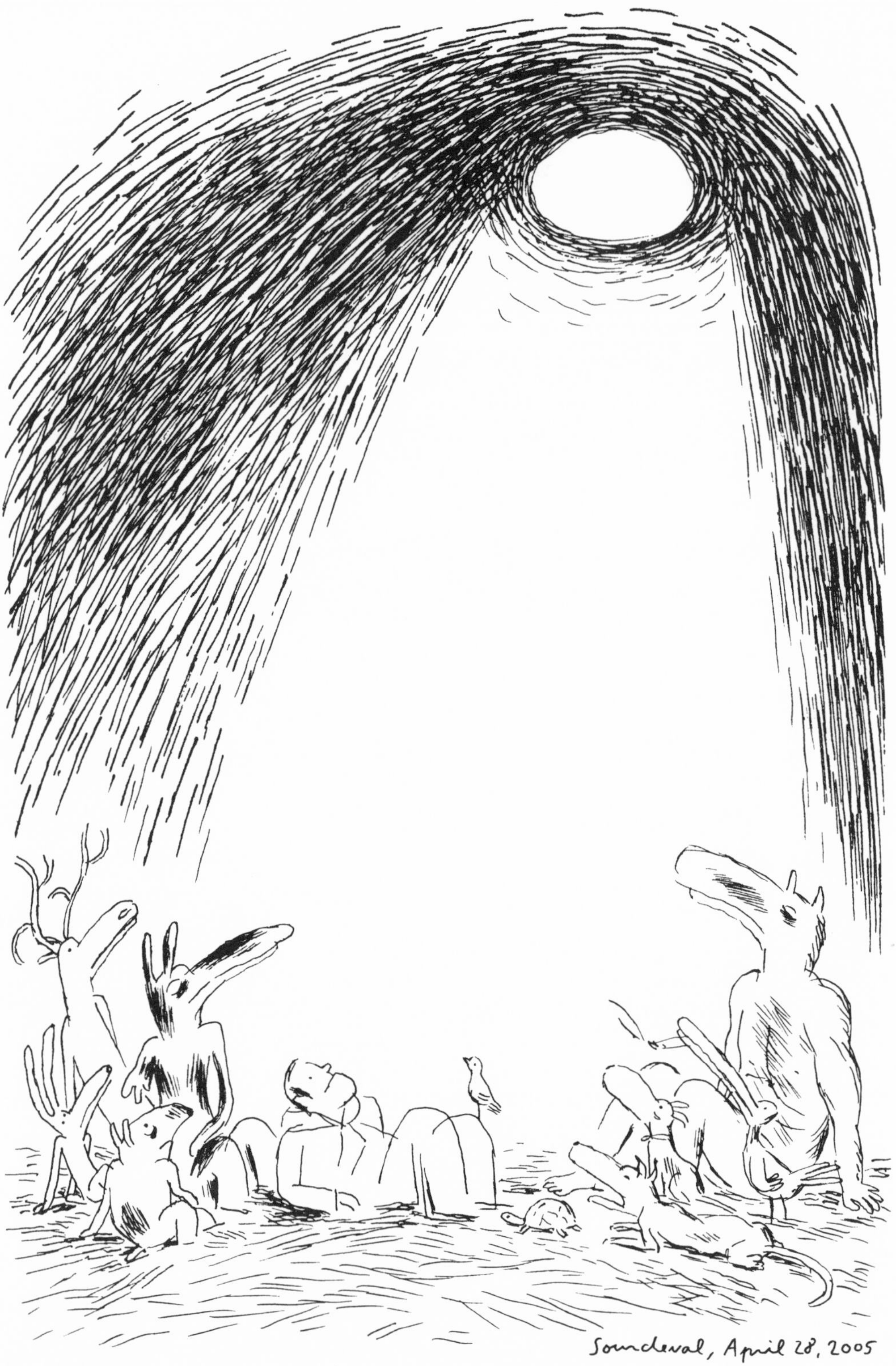
Sourdeval, April 28, 2005

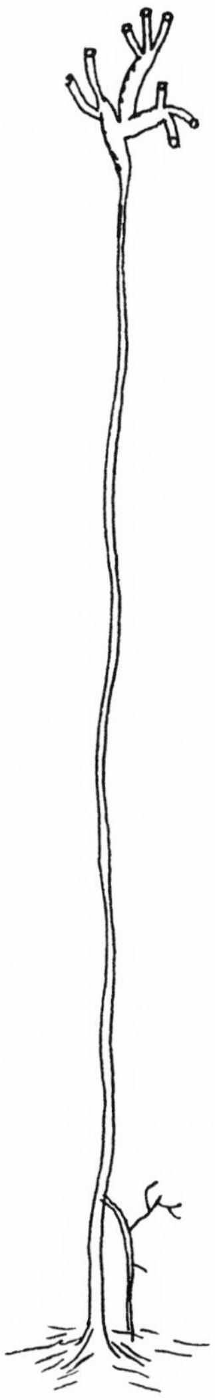

Born in Paris, Philippe Dupuy has been working in comics for nearly 30 years, mostly in collaboration with Charles Berberian, creating strips about their well-known character Mr. Jean (published in English as *Get a Life* (Drawn & Quarterly)). His other work includes *Maybe Later* (Drawn & Quarterly) and a book with Loo Hui Phang about mexican drag queens, Arizona and the reelection of President George Bush: *Une élection américaine* (Futuropolis), published in France in 2006.

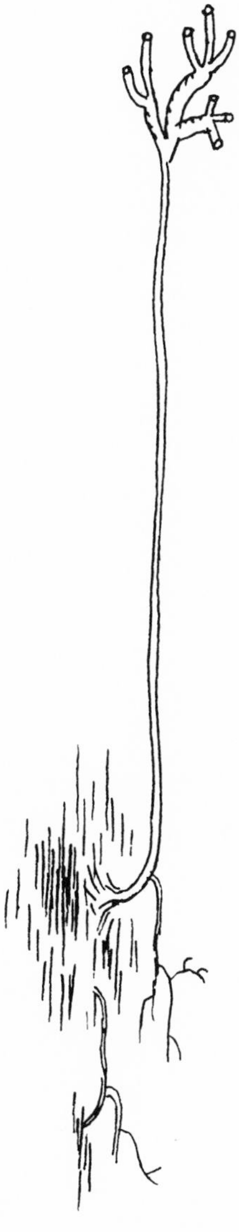

Haunted by Philippe Dupuy. Originally published as *Hanté* by éditions Cornélius. First Hardcover Printing: March 2008. 10 9 8 7 6 5 4 3 2 1. Library and Archives Canada Cataloguing in Publication; Dupuy, 1960-; Haunted / Philippe Dupuy. Translation of: Hanté.; ISBN 978-1-897299-26-5; I. Title.; PN6747.D86H3613 2008 741.5'944 C2007-904707-6; Translation: Helge Dascher with thanks to Anne Billy and Mark Lang. Lettering: Dirk Rehm. Drawn & Quarterly; Post Office Box 48056, Montreal, Quebec, Canada H2V 4S8; www.drawnandquarterly.com; Distributed in the USA and abroad by Farrar, Straus and Giroux; 19 Union Square West, New York, NY 10003; Orders: 888.330.8477; Distributed in Canada by Raincoast Books; 9050 Shaughnessy Street, Vancouver, BC V6P 6E5; Orders: 800.663.5714. Printed in Canada.

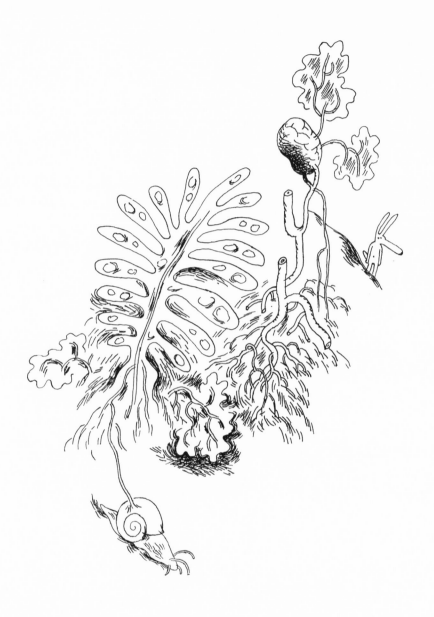